WITHDRAWN

AN ILLUSTRATED ENCYCLOPEDIA OF
ABORIGINAL LIFE

AN ILLUSTRATED ENCYCLOPEDIA

OF

ABORIGINAL LIFE

by

A. W. REED

illustrated by

E. H. PAPPS

A. H. & A. W. REED

Sydney   Wellington   London

First published 1969
Reprinted with corrections 1974

A. H. & A. W. REED

51 Whiting Street, Artarmon, NSW
182 Wakefield Street, Wellington
11 Southampton Row, London
also at
29 Dacre Street, Auckland
165 Cashel Street, Christchurch

© 1969, Literary Productions Ltd

Printed and bound by
Dai Nippon Printing Co (Hong Kong) Ltd

National Library of Australia
Cataloguing in Publication data
Reed, Alexander Wyclif, 1908—
  An illustrated encyclopedia of Aboriginal life/ by A. W.
  Reed; illustrated by E. H. Papps. —
  Artarmon, N.S.W.: Reed, 1969.
  ISBN 0 589 07034 7.

  [1.] Aborigines, Australian — Social life and customs —
Dictionaries and encyclopedias. I. Title.

390.091749915

INTRODUCTION

It is obvious to all who know something of Aboriginal life that it is impossible to generalise about the physical characteristics, life, customs, material possessions, languages, and religious beliefs of the Australian Aborigines. In environments such as the central and western deserts, life was, from a white man's viewpoint, a struggle for survival and vastly different from life in the fertile tropical regions of parts of Queensland and Arnhem Land, or the more kindly climate of New South Wales, Victoria and South Australia. It is natural that there should have been differences between north and south, where the contrast was greatest, and even on occasion between adjacent tribes living in different environments.

For this reason variant aspects of life and custom have been outlined in the following pages, but whenever a generalisation is made it should not be assumed that the statement applies to Aborigines in every part of Australia. Further, the account of their lives is based on conditions that existed before the coming of Europeans, and which remain today only in a few isolated groups farthest removed from white influence. The Aboriginal came into sudden conflict with an advanced civilisation that debased his spirit and robbed him of the comfort and discipline of the Eternal Dreamtime. It is to the credit of a few humanitarian leaders drawn from the ranks of missionaries, doctors, legislators, civil servants and dedicated anthropologists, that there have been active endeavours to find a place for these people in the world of today. To the anthropologists of the present day and of an earlier generation we owe a debt for their researches into the lives of the people of the Stone Age, and for recording their struggle against the hostile forces of Nature, their advanced religious beliefs, and their acceptance of the unity and cohesion of life. Special recognition should be made of the work of the Australian Institute of Aboriginal Studies which was established in 1961 by the Commonwealth Government to carry out a programme of urgent field research on Aboriginal customs. In addition to academic works, many books of a more popular nature have been published in recent years. The present compilation does not pretend to add anything to the information that may be found in other works, but attempts to present it in a handy form which enables the reader to refer at a moment's notice to any of the major and many of the minor aspects of Aboriginal life.

No matter how contradictory or confusing different tribal practices may at first appear to be, it should be made clear that beneath them is a basic pattern. In spite of the way Aboriginal man was affected by his environment, his religion or philosophy (call it what we will) sprang from the noble concept of the Dreamtime. Without some understanding of this important universal principle we cannot begin to appreciate the discipline of initiation ceremonies, the abandoned joy of dance, mime, and song, the intense loyalty to tribal land, the ceremonies connected with the power of the medicine man, the mythology and influence of the tribal and totemic ancestors, the controlled social life, rigid customs, and kinship obligations of every tribe. For this reason emphasis has been placed upon religious and ritual matters throughout this book.

Although writing at an elementary level, and admitting the inadequacy of the articles on such subjects as totemism and kinship, the compiler has sought to avoid shallow judgments and to penetrate a little into the mysteries of life which were the motivating force of the Aborigines and to share them with the reader.

Information has been drawn from a wide variety of books and periodicals published over a long period of years. Particular acknowledgment is made to the following works which range from the scholarly to the popular. I express my thanks to the authors and publishers for their consent to the inclusion of a number of extracts from these books, all of which are recommended to the reader:

Daisy Bates, *The Passing of the Aborigines*. Heinemann and Murray, 2nd edn 1966.

R. M. Berndt (ed.), *Australian Aboriginal Art*. Ure Smith, 1964.

R. M. and C. H. Berndt, *The World of the First Australians*. Ure Smith, 1964.

R. M. and C. H. Berndt (ed.), *Aboriginal Man in Australia*. Angus and Robertson, 1965.

Charles Duguid, *No Dying Race*. Rigby, 1963.

A. P. Elkin, *The Australian Aborigines*. Angus and Robertson, 4th edn 1964.

Mrs Aeneas Gunn, *The Little Black Princess*. Robertson and Mullens, Angus and Robertson.

Ion L. Idriess, *Our Living Stone Age*. Angus and Robertson, 1963.

Australian Aboriginal Studies. Oxford University Press, 1963.

Special thanks are accorded to Emeritus Professor A. P. Elkin for reading the manuscript and for saving the compiler from perpetuating errors and misunderstandings; also to Mr F. D. McCarthy, Principal of the Australian Institute of Aboriginal Studies, who has offered many constructive suggestions and contributed much additional information.

A. W. REED

Dedicated to June and John

CROSS REFERENCES

The lines set in italic that follow many
entries give other headings that may
usefully be consulted for related information.

A

ABORIGINES. The original inhabitants of a country seldom have a name for themselves as a race. This is particularly the case in the Southern Hemisphere, where the need for national identification did not arise until contact was made with the outside world. Even then, while a country is small and its native population still dominant, there is no ambiguity in calling the inhabitants by the name of the country, e.g. Tahitians, Papuans, Nauruans. In Australia and New Zealand white settlement developed so quickly that the terms "Australians" and "New Zealanders" soon came to be applied to the newcomers. The first explorers called the native inhabitants Indians, and then Australians and New Zealanders. In the 1850s the term Maori gradually came into use in the smaller country. It was a useful adaptation of a word that meant native, ordinary, or normal. The dark-skinned inhabitants of Australia had no common language from which to draw such a descriptive

ABORIGINES

word. They were known for a long time as blacks, but this had almost become a word of opprobrium (unfortunately many uncomplimentary epithets have been applied to them by the usurpers of their land), and all that is left is to use the generalisation "Aborigines" as a particular term for the first inhabitants of Australia and their descendants. The singular form is Aborigine or Aboriginal (as a noun) and Aborigines the plural. A distinction is made by anthropologists between the Australoids, the inhabitants of the continent, and the Tasmanians who by some were believed to be the first to occupy part of the mainland.

In spite of their simple material culture and in many places their nomadic type of existence, they had developed a co-ordinated social system. Their lives were governed by an implicit belief in the enduring influence of their heroic ancestors. They lived in what appears to us as a hostile environment with courage and ingenuity. As semi-nomads they were burdened with few material possessions. As F. D. McCarthy writes in *Aboriginal Man in Australia*: "An outstanding feature of Aboriginal culture is the adaptation of a narrow range of basic methods and gear as widely as possible in hunting and fishing, rather than the invention of new methods, demonstrating an intelligent approach to the use of equipment. The immense contrast between the equipment of Arnhem Land and Cape York coastal tribes, with the dugout and detachable harpoon complex, and the coastal tribes of Western Australia lacking nets, traps, hook and line, harpoon and canoes, is one of the finest examples of the rapid and immense additions that diffusion can make to a culture."[*]

In developing a unique religious system, in adapting himself to diverse environments, and in establishing an economy ideally suited to his needs, the Aboriginal has proved that the adjective "primitive", which has been applied so freely, is a word that must be used with discretion. In the *Australian Encyclopaedia* of 1926, the Aborigines were described as polite, proper in their behaviour according to their rights and

[*] Angus and Robertson, 1965, page 93.

teachings, unassuming and gay, fond of jokes and laughter and skilful in mimicry, by nature frank, open, and confiding, of a lively disposition, and cheerful under all sorts of privations. Such a statement today may be considered too flattering (it would certainly be so if applied generally to a European community) but fundamentally it is correct, and indeed less than the truth. Life for them was once more disciplined than it is today; but the intelligence that evolved the concept of totemism, rules of kinship, tribal and inter-tribal etiquette, and the skills employed in bushcraft, food-gathering and hunting, enabling the group to move across an apparently sterile desert with a relaxed mind and confidence in its ability to survive, scarcely merits the use of the term primitive. The tragedy is that recognition of these outstanding qualities has come only when the old way of life has been completely changed by western civilisation.

Ancestors, Australoids, Dreamtime, Introduction, Origins, Physical characteristics, Possessions, Relationships, Religious beliefs, Totemism.

ADZES.
Axes.

ANCESTORS. There was a universal belief in the existence of ancestral spirits. Amongst many of the tribes the sky cult-hero, the All-Father, was by his various deeds in the Dreamtime responsible for the natural features of the world and for bringing plant and animal life to it. Elsewhere the ancestral spirit heroes performed the same role and, through ritual, provided for the people who were their spirit descendants.

These ancestors made lengthy journeys across the continent. Their mythical tracks, extending for hundreds of miles, were shared by many tribes. Wherever they paused they left in stones, trees, waterholes, and other natural features the spirits of living creatures. Thus fish, animals, snakes, insects, and birds became part of each "country" and had totemic significance because they were emanations of their totemic ancestor.

In many tribal myths, especially in Central Australia, the ancestor could transform himself from human to animal form at will. It is sometimes difficult to separate the human likeness from the animal form. The animals of which the ancestor was the prototype were all de-

scended from him because every particle of his body was a life cell. For the same reason he was the totemic ancestor of men and women who were descended from him; and so there were links, both material and spiritual, between all three. The vitality of man and the fertility of plant and animal life were all dependent on the ancestor, whose guardianship was kept alive only by the observance of proper ritual. Without these intimate, other-worldly bonds, life would have ceased.

Each tribe owned some part of the myth of its ancestor. It might share the whole journey (or myth) with other tribes, but only a part of it belonged to an individual tribe. This portion was all-important, for it was in the hunting grounds, the recognised territorial region of that tribe, that the ancestor left pre-existent spirits of man and natural species. The Aboriginal who left his own territory was never at ease until he returned to it; unless he died there his spirit could not remain at rest.

Recognition of the ancient deeds and the continuing spirit of the culture heroes or ancestors was expressed in art, dance, song, ritual, and drama. The spiritual ancestors welded the tribe to its own territory and through the totems they created they linked each social group to a portion of this territory. The ancestors were present in individual totems as well as in the natural features on which they depended for their existence.

Boundaries, Dreamtime, Gods, Mythology, Personifications, Pre-existence, Religious beliefs, Spirits, Totemism.

ANIMALS. It was fortunate that Australia abounded in animal life. Boys were trained in hunting from an early age. As adults they devoted most of their lives to the chase. Kangaroo and wallaby skins were occasionally used in the southern regions as rugs, and bone, sinews, and fur had many practical uses. The importance of animals was expressed in totemism which pervaded life, linking men and women with the animals upon which they depended and with whom they had a common origin; this no doubt accounted for the frequency of their appearance in folklore.

In mythology many of the animals were originally men. They were changed to their present form but retained some of the characteristics of their progenitors. Conversely, there are legends which relate how animals were transformed into men and women. Animals provided inspiration in art, songs, dances, and games.

Cooking, Creation, Food, Hunting, Mythology, Totemism.

ANTS. Honey ants provided a welcome change of diet among the desert tribes. Black and red ants stored honey in their bodies. The Aborigines were quick to detect nests by tracks in the sand, and by observing the ants, but the task of digging out the nest was long and tiresome. The usual time to unearth them was in the late afternoon, when the camp was near at hand, and others could commence preparations for the evening meal while the diggers turned up the ground with their sticks.

There were several species in which the bodies became enormously distended with the food supplied by the worker ants, which used them as food stores.

ARCHAEOLOGY. The application of systematised archaeological research to the Australian continent is revealing many unsuspected facts about the pre-history of the Aborigines.

It has already been shown that the antiquity of man in Australia extends further than early research workers imagined. Radio carbon dating is a comparatively new science which is penetrating the secrets of the past, confirming and extending the findings of the geologists.

Middens are the happy hunting grounds of the archaeologists, who have been able to date stone flakes, shells, and charcoal remains as accurately as 585 years ago in coastal districts in Victoria, and to extend the date back more than 1,000 years on an ancient shoreline at Port Fairy. In Cape York Peninsula, remains which are proof of human occupation have been dated with some accuracy to about 1000 BC.

Even more spectacular results show that the ancestors of the Aborigines inhabited parts of Victoria from 6,000 to 8,000 years ago, with the speculation that cooking hearths at Maribyrnong may date back to more than 12,000 BC. It has been stated that a similar hearth at Lake Menindie on the lower Darling was used in 16,800 BC.

It seems certain that Aborigines occupied the central and some of the eastern regions, including Queensland, 16,000 years ago. As the invasion of Australia began in the far north and spread southwards, it is expected that excavations will show even greater antiquity in the northern regions.

An equally important result of archaeological investigation is the determination of successive periods of occupation, and the characteristic changes in culture as revealed by the artifacts that are exhumed. Already it has been possible to separate different stages of culture by an examination of varying types of spearheads. Gradually a composite picture is being put together as the archaeologists make further discoveries, and these in turn are integrated with the results of geological and anthropological research.

Carpentarians, Origins, Tasmanians.

ARMBANDS. Armbands made of cane, human hair, and animal fur twine were worn more commonly by men than by women, on the upper arm. Feathers and other ornaments were added for corroborees and ceremonies. On Bathurst and Melville Islands women wore a large decorated bark armlet in mourning ceremonies.

Ornaments.

ART. Visual art, wrote Professor Elkin in *The Australian Aborigines**, "is an expression of Aboriginal philosophy in form and colour and in design, which has an aspect of beauty according to the tradition of the tribes concerned. It is not primarily an attempt to produce the beautiful for its own sake, though it does reveal aesthetic appreciation. Aboriginal art is first and foremost a ritual activity, correlated with chanting, dancing and acting. . . ."

The quotation serves as a reminder that manual art (painting, engraving, sculpture, featherwork, etc.) is but one form of art. Reference to other art forms will be found in separate entries. Dr Catherine H. Berndt provides a clear and salutary statement on this subject, warning against a too narrow concept when she defines the complex of expressive symbolism:

"Without being pedantic about definitions, we can take this to include not only visual art but also myth, story and song . . .; dancing and dra-

* Angus and Robertson, 4th edn 1964, page 278.

matic representations . . .; and, peripheral to our central concern here, humour and play. Any or all of these can be looked at from other, divergent, points of view; and to talk about their expressive aspects is not to underestimate their instrumental significance, their importance as means to ends. . . .

"The distinction between 'artist' and 'craftsman' is not relevant, traditionally in Aboriginal Australia. There is not a special category of behaviour or expression which is referred to by an equivalent of the term 'art'. In other words, the Aborigines are not self-conscious about this aspect. But what we may call an aesthetic element, a quality of aesthetic appreciation, permeates much of their activity in everyday as well as in sacred affairs. It enters into their sacred designs, or patterns of mythological significance, as well as into ordinary objects like dilly bags and pipes, and into their songs and dancing, including 'playabout' ceremonies where entertainment and amusement is the main aim of the proceedings. This quality of aesthetic appreciation is part of their recognition of what is good in any of these spheres."*

At one time students divided Aboriginal art into two distinct categories, "ordinary", secular, or that delightful term already used by Dr Berndt, "playabout", and sacred. It cannot be denied that a creative and light-hearted element entered into some art forms, but the underlying theme of the sacred, the mythological, the ritual, was an integral part of the purpose and meaning of most forms of art. Elkin showed how the sacred and secret life not only inspired but permeated the practice of art in its many manifestations. He referred to chanting over bull-roarers incised with decorative designs, the manner in which the grooves were rubbed with fat and stroked on these and other types of churinga, the painting of totemic designs on sheets of bark, and the painting and carving of figures to bring the Dreamtime past into the Dreamtime present. "The painting is the visible sign and sacrament of the 'dreaming', just as the chanting is its audible sign, and the acting by the painted and transformed actors its dramatic form."†

Although the various forms of art give release

to creative and emotional urges, they were often controlled by convention as well as by the limitations of the medium. The picture or decoration followed a traditional formula which varied greatly in different parts of the continent. It has been said that Aboriginal art was basically utilitarian; this was true when it implied a deep purpose in living, and the linking of the artist and his fellow-tribesmen with the continuing spirits of survival, fertility, and increase. A great deal of art was ephemeral, especially bark and body painting, but rock carvings and paintings and decorated sacred boards were of a more permanent character.

Because of the hidden or symbolic meaning in art, it is not always possible to judge it by European standards. There is a good deal of meaning in the most highly stylised painting and carving. Mythology entered into large areas of art. Understanding of the local knowledge of the sequence of a culture hero's journey is necessary to provide an understanding of the designs of a particular tribe. Though cast in a mould of tradition, such paintings often show a lively imagination. Others which to the uninitiated seem only a random pattern of zigzag lines and circles may in fact tell a story that can be read with ease, provided that the "shorthand" of the artist is understood and fitted into a known context.

Not all the designs are symbolic. Some are surprisingly realistic. When we look at them through Aboriginal eyes we realise that a series of small marks separated by a straight line indicate the tracks of a wallaby with his tail trailing on the ground, and that a circle with two U-shaped marks on either side represents men sitting round the fire. Lindsay and Tindale tell of the design which has been adopted as the badge of the Adelaide Bush Walkers. The original design appears on a shield in the South Australian Museum. There is a broad band representing a track surrounded by dots, which are trees. There are several U-shapes, the whole design portraying a party of people travelling along a track through the bush and camping several times on their journey.

Apart from stylised animal drawings on shields in south-eastern Australia, and bark and rock drawings where animals, plants, and mythological events were pictured, most designs, whether used in the ornamentation of weapons,

* *Australian Aboriginal Studies*, published for the Australian Institute of Aboriginal Studies by Oxford University Press, 1963, pages 256-7.

† A. P. Elkin, *The Australian Aborigines*, page 278.

implements, and sacred objects, or the human body, consisted of conventionalised patterns. There was nothing haphazard about the work. Elkin has stated that anyone who has been privileged to see an Aboriginal painter at work will realise that the whole picture is in his mind before he begins, and that he does the actual work with a sure hand, knowing where every line and dot will go.

Even the "geometrical design" must not be dismissed too lightly as an exercise in formal art. Elkin as usual goes to the heart of the matter: "The meander and the maze; the spiral; the concentric circles and diamonds; the wavy or the angled lines; the U and the arc; the tracks and other markings; and often, too, the figures of man, animal, plant, and inanimate objects; what are these but the symbols of the deeds of ancestors and culture-leaders, and signposts along the way they followed—the way which must be followed by each generation of men, even as they rub their fingers along the grooves and over the paint, chanting as they 'go'!"*

Paintings, whether naturalistic or formal, were confined to only a few colours, owing to the lack of suitable materials. The principal pigments were red and yellow ochre, white pipeclay, and black charcoal. The use of the third primary colour, blue, was rare, though it is found in northern Kimberley and Groote Eylandt; but a light-grey tint was occasionally achieved by using powdered oxide of manganese. The use of white down from birds, and of wild cotton, should also be mentioned, because they were employed so freely in decorative designs on the human body and on sacred objects. They were often coloured with red ochre and stuck on to the skin and other surfaces with human or kangaroo blood. The materials used were not in fact confined to pigments, but were often of the same type as children use in school, and which are known as collage. Blood, feathers, flowers, twine made of human hair, down from plants and birds, and animal fur were all used in the different types of art. Paint brushes consisted of sticks frayed at the end by chewing, or of feathers tied on sticks. Finger painting was also used.

The paints were used on sheets of bark, on the human body, on cave walls and overhangs, and on the ground, but painting was not the only form of pictorial art. Wooden objects were frequently carved and painted, and rock carvings are found in many parts of the continent. The making of baskets and bags, feathered strings, and the moulding of beeswax into figures should be numbered amongst the arts. These various art forms should be considered in a little more detail.

As most Aboriginal art has some sacred significance it is necessary to study the forms it has taken in different parts of the continent.* Sacred designs, probably universal, are best known from the central and northern regions. The design was used primarily on the body, being constructed with lines and circles of red and white down stuck to the skin with blood, but was also used in emblems employed in ritual. Many totemic groups also drew their distinctive designs on rocks and at places where ceremonies

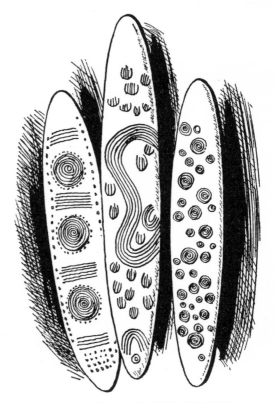

DESIGNS ON SACRED BOARDS

* *Australian Aboriginal Art*, ed. R. M. and C. H. Berndt, Ure Smith, 1964, page 16.

* See McCarthy, *Australian Aboriginal Decorative Art* and *Australian Aboriginal Rock Art*.

were held, and where their sacred emblems were stored.

Ground and earth drawings were made in some places. The snake totem of the Warramunga tribe (Northern Territory) provides a typical example. The sandy soil was moistened, smoothed, and coated with yellow ochre. A series of concentric circles represented the waterhole where the snake lived, surrounded by trees. The whole length of the painting was occupied by the snake's body, together with the footprints of the elderly man who was its guardian. The 18-foot rectangle was completed by a design of white spots and black bands. Elsewhere similar designs were painted or constructed on low mounds in the same fashion.

Sacred objects were either permanent or temporary. They were held in great reverence, and displayed only during religious ceremonies. Frequently they were ornamented with carvings, patterns of grooves and ridges, or paint and down. One of the most interesting was the waninga made by tribes in the Central Australian region in a wide variety of forms to represent different subjects, usually connected with increase rites. An early description of a rain waninga tells us that it was a wooden spear, 10 feet in length, with two shorter pieces of wood lashed to it at right angles some 2 feet from each end. Lengths of human hair cord were attached to the ends of the cross-pieces, running parallel with the shaft of the spear. Further lengths of string were taken diagonally across the structure, the rest of the space being occupied by bands of string with a triangular pattern at each end. A band nearly 2 inches in width made of possum fur string whitened with pipeclay, and another impregnated with red ochre, were tied to the sticks, and bands of white down used to complete the basic design. Bunches of red-tipped tail feathers of the black cockatoo were then tied to the ends of the spear and the cross-pieces.

The waninga was therefore an art which would have appealed to modern sculptors, but it had a serious purpose. The red string on the specimen mentioned above represented thunder, the white band was the lightning, the white down the clouds, and the black strings of human hair falling rain. Each part of the waninga had some significance. The red feathers, for instance, represented the discoloured scum floating on the surface of flood waters; the cockatoo feathers indicated the presence of a waterhole, because the tribes were able to identify the presence of water from the call of these birds.

Such a construction was the work of one or more artists, the labour being justified by the use of the waninga in rain-making ceremonies. This aspect was important, and extended to other waninga used in ceremonies of different types, and to most forms of art. Many hours of work were involved in the construction, while the actual ritual was comparatively short.

Many rock drawings and paintings were similarly connected with magic and sorcery. They can be divided into the categories of imitative magic, especially of fertility in relation to men and women; or sorcery, designed to cause sickness and death; and mythological paintings portraying the portions of ancestor journeys known to the artists. Rock drawings and paintings depict totems and food animals, hunting and fishing, combats, mortuary scenes, corroborees, and musicians, magic, and ritual subjects.

The types that may be regarded either as sacred or secular cover the complete range of Aboriginal art in various media. Decoration by incision was found mainly in New South Wales and Victoria, Lake Eyre region, and north-west Australia, and ranged from simple grooves cut in weapons and implements running the length of the object, to complex designs incised on weapons, sacred boards and stones, pipes (Arnhem Land), and deeply carved on trees and rock faces. In addition to linear and geometrical designs the motifs included animals, birds, lizards, and fish. A more elementary method of indelibly inscribing a surface was by the use of a fire stick, but it was used only occasionally. Decoration by incision was secondary to painting in northern Queensland and Arnhem Land, but was an important art technique elsewhere in Australia.

Painting with various kinds of pigment was applied to human bodies, wood, bark, rocks, and earth—in fact, to every kind of surface. The subjects range from naturalistic representation to symbolic and geometrical designs. Weapons, ritual objects, grave posts, dilly bags and, on Melville and Bathurst Islands, large bark baskets, were all decorated in this way. A great deal of imagination was used by some artists, indicating an intimate acquaintance with Nature in all its moods and forms that would be expected of people whose life and health depended on it. Impressionistic motifs of an emu sitting on an egg or a kangaroo sitting down, as though seen from beneath, occur in the rock art.

A frequent practice was to rest the hand against a rock or bark surface and silhouette the shape by blowing white or red ochre round it. There have been many references in past years to "the red hand", but white ochre or ground charcoal were used in the same manner and much more frequently; both red and white stencilled hands occur in large numbers, yellow commonly in some areas, and black rarely. Weapons, fish, lizards, snakes, bowls, leaves, emu and kangaroo feet, and even a full-sized man were also stencilled.

The portrayal of animal figures showing internal organs, known as X-ray art, is limited to western Arnhem Land. These drawings, indicating an intimate knowledge of anatomy, are found mainly in rock shelters and caves. They sometimes occupy a large area, up to 700 or 800 square feet, crowded with detail, and portraying many forms of animal life, which include kangaroos, barramundi fish, geese, lizards, and snakes. The human figure is rarely included.

Another interesting feature is the match-like figures of men and women engaged in various activities, painted with red and other ochres. In spite of their skeleton form they are often graceful and striking, not infrequently portraying legendary events and important phases of mythological significance. F. D. McCarthy describes this as the most graceful and elegant style in Australian rock art. It occurs prominently in western Arnhem Land and also in the Kimberleys and in eastern Australia.

There are eight main regions of art forms in Australia, as noted by Professor Elkin and others, but it will be realised that they overlap and must not be regarded as being in watertight divisions.

Arnhem Land: This was a very productive area, most of the art forms being found here, including cave and bark paintings and rock carvings. In addition there were unique features such as decorated baskets and weapons, painted grave posts, and many examples of X-ray art.

Kimberley: Especially rich in cave paintings, brightly coloured and extensive in area, containing many examples of the deeds of culture heroes.

South-western region: Rectangular designs and silhouette hands are characteristic of this area, together with some simple cave paintings.

Central and northern-central regions had little pictorial art except the painting of the human body.

Southern and western districts: Mostly desert with little opportunities for the Aborigines to develop art in any form. Trading with other tribes was responsible for most of what has been preserved.

Lake Eyre district: Another area of sand and desert, which did not encourage art except in the form of incised weapons, and an unusual development—brightly coloured signposts which showed the paths taken by the ancestors of the Dreamtime.

North-eastern Queensland: In this region pictorial art was confined to painted weapons, implements, and sacred objects.

South-eastern region: Another area which was rich in art, embracing rock shelter and cave paintings and carvings, figures fashioned from earth used in connection with initiation ceremonies, and designs carved and painted on weapons and implements, sacred objects, and trees; most of these were of the conventional, geometrical, or symbolic type.

The final development amongst the people whose inner life was so largely expressed in the visible forms of painting, carving, dance, and mime, has been shown by a small group of modern artists. The most famous is Albert Namatjira, a member of the Aranda tribe of the Centre. The Pareroultja brothers have followed this tradition. The first of the modern artists was Barak, the last survivor of the tribes which inhabited the Yarra River area, and who died in 1903. His landscapes are to be found in a number of art galleries.

There was no word that we know of in Aboriginal languages either for art or artist. Art was a part of life for everyone. It was indistinguishable from the Dreamtime, just as story-telling, song, and dance were parts of that mystical life; and there were no professional artists, for every man was himself part of that Eternal Dreamtime and an expression of it.

Carving, Caves, Drawings, Paintings, Pigments, Sacred objects.

ARTIFACTS.
Possessions, Tools, Weapons.

ASHES. The ashes of the fire had many uses. Mixed with oil or fat they were a protection against sunburn, especially for young babies, and as a healing agent for wounds. Many foods, especially fish, and small animals such as lizards, mice, rats, shellfish, and also dampers were baked in the hot ashes of a fire. Charcoal was an important pigment.
Cooking.

ASTRONOMICAL KNOWLEDGE. The Aboriginal who lay all night in the open air, moving only to push the smouldering logs of his personal fire together (or leaving his wife to do so), gained an intimate knowledge of the moon and stars as the hours marched slowly onwards. The elders, whose sleep was no doubt more fitful than that of younger people, studied the constellations, in due course passing on their knowledge of the astronomy and mythology of the heavens.

The sun, a female, was known to the Iuwalarai tribe as Yhi, and the moon, a male, as Bahloo. Amusing legends were told of Yhi's pursuit of the moon god, who had the responsibility for creating girl babies. There were ingenious explanations of the waxing and waning of the moon. In one of the legends there was a fertile valley in the sky, peopled by round shining moons which came out one by one, only to fall victims to the sun who reduced them in size each night by thin slivers which were cut up into sparkling stars.

There were other legends to account for the stars. The Southern Cross, in the version of one tribe, for example, was composed of the eyes of two cockatoos which fled into the sky in a hollow tree; the seven sisters of the Pleiades were the women who had many adventures on earth and finally took refuge in the sky. Aboriginal folklore was especially rich in the mythology of the heavens, and much of it was connected with the creation. The constellations were all named and their origin linked with spirit people of the Dreamtime. The great culture heroes, Baiame, Daramulun, and others of south-eastern Australia lived in the sky and some tribes believed that it was the final home after death.

These were the normal folklore explanations of celestial phenomena which would be expected of a primitive people, but they were highly imaginative and remarkably convincing in a pre-scientific age.

The study of the stars was of practical importance in foretelling the seasons, and preparing to reap the fruits of the earth; not so much perhaps as to an agricultural people, but important because of the need to observe the appropriate increase rites before the harvest season, and to know when certain plant and animal foods would be available. The coming of the new year was indicated by the appearance of the Pleiades in May. It was the sign for the commencement of increase rites in order to ensure a plentiful supply of food during the new year. At this time, and in winter, the elders, observing the night sky, would cry, "The earth is turning itself about."
Seasons.

AUSTRALOIDS. The name of the division of mankind which includes the Aborigines. The human species falls into three distinct categories or types—Caucasoid, Mongoloid, and Negroid; but the Australian Aboriginal does not belong to any of these groups. Theories have been advanced to the effect that he was an earlier European type, or that he was a survival of primitive mankind from which all races originally descended.

Whether or not he is a survival from an earlier era, or a primitive modern type, the fact that he cannot be identified with the three great divisions of the human race has led to the classification Australoid. There are indications of Australoid elements in parts of India, Malaysia, and the islands north of Australia, but it was only in Australia, with its isolation from the south-easterly migrations of Melanesians, Micronesians, and Polynesians, that the type remained comparatively stable. Nevertheless there were occasional modifications of the primal stock in northern and eastern coastal areas and, according to one school of thought, some major differences in the physical characteristics of the successive waves of migration.

As early as 1878, E. B. Tyler wrote: "He [Professor Huxley] distinguishes four principal types of mankind, the Australioid [a variation of Australoid no longer in use], Negroid, Mongoloid, and Xanthochroic, adding a fifth variety, the Melanochroic. The special points of the Australoid are a chocolate-brown skin, dark brown or black eyes, black hair (usually wavy), narrow (dolichocephalic) skull, brow-ridges strongly developed, projecting jaw, coarse lips and broad nose. This type is best represented by the natives of Australia, and next to them by the indigenous tribes of Southern India."*

Aborigines, Origins, Physical characteristics.

AXES. The study of all types of cutting implements—knives, chisels, adzes, and axes—is one of the methods employed by scientists to determine the dates of the different periods and regions of culture.

The simplest form of manufactured cutting tool is the knife or chisel, consisting of a knapped stone with a cutting edge. In time men learned to sharpen the edge by grinding, making it more comfortable to hold by setting it in gum which hardened to form a hand-grip, and finally tying the blade of basalt to a wooden handle by means of cord or sinew, fixing it in place with gum, or by bending a flexible length of wood double and holding the blade at the bend by means of gum. In Australia the two types of implement, the knife or chisel, and the blade with a handle, were frequently contemporaneous.

Development of the hafted tool marked an important stage in culture, and determined the shape of the implement. It was necessary for the blade to have a sharp cutting edge and a broad butt to enable it to fit snugly to the shaft. Gum from grass trees and other plants was moulded to shape. The blade was set firmly in the soft mass, which hardened and held it securely in place, enabling the user to cut the hardest timber.

Much time and patience were needed to make the blade. Several methods were employed. A large flake could be chipped from a rounded stone. One side was convex, the other flat, thus forming an adze-like blade which could be sharpened by chipping or grinding, and resharpened as it wore down. Similar tools were made by chipping an irregularly shaped stone until it was properly shaped. Smaller blades were fashioned from flakes of rock. Whatever the size or method of manufacture, remarkable skill and patience were displayed by the maker.

Adze blades have a surface which can be ground down on one face only to provide a keen cutting edge, and are usually mounted at right angles to the handle. Axes are ground on both faces, and it is noteworthy that some of these blades had a thin, rounded butt which was held firmly in the gum at the head of the shaft. This in itself was a remarkable accomplishment for the early inhabitants of the continent.

Specimens have survived which have served the double purpose of a cutting tool and a hammer. In these cases the blade projected from either side of the shaft, one end of the blade having a cutting edge, the other being flattened as a striking tool.

Axes and adzes were sometimes thrust through a string belt as a handy means of carrying them. Although they were almost invariably used as domestic implements, stone-bladed picks were occasionally used as weapons.

Knives, Tools.

* *Encyclopaedia Britannica.*

B

BABIES. In common belief, babies were born because pre-existent spirit children entered a mother's womb or through the participation of supernatural beings, such as the Rainbow Snake or the moon. Walking under trees, or near a totem centre, where spirit babies were waiting, was the most frequent cause of conception. In certain tribes women who became sick after eating food knew that the spirit child had entered their bodies, especially if they had a dream about the spirit at that time. In such cases the food that had been eaten became the child's totem. When the mother felt the child stirring in her body, she informed the elders, who then studied the sacred objects of the tribe to determine its totem.

When the babies were born their skin was light in colour and had to be protected from strong sunlight by applying ashes and charcoal mixed with goanna fat, or with the mother's milk. Protected in this way, the delicate skin was not burnt, and in a few days the child's skin became dark. The thick mixture of fat and ashes protected the child against heat, cold, biting insects, and to some extent against flies—but it was often impossible to keep the latter away from the infant's eyes, so causing disease and sometimes blindness.

The babies were breast-fed up to three years of age, for no animal milk was available. In dry seasons when food and water were scarce, the child might reach the age of four before being completely weaned. If the mother gave birth to a second child during this period, she had to decide whether to kill it or not. When the tribe was on the move from one waterhole to another it would be impossible for her to carry and feed both children. Infanticide was not commonly practised, but the stern realities of existence (the long period of weaning and the many tasks that women had to perform) allowed no false sentimentality. On occasion the elder child might be killed, if it were weak and sickly, but it was usually the second-born who suffered. The one who was put to death would be reincarnated.

Mothers carried their babies with them everywhere. One method was to hold the child across the small of the back with its feet through one arm and its neck through the other. Babies slept peacefully in this manner. Their mothers were able to dig for roots with the baby held on the mother's hip or under one arm. Coolamons, or shallow wooden dishes, were used as carrying cradles which could also be placed on the ground in the shade of a tree when the mother needed both arms free. Sometimes paperbark bowls were used.

When the weather was cold and the mother busy food-gathering during the daytime, she scooped a shallow hole in sand or earth in a sheltered place, lit a small fire in it, and when it had burned down, covered the baby, still in its cradle, with the ashes, placing it in the hole where the fire-warmed earth would keep it comfortable while she went on with her work. The

ABORIGINAL INFANT

same procedure was adopted at night, when it was necessary to prevent it from crying lest evil spirits should be attracted to the camp.

As the child grew older it sat with its legs round its mother's neck, holding on to her hair, and could sleep in this position even when she took part in tribal dances.

The young baby was surrounded by love and affection and was seldom left unattended by its mother and father, who petted and fondled it. During its second year the mother's milk might be supplemented by a diet of witchetty grubs, which were soft and fat, and by specially selected portions of meat chewed by the mother, eggs when they could be found, marrow from bones, and the softer part of lizards' tails. By the time it reached its third or fourth year it was wholly dependent on solid foods unless they were in such short supply that they had to be reserved for adults.

On the few occasions when the mother had to go away, the child was cared for by older brothers and sisters, the mother's sister, co-wives, or grandmother. It spent its life from its earliest years in the closest possible contact with the members of its group, and other men treated it as affectionately as its own father.
Birth, Carrying, Children, Conception.

BAGS. Dilly bag is the common term for a string bag. The Aboriginal name, used in one area only, was dilli, but there were a number of variants, such as dhilla, dirrang, jirra, etc. Dilly bag is therefore a tautological expression, but one that has come into common use since European settlement.

Dilly bags constituted the luggage of the Aborigines, and in them all material possessions were carried except weapons and implements such as digging-sticks and fire sticks. In the large bags women carried rushes, yams, shell-fish, and other foods; in the smaller ones men carried magic stones, feathers, down, and small implements. They were made mostly of bark string, pandanus fibre, and grass. The shape was much the same everywhere, the size varying according to the needs of men and women. The techniques (simple loop, loop and twist, hour-glass, knotted) were more advanced in northern areas. The essential thing was to make them strong and suited to their many uses.

Most dilly bags were loosely woven, but

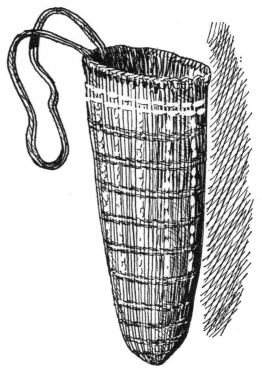

DILLY BAG

some were so closely knitted or plaited that they could be used as honey and even water bags. Small kangaroo and wallaby skin bags were used for carrying water. In Arnhem Land, men also used fighting or spirit bags as necklets.
Baskets, Bowls.

BAIAME.
Gods.

BALL GAMES. The universal popularity of games played with balls was shared by the Aborigines. The balls were usually made of grass or fur, tied with vines or hair cord, and covered with beeswax. Made in this way they could stand rough handling. Stone balls were hit with bent-ended sticks in a hockey-like game in Queensland. In Victoria and on the coast of the Gulf of Carpentaria ball games entered into the ceremonial of initiation rites. Elsewhere they were played purely for recreation. One of these games was played only with the feet, for no one was allowed to handle the ball. It was kicked into the air by the first player, the object of the game being to keep it from touching the ground.

Another game played in certain areas was called pulyugge and was a favourite sport amongst men and boys. Two teams each containing about half a dozen players were chosen. Each team threw the ball from hand to hand and tried to keep it from the opposing players. If it was intercepted by a member of the other team, the ball was kept in play by his team as long as possible. It is said that the game was so popular that it went on until the players were too tired to continue. If the sun set, the game was frequently continued the following day.

It is fairly obvious that such sports could seldom be indulged in when a tribe was attempting to gather food in a lean season, when all its energies would be devoted to hunting and food-gathering, but in plentiful seasons it no doubt formed a pleasant kind of relaxation.

Nature provided seed pods and "melons" ready-made for balls. Home-made ones were often fashioned in clay and baked in the ashes of the fire, or in the hot sun. In the Lake Eyre region clay balls were sometimes decorated with gaily coloured feathers which were inserted while the clay was still soft.

BARK. Tree bark had many uses. Large rectangles of bark stripped from the trunks of red gum trees were folded in two to form a tent or hut. Single sheets were supported against a branch to form a lean-to. Folded and tied, or with the ends sewn together and made watertight with gum, they made light canoes for use on rivers and lagoons. Bark also provided a "canvas" for painting, and was used to make baskets and bowls for carrying seeds, or water, and as cradles for babies. In northern Kimberley bark baskets were used as "carry-alls".
Art, Bowls, Canoes, Huts, Painting.

BARTER. A system of barter or exchange of gifts was widespread throughout the continent and had an important effect on the growth and diffusion of culture. In its simplest form it consisted of an exchange of gifts between adjacent tribes, enabling them to share the resources that were found in different types of country. A coastal tribe or one whose territory was enriched with lagoons and streams, for instance, was in a position to exchange the products of the waterways, such as fish and wildfowl, with a "bush" tribe which could provide grubs, herbs, honey, and game.

The barter routes extended over immensely long distances, mainly from north to south, and to a lesser extent from east to west, and also in a circular manner. Climate and vegetation were so widely divergent over the whole continent that the principle of barter added greatly to the comfort of the tribes. The trade routes tended to follow chains of waterholes, intersecting at many points. Tribes in eastern South Australia exchanged red ochre from Parachilna, and stones selected for grinding seed with axeheads made of stone found in north-western Queensland. From Kimberley there came pearl shell, bamboo necklaces, and boomerangs, while from the eastern parts of the continent there flowed a stream of spears, special types of boomerang, wooden coolamons, dilly bags, and red ochre; from Arnhem Land came shovel-bladed spearheads. Pearl shell and pitcheri leaves were traded over a wide area. Articles of trade also included bamboo, shell ornaments, sacred objects, and artifacts of many different types. There were also more intangible elements in the universal system of barter, such as chants and different kinds of ceremonies, and the words that went with them.*

It is necessary to differentiate between the giving and receiving of presents, and of barter. Gifts were usually made on a person-to-person basis; barter was a group activity which could occur even between hostile tribes. Among the Wuroro it was usual for the host group and the visitors to sit on the ground, the latter with their goods placed in front of them. Members of the resident group then heaped their own products in front of them until there were two lines of offerings, after which the visitors would come forward one by one to make a selection of goods in exchange for their own.

Some trade routes extended for thousands of miles, and trade could be engaged in satisfactorily only if the goods were passed from one tribe to another. There was no chance of a group or even of an individual travelling such long distances to barter with the original owners of coveted possessions. Language was one of

* F. D. McCarthy has mapped the local and trunk trade routes in Australia (*Oceania*, Vols IX-X).

the barriers. Most tribes were able to speak their own language and the language or dialect of the adjacent tribes, and this provided a means of communication over the whole route, as the goods were passed further and further afield. It avoided the necessity of a man's going outside his familiar territory, to places where he felt himself to be a stranger, severed from his kinship and clan ties.

It might be thought that the assets would waste as they passed through so many hands, but tribal prestige was always at stake. This was exemplified by the merbok and kue types of exchange in the Daly River district. Essentially the merbok system applied to individuals rather than to tribes or clans, but the principle behind it was constant. A gift might be given to a relative in the same or in another tribe. It was kept for a while, and then passed on; but the receiver of the gift had placed himself under an obligation to the donor, and in time the obligation had to be repaid. In fact, personal and tribal prestige was involved to such an extent that it was incumbent upon the recipient to return a gift of greater value than that received. Tribal prestige being of equal or greater importance than that of the individual ensured that the gifts that were eventually given in exchange were of sufficient value.

The system was of great benefit to all the participants, and was the only universal link (except for the journeying tracks of the ancestors) between the tribes. It resulted in the diffusion of culture, as well as of objects of immediate material value. It even encouraged an influx of new cultural elements from as far away as New Guinea and Indonesia whence annual and periodic visits were made for trade and ritual purposes.

Gifts.

BASKETS. Generally speaking, baskets were more or less rigid, and made of reeds, pandanus fibre, cane, or bark, whereas bags were flexible and made of string or animal skins. There were three main basket-making areas—Arnhem Land, Cape York, and south-eastern Australia. Bark baskets were made in north-eastern Queensland and on Bathurst and Melville Islands.

Baskets were necessary for the preservation of treasured possessions, including domestic implements, and were made in districts where climatic conditions permitted settlement in one place, even if only for part of the year. Nomadic desert tribes that could not be encumbered with impedimenta had to be satisfied with pitchis or shallow bark carrying-bowls.

The materials used in the manufacture of baskets varied with the district. The simpler types were plaited from palm or pandanus leaves with the stalks folded over. Other materials commonly employed were bark, plaited grass and string, reeds, and split cane. With such a variety of types it is impossible to differentiate between bags and baskets. Some were so closely woven or netted that they would hold honey and water. Generally speaking, the baskets manufactured in the northern part of the continent were more elaborate and artistically constructed. The rush baskets of the southern regions are notable for their unusual shapes and fine craftsmanship.

In quite a number of districts the baskets were decorated in different ways and showed a high degree of artistry. In Arnhem Land the designs varied from plain geometrical patterns to stylised human figures, and the decorations included feathers, patterns of human hair, string and down, pandanus fibre, and feathered pendants. The contrast of red feathers and white down provided a striking effect.

Bark baskets were used in the Kimberleys and on Melville and Bathurst Islands. They were masterpieces of art, the sides joined or tied with split cane and waterproofed with wax or resin. These baskets were highly decorated with bright stylised patterns.

Baskets were made for men as well as for women, the former often having special significance in sacred rites. As well as their primary purpose as containers for personal possessions, small baskets or pouches were made for carrying pitcheri leaves (these sometimes being suspended from the neck), as cradles or "carry-alls" for babies, and larger ones of paperbark in the Cape York Peninsula for a variety of uses.

Bags, Bowls, Carrying.

BELTS. Girdles or belts made of plaited human hair, often that of deceased relatives, were worn by men and women of many tribes. The usual style of decoration was to interweave feathers with the hair, though the belt was frequently plain. There was a belief that a man's headache could be cured by wearing his wife's headband or belt. It was a test of her faithfulness, for if the headache remained he knew that she had succumbed to another man's flattery, and in that case the husband was not slow to mete out punishment. Belts were also made of animal fur, plant fibres and cane.

On Melville and Bathurst Islands, which were notable for their material culture, the apparel worn at initiation ceremonies included belts with panels of human hair and bark string, the edges being sewn with split cane. The belts were painted with white pipeclay and covered with conventional designs.

Men carried stone axes and boomerangs in their belts, leaving their hands free for holding spears and throwing-sticks and, in time of war, the heavy nulla nullas. Amongst women the dilly bag, their mop of clay-daubed hair, and

BELT

their hair belt carried all the utensils and implements needed on long journeys.

One of the most important gifts that a young man received at the time of initiation was the belt made by his mother or other relatives from the hair of his relations.

In Arnhem Land white down and parrakeet feathers were interwoven in twine; human hair belts were plain, or had painted end panels. Wide bark belts were worn by the men in western Arnhem Land. A grass, leaf or twine pubic apron was suspended from the belt, and occasionally from the back as well.

BETROTHAL. A girl was usually promised as a wife when still a child; in fact it was normally during babyhood that the promise was made. There were tribes in western Arnhem Land in which the ideal time for the betrothal was before the afterbirth had ceased to flow. The emphasis placed on early betrothal is explained by the fact that the marriage was prescribed by kinship rules and reciprocity. It was not decided lightly or impulsively by the parents.

There were several economic reasons for a system which resulted in a young woman being married to a much older man who as a rule already had one wife. As the betrothal was made to a warrior who had completed the tests of manhood, the girl was assured of protection until she reached the age of puberty. The parents, who congratulated themselves in providing for her welfare, had also subscribed to an insurance policy in their own favour: their future son-in-law had reached the age when he had proved his skill as a hunter. He was therefore expected to provide his future bride's parents with regular gifts of food in acknowledgment of the declared relationship. When the baby was promised to him in marriage, the prospective bridegroom had a long period of gift-making ahead of him. If the girl ran away or refused to obey her parents when she reached maturity, the unhappy "husband" had a legitimate grievance to work off. The possibility was somewhat remote, because tribal opinion would be against her, and any disciplinary measures taken (and they would not be light) would be condoned, and no one would be likely to interfere.

The system of family relationships governed the choice to a large degree. The most common method was for the arrangements to be made by parents, mother's brother, or maternal grandmother's brother, and the mother's brother. In some tribes it was virtually compulsory for a married man to see that his sister's daughter was married to his wife's mother's brother. As

Elkin has shown, this exchange of nieces between two men of succeeding generation levels left no choice for a girl to express her preference for a man of her own age and choice.

The effect on young men who had reached the full strength of manhood, and whose majority had been recognised, must not be neglected. It must have been frustrating, to say the least, for such a young stalwart in the full vigour of life to realise that the young women of his own age, whom he longed to marry, were committed to much older men, and indeed often to grizzled veterans who already had more than one wife and who looked to the young women to work for them. This in turn accounted for elopements, and for marriage raids on a neighbouring tribe, where the dangers were equally severe, but did not usually merit the disapproval of their own people. In other words, if the young man got away with his life and the young woman he had seized, it was regarded as the fortune of war.

Even when the age-level was equal the woman had little say in her destiny, for she might be given as a wife or simply "lent" to turn aside the anger of members of an avenging expedition. If her betrothed husband died before the marriage was consummated, she was normally given to one of his brothers. Yet in spite of a woman's subservience to older relatives, lack of courtship, and marriage to a husband much older than herself, most unions were happy, and real affection was displayed by husband and wife.

BILLABONGS. In the Wiradjuri dialect of New South Wales, billa is a river, and bung is a root word "to cut" or "to cut off", hence the term billabung or billabong is properly applied to a stretch of water isolated from a river (river cut or broken). In 1862 W. Landsborough wrote: ". . . a dried-up tributary of the Gregory, which I named the Macadam. Note: In the south, such a creek as the Macadam is termed a *billy-bonn*, from the circumstance of the water carrier returning from it with his pitcher (*billy*) empty (*bong*, literally *dead*)." It was an ingenious explanation, but there seems no reason to doubt the correctness of the term "dead water" to define a pool isolated from its parent river, and filled intermittently in time of flood. Such pools made fruitful hunting grounds, providing fish, waterlily roots and other vegetable food, as well as wildfowl which came to the water to drink. Regularly used seasonal camping places were established near them. The word is also used loosely for ponds and small lagoons.

BILLABONG

BIRDS. Birds were prominent in many of the creation legends, and some ingenious explanations were provided for their individual characteristics. The Native Companion, for instance, was supposed by one tribe to have been a young woman who danced divinely. She was captured by the Wurrawilberoos, the whirlwind spirits, and was never seen again. Some time later, when a Native Companion was seen stepping lightly as though in a dance, the tribespeople knew that the greatly admired girl had returned to them in this form. The most mischievous bird in many folklore tales was Wahn the Crow, whose great antagonist was Mullyan the Eaglehawk, the messenger of Baiame.

Birds were one of the more important elements in the food supply of the Aborigines.

Chief among them was the emu, which provided a satisfying meal for a large family. Emus were captured with nets, killed with spears and boomerangs, or trapped in pits.

Smaller birds were killed with throwing-sticks or clubs. Parrots, parrakeets, ducks, and other flock birds were captured in nets. Tribes which used boomerangs sent them circling like hawks, so that the bewildered birds dived into nets suspended from the branches of trees across a break in the forest.

Ducks were caught in an ingenious manner. The hunter submerged himself in a lagoon or river, sometimes breathing through a hollow reed, the end of which was above water. In this way he was able to creep up unsuspectedly, drag the duck under water by its legs, and drown it, or wring its neck. This was done so quietly that several birds could be killed without disturbing the others.

Cockatoos were caught in Queensland by smearing a viscous gum on the branches of trees. The birds alighted on them and were unable to escape.

Feathers and down of various birds were used for decorative purposes. While the emu is one of the commonest subjects in Aboriginal art and ritual, other birds were comparatively rare motifs.

Art, Food, Hunting.

BIRTH. Before the birth of a child a number of tabus had to be observed by the mother and father. They varied in different regions. One example of this was a prohibition against eating fish which had been caught with a hook and line, lest the child should be strangled. Magic in several forms entered into the period of waiting, and was sometimes employed to determine or influence the baby's sex before it was born. In some tribes women wore a small bag round the neck at this time. If a boy was wanted, it contained a miniature spear; if a girl, a small representation of a dilly bag. In the event of these preparations failing to give the desired result, it was imagined that their power had been defeated by a superior magic, or that the birth spirits were more powerful than the medicine man, and that his ideas differed from theirs.

Births occurred not infrequently when a group was on a walkabout. The expectant mother remained behind with a female companion, or by herself. After the baby was born and she had rested briefly, she hurried after the others to reach camp before darkness fell, carrying the baby in her wooden coolamon. Daisy Bates wrote that on the day of the child's birth the mother might go on a journey of 30 miles when the group was travelling.

In more settled conditions, when the group was camped round a waterhole or at a permanent camp site, the birth took place at a little distance. No men or unmarried women were allowed to be present. A small shelter or windbreak was built if the weather was wet or cold, but this was the only protection. Birth usually came easily, whether in camp or on the march, but if help was required, the woman's mother or other female relatives gave assistance. In the few difficult cases, a medicine man was called on to recite spells.

Although an important event in the experience of the family group, little attention was paid to it, and in only a few cases were rites of any kind observed.

In such a simple and natural act there is little to tell of the procedure, but it has been recorded that among the tribes of the Great Victoria Desert the mother squatted over a hole in the ground and had her back rubbed by an old woman. When the child was born the umbilical cord was twisted, cut with a sharp knife, and made into a ring which was placed round the baby's neck to keep it from crying, or put in a bag and worn round the mother's neck.

The child's delicate light skin was rubbed with a mixture of fat and ashes to protect it from the sun until it turned dark in colour. When infanticide was necessary, as when the group was on walkabout, food was scarce, or an older child had not been weaned, it was dispatched mercifully with a blow on the head, or by some other means.

Families varied greatly in size, perhaps with several wives and a dozen or more children, but usually there were four or five, and in times of drought and food scarcity families were much smaller.

Babies, Conception, Children, Pre-existence, Reincarnation.

BLOOD. Blood was the symbol and source of life; it was sacred, linking physical life with spiritual powers, giving vitality and strength to men. For this reason it entered largely into religious ceremonies, especially of fertility and initiation rites. In the latter case blood-letting occurred invariably, either from the arm or the genital organ. It was smeared over the participants or drunk sacramentally, in which case it symbolised the life-spirit of the totemic ancestor of the group. In a few cases red ochre was used in a form of sympathetic magic.

It is difficult to overestimate the importance of blood in increase and manhood rites. Not only did it impart new life to young men, who had died to their immature past, it also admitted them into the secret society of their elders. It conferred power to endure the sacred rites and to absorb the secret knowledge into which the young men were being initiated.

In many cases the thighs of the participants became splashed with blood as they took part in the sacred dances, while their bodies were painted in symbolic patterns with red ochre and down which was fixed to the body with blood. Blood from a novitiate's arm was sometimes allowed to drop on to a sacred object which represented his totemic lodge, thus vitalising it and conferring the power within it upon the donor of blood.

Blood was used to anoint the stone symbols which marked and perpetuated the presence of the totemic ancestor of the region, or of the animals associated with him. In the increase ceremonies the sacred stones were cleaned and blood was allowed to drop on them to represent new life given to the ancestral spirit. In return the ancestor gave life to the tribe and to the animals and other food products on which it depended.

Blood taken from the heart was dried and preserved as a means of restoring vitality to others. This was one of the secret acts performed by sorcerers, who believed its power to be effective in black magic, especially when they had removed the kidney fat from a victim and wished to keep him alive until his second death a few days later.

Increase rites, Initiation rites, Rainbow Serpent.

BOARDS, SACRED. Ranging in length from several inches to many feet, these sacred objects had an important part to play in ceremonies. They were usually painted red and carved in naturalistic or linear designs and kept in secret hiding places when not in use. The painted designs represented the sacred pathways of the ancestral spirits.

Sacred objects.

BONE. The heads of spears and a few knives were sometimes made from bone. Bone was especially efficacious in sorcery, the most notable use being that of "pointing bones", which were made from kangaroo or human bone.

Marrow from bones of animals and emus was often the first solid food given to a baby. In districts where tribes had permanent camps, human bones were sometimes preserved after death until their final interment, and often carried about for several months until this occurred.

Burial, Knives, Magic, Pointing bones, Spears.

BOOMERANGS. Contrary to popular belief this typical and almost unique type of weapon was not in universal use throughout the continent, and the majority of boomerangs were not of the returning type.

Returning boomerangs were used in eastern and western Australia but not in Central Australia or the Northern Territory. The boomerang was usually flat on one side and slightly convex on the other, thin, and curved like a eucalypt leaf. Its shape enabled the non-returning boomerang to travel in a comparatively straight line, achieving accuracy in aim. It was longer and heavier than the returning type, and was used in fighting and hunting. The returning boomerang had a longitudinal twist so that the two arms were in different planes. It has been suggested that the purpose of this development was to ensure that, when hunting wildfowl, the weapon would not fall in the water and sink, the wood being too heavy to float. According to this theory, the birds were startled by the sound of the boomerang as it whirled through the air. They flew to the shelter of the reeds by the bank of the billabong or river and so were driven into a net, and the boomerang returned to the thrower at the end of its flight. Although it was used in this way in the Murray and Darling River districts and elsewhere in eastern Australia to frighten birds into a trap, the returning boomerang was generally regarded more as a plaything than as a weapon. Skilful throwers were able to make it describe up to five decreasing circles as it returned to their feet. The weapon was thrown directly into the air or made to bounce off one end, thus giving added force to the flight.

The boomerang developed from its simple throwing-stick form in two or three distinct directions. One of the variations was a plain stick rounded in section, as used in South Australia and western Queensland for killing birds and small animals, and in hand-to-hand fighting.

Another variation in northern and central areas had a hooked end, and was known in some places as a warradulla; it has been described as a "diabolical weapon". One end was shaped into a flat pick or hooked projection. The weapon was thrown at an opponent. If he attempted to parry it, it is said that the weapon would catch on the edge of his shield and swing round with lethal force. It was probably also used as a fighting pick.

The third type was the returning boomerang, unknown in the western half of South Australia, Cape York, northern Kimberley and Arnhem Land. Throwing the returning boom-

erang was a favourite sport for men and boys, and where it was in use, frequent contests were held. Spectacular feats were performed, both in the length of the throw, accuracy of aim, and in the complexity of the manoeuvres. A skilful player could throw his boomerang 70 or 80 yards, after which it would make a sharp turn, fly over his head and behind him for another 30 or 40 yards, turn again and gradually curve round, losing height until it fell at his feet. Another test of skill was to make the boomerang fall within the compass of a small circle, or near a peg, at the conclusion of its flight. The ingenious development of the returning boomerang was a remarkable achievement unique to Australia. A popular feature of these contests was to see men and youths dodging the boomerang as a test of skill in avoiding weapons in combat.

In 1830 R. Dawson, in *The Present State of Australia*, wrote: "We gambolled all the way up, throwing small pieces of bark at each other, after the manner of the native youths, who practise this with a view of strengthening their arms, and fitting them for hurling a curious weapon of war called a 'bomering'." It should be noticed that boomerang was pronounced bummerang in many districts. Some students have thought it might have a connection with the word for wind, which in the Hunter River district was boomori. In southwestern Western Australia, the weapon was known as a kylie.

To make a good boomerang required experience in selecting the right branch of the tree, and patience and skill in shaping it to the desired curve and thickness. For the returning type the wood was heated and bent over the fire until it assumed the right degree of twist. The weapons were usually decorated by painting or inscribing; they were used as sticks for beating time for the rhythm of a dance as well as for hunting and sport, the ends for digging and cutting meat, the edge as a fire-saw. The word boomerang came from the George's River, Sydney, but different names were given to it in other tribal languages.

Clapping-sticks, Drums, Throwing-sticks.

BORA GROUNDS. The sacred place reserved for initiation or bora ceremonies usually consisted of two cleared circles connected by a

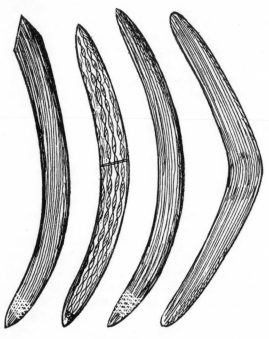

BOOMERANGS

path. Carved trees, ground figures and other sacred objects were a feature of the south-east Australian bora grounds. The inner circle was so sacred that women were not allowed near it. Originally it was a term used by the tribes of New South Wales, but it is now applied generally to the secret ground or ring in eastern Australia. Elkin believes that the smaller bora represented the sky world.

BORA GROUND

The bora itself was the rite of initiation, and may have been derived from bur (Kamilaroi tribe), which meant circle or girdle. As the bora ground was circular, and the girdle was the insignia of manhood, there may well have been a double meaning in the word.

Initiation ceremonies.

BOUNDARIES. While each tribe had its own recognised territory to which it was bound by the strongest ties, the boundaries were seldom clearly recognised. Inadvertent trespass of neighbouring country was not regarded seriously, unless the trespass threatened the economy of the home tribe. Visits for hunting and social purposes were customary but serious invasions, such as a party of young men intent on capturing wives for themselves, led to bloody fighting. The boundaries were frequently defined by rivers, mountains, and other natural features, but it was the recognition of mythological and totemic sites which really defined the territorial rights of a tribe or subtribe.

The ancestral spirits and heroes travelled along well-defined routes, marking their progress by forming natural features. Each tribe owned part of the myth, which consisted of the deeds of the ancestor, songs, dances, and mime associated with that part of the journey and, in particular, the totemic and other sacred sites which were consecrated by his continuing presence. The boundaries, therefore, were roughly defined by geographical features beyond which the sacred part of the journey— legend, song, and dance—could not be told or performed.

These religious beliefs prevented disputes over the possession of land. Every waterhole, stream, lagoon, hill, depression, and plain was not only known and named but was also a place of peculiar spiritual or economic significance. It could not be claimed by another group, for its leading man had no authority within its mythology, ritual, and sacred rites.

Hunting rights over part of the territory might be accorded to another local group, but there was never any temptation for visitors to linger or outstay their welcome. They were not "at home" away from their own sacred country, to which they were firmly bound by links with their totemic sites. Without religious associations boundaries were practically nonexistent; in fact there were sterile areas of no importance simply because they were either barren, too rugged, or were not on the tracks of the ancestors. Such areas could be mutually occupied by adjacent tribes. Outside the known localities of the spirit ancestors there was also territory for hunting and collecting food.

Tribal territory varied greatly in size, depending on the fertility of the land and the number of groups it was able to support.

Ancestors, Smoke, Tribes.

BOWLS. The commonest type of bowl used for domestic purposes was the oval, shallow, wooden or bark dish generally known as a coolamon. It was an all-purpose utensil, used for carrying water, honey, grass seed, and other foods, and as a portable cradle for babies. When a group was on walkabout it was one of the few possessions essential for daily life. Amongst other things it was essential for winnowing seed for flour-making. Women carried it under their arms or on their heads.

The interior of the bowl was hollowed out and kept as light in weight as possible. Some were patiently cut from gum trees, or more easily from a soft timber such as that of the bean tree in north-eastern Queensland. Where possible a swelling on a tree trunk was hacked

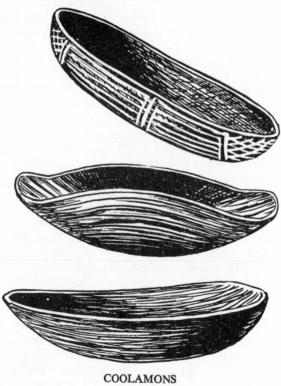

COOLAMONS

off with a stone tool, so that the bottom of the bowl was roughly the proper shape before the interior was hollowed out. Roughly made bark coolamons were quickly made but the wooden ones involved considerable labour. They varied in shape from shallow dishes under a foot long

to large elongate bowls 3 feet in length. The wooden and bark vessels were used largely in central, north-western and eastern Australia. The baler, helmet, and nautilus shells were also used for holding water.

Coolamon, coolaman, or kooliman was a word in use in the Wiradjuri language of New South Wales. It may have been derived either from kulu (seed) or kolle (water), for the vessel was used to contain both. Early writers say that coolamons "were made of the inner layer of the bark of the stringy-bark tree", and that they were "made out of the bark which covers an excrescence peculiar to a kind of gum-tree".

The gnarl which grows on certain eucalypts was cut off and cleaned out to form a deep bucket-like container in eastern Queensland and New South Wales. Stringybark sheets were folded and tied (and also skewered) in eastern Australia and Arnhem Land, while temporary bowls were made from sheets of paperbark in the same way.

Babies, Baskets, Seeds.

BOYS. The Aboriginal boy had a carefree existence in his early years. A baby boy was welcomed by the parents as a potential warrior, hunter, and food provider for the future, and because he would eventually become the recipient of the age-old lore and ritual passed on from one generation to another. But unless he had been preceded by a number of sisters he might be no more welcome than a girl baby who, in her own way, could provide food, and whose future husband, to whom she was dedicated from birth, would be required to make gifts of food to the parents.

From a very early age the hunting instinct was encouraged amongst boys. They played at being men, and began to develop their powers as hunters. At first their energy was devoted to hunting small game—lizards, spiders, and insects—tracking them to their lairs, killing, roasting, and eating them. From such small beginnings they developed the skills on which the group to which they belonged would some day depend. They loved to imitate their fathers, but seldom had the opportunity to accompany them on hunting expeditions until they had developed the strength and endurance that came with adolescence.

Boys threw grass reeds and sticks as soon as they could handle them, and thin short spears until they were initiated. Part of their daily life was this play training in the handling of the weapon, balance, and dexterity in throwing. Gradually their toy armoury increased until they were familiar with several kinds of striking and throwing weapons; then they began to use them in contests with other boys. Pitched battles were held, watched over by observant elders who cared little if a boy was hurt, but very much indeed if he were inexpert, showed signs of fear, or winced when he was injured.

This carefree existence suddenly came to an end about the age of 12. As he approached puberty the boy became more self-assertive and rougher with his companions. His mother, and other women in the group, were quick to note the change. As a small boy he had been almost entirely dependent on them, though he had always been proud when his father or other full-grown men took notice of him.

There came a day when his mother, ably supported by her friends and relatives, picked up their sticks and drove the boy, together with companions of his own age, to a section of the camp to fend for themselves. It may well have been a moment of disillusionment when, severed from the comfort of the camp fires and the reassuring presence of others at night, fed from the communal store of food, he had to support himself by his own efforts. Alone, or in the company of two or three friends, he had to apply the make-believe play of childhood to real life. A handful of insects and small lizards were not enough to keep hunger at bay, and if he needed to build a windbreak, or light a fire to cook food and to keep him warm at night, he had only his two hands to help him.

He soon found that it was a man's job to capture a nimble wallaby or a fleet-footed emu, but he was forced to keep at it until the moment of triumph when his spear or boomerang was red with the blood of his prey. But further disillusionment was in store. Staggering proudly into the camp with the limp body on his shoulders, it was quickly taken from him, cooked, and shared amongst others, while his own portion was one of the less palatable morsels.

He was not to know with what pride his mother and father had observed him, nor to hear the favourable grunts of the elders. In their eyes he was learning to become a man, and these were the disciplines which led to true manhood. Already he had probably endured the pain and discomfort of one of the bodily initiation operations, such as nose-boring, tooth evulsion or, in some regions, circumcision; and so the young boys in a camp continued to improve their skill in the chase and to become entirely self-reliant and self-supporting. Physically and mentally each had changed during the period of trial, until he was ready for the most important step of his life. Before him lay the later ordeals of the initiation rites—after which he would be a man.

Babies, Children, Circumcision, Games, Initiation ceremonies.

BULL-ROARERS. The toy which is known to most children as a bull-roarer consists of a thin, flat piece of wood suspended from a string at one end. It is whirled round and round at arm's length, turning on its axis, and making a whirring sound which grows louder the faster it is swung. It is used in many parts of the world, and frequently has some sacred significance, but to no one more than to the Australian Aboriginal. To him it was the voice of a great ancestral spirit and so holy that it might not be seen by women in most areas. In speaking of it the women used a different name to that used by men. In one district men and boys called it gayandi, the women gurraymi. Both words meant bora spirit; but amongst many tribes women and children were ignorant of the cause of the sound, believing that it emanated direct from spirits or devils.

The bull-roarer was a sacred object which must be hidden from sight and used only during initiation rites and other important ceremonies. Even its hiding places were so sacred that a hunted animal which took refuge there was safe from harm.

There have been occasional examples of stone bull-roarers, but normally they were made of wood, varying in length from 6 inches to 3 feet, and from one to 4 or 5 inches in width. They seldom exceeded a quarter of an inch in thickness, and were made in various shapes, some being thin and slender, others in the form of a broader oval. Because of the reverence in which they were held, it was customary for them to be decorated with paint, or more usually with incised totemic designs in which spirals were a dominant feature.

Small bull-roarers were known as "woman-drawers", and were termed nurmi or nama. Their notes were thin, like high-pitched singing. In "The Song of the Woman-Drawer" Dame Mary Gilmore wrote:

> I am the woman-drawer;
>   Pass me not by;
> I am the secret voice,
>   Hear ye me cry;
>
> I am that power which night
>   Looses abroad;
> I am the root of life;
>   I am the chord.

In this way men used spirit powers to draw women to them; but the purpose of bull-roarers was normally far more important than this. Only men who were fully initiated were allowed to use them; only the wisest men were able to understand what the voice of the bull-roarer said.

At the time of initiation the candidate left the women's part of the camp and heard the bull-roarers wailing in the distance. The sound was the voice of the spirit or god to whom he was to be dedicated, who would swallow him and reject him; this was the ritual of death and rebirth into the sacred life of a grown man.

These sounding instruments, which did not sing but spoke with the voices of the Dreamtime, served several purposes. They warned off the uninitiated from the bora ground, expressed feelings of friendship between initiated men, thereby proclaiming a unity and purpose in common life, and symbolised the totemic ancestors of the tribe, or of the Creator spirit himself. Mrs Bates has recorded that bull-roarers, which were the most sacred objects of Central Australia, were traded by the Bibbulmun of south-east Western Australia, and their children used them as playthings; but this was most unusual.

Ceremonies, Love magic, Reincarnation, Sacred objects.

BUNYIPS. Monsters which were supposed to haunt swamps and billabongs. Many legends feature these fearsome creatures, which appeared in several forms. A typical bunyip was Moolgewanke which lived in the waters of Lake Alexandrina, and had a booming voice which caused rheumatism among the people who were unfortunate enough to hear it. Moolgewanke was half man, half fish, with a thick mop of reeds in the place of hair. But there were many other descriptions, such as half horse, half crocodile; bigger than an elephant, in shape like a bullock, with eyes like live coals, and tusks like a walrus's; a monster with countless eyes and ears, with sharp claws, and able to run so fast that it was difficult to escape him. The hollow booming so often heard on the margin of reedy swamps, more hollow and louder by night than by day, was the voice of the bunyip—even though sceptical white men might ascribe it to the lonely bittern. The Aborigines' belief in such powerful spirit beings as the Rainbow Serpent which dwelt in waterholes and rivers may be the basis of legends of the bunyip.

BURDENS.
  Carrying.

BURIAL CUSTOMS. There was no universal procedure for the disposal of the dead. The main methods were interment, cremation, platform or tree disposal, mummification or desiccation, and exposure. In some cases there were forms of temporary burial, in which one or more of the above processes was employed. In a few instances ritual cannibalism, an eating of a small portion of the dead, was one of the rites observed by the mourners, but in some areas part of the body was eaten as the first stage in delayed disposal.

Prior to burial of any type it was usual to make some preparation of the corpse, but here again there was no uniformity in treatment. The following procedures were observed by different tribes. The deceased's hair was cut off and woven into a girdle which was worn by the man who sought to avenge his death, finally being preserved as a sacred object. The body might be painted with the totemic design of the clan, or coated with red ochre, a practice that was observed in Arnhem Land. Amongst some of the tribes in New South Wales a man's body was wrapped in a possum skin rug and his weapons placed by his head. In Queensland a few treasured possessions were given to close relatives, and the remainder buried. Elsewhere they were burned. It was not uncommon in eastern Australia for the internal organs to be removed, the body cavities packed with grass, dried, bound, and painted before disposal. An extension of this practice was to treat the body as though the deceased were about to take part in some ceremony.

In parts of Arnhem Land the decorated body was tied to a post in a sitting or standing position, while the relatives danced and sang round it as though encouraging him to return and share their life with them again. In fact the corpse was encouraged to take part in the dance. It could not do so, and so the departure of the spirit was confirmed. The invitation had been given, the deceased had rejected it, and therefore no blame could be attached to those who remained. Dancing around the body was an act of mourning, and took place nightly. It kept the deceased among the group until satisfaction for the death had been obtained.

Simple earth burial was probably the most usual form of disposal, and was practised in all parts of Australia. The body was frequently buried in a sitting position with the knees drawn up to the chin. When the earth was piled above the body in a mound, an aperture was left open to permit the spirit to escape. In the Arunta tribe the ceremony of trampling twigs on the grave a year or more later was observed. The widow, who had been forced to remain silent all the time, covered with pipeclay and wearing a head-dress of small bones, went first to the old camp, and then to the grave, yelling at the top of her voice to drive the spirit away. This convinced the lingering, disconsolate spirit that the mourning was over, and that it might take its departure.

In western districts the body was also buried in a sitting position, a woomera or shield being used as a head-rest for men, a coolamon for women. In South Australia the grave was usually dug in the side of a sandhill, the excavation lined with sticks, and the body placed in a sitting position as though crouching by a camp fire. In many places the grave was dug in the old camp site, and a new one formed at a little distance in order that the group might not be harmed by the spirit of the dead person. His name was not mentioned, and after a time the burial was forgotten, the spirit had de-

parted, and the old site could be used again with impunity.

Concern for the welfare of the departed warrior was sometimes shown by putting all his possessions on top of the grave and covering them with a sheet of bark to protect them from the weather. The bark was anchored with large stones and a bark hut built over it, where the spirit was able to live for a while in comfort after the clan had taken its departure. Fires were lit in some places to keep the spirit warm at night.

In parts of Victoria and eastern New South Wales and in northern Queensland the body was burnt and a mound of earth built over the ashes. The calcined bones were sometimes placed in a hollow tree. There were occasions when an emergency prevented earth burial, and the body was disposed of in this way. More frequently cremation was the last act in the funerary sequence.

The practice of platform or tree-stage disposal was widespread in the north-western third of the continent, but was performed in many different ways. In northern Central Australia, for example, the body was placed on a platform erected in the branches of a tree. In a few localities there were groves of trees which could be described as cemeteries because of the number of bodies there disposed of in this manner. Frequently it was only one stage of a delayed burial rite. In Arnhem Land the body was smeared with red ochre and then painted with the clan totem symbols and was placed in a tree so that when the spirit went to the afterworld, other spirits would know what tribe it came from, and what sacred places it had frequented while on earth. At times the body was wrapped in sheets of bark.

Mummification or desiccation was an important element in platform disposal, and was often observed in the Torres Strait area and northern Queensland. After exposure the bones were placed in a bark coffin painted with the clan design of the dead person. It was carried by the women to all the places visited by the deceased person when he was alive until it was handed over to the men for the final rite, which consisted of placing it in a cave or waterhole spirit centre. Amongst some Arnhem Land tribes the bones were smashed and thrown in a hollow and beautifully decorated post. On the Lower Murray the body was placed in a sitting position, with arms outstretched, on a low platform, and a fire lit underneath. After a while the corpse was removed, the body apertures closed, and rubbed all over with fat, after which it was returned to the platform and placed in a hut which had been built on it. The fires were kept going until the body was completely dried. It was carried from place to place as the tribe moved about, and then wrapped in a mat and placed on another platform. Eventually the body disintegrated, and the skull was broken and used as a drinking-vessel. Sometimes the exudations of the drying body were rubbed on to young men to confer the good qualities of the deceased upon them.

The final stage of mummification varied from tribe to tribe. The body was mourned over for a long while and eventually disposed of by interment, cremation, or by being placed in a hollow tree. There was never any attempt at permanent mummification, for at the last the spirit returned to its ancestors, and the living person who was known to all was forgotten.

A simpler form of disposal was exposure to the elements, but this was rarely practised except after battle, when the bodies of the slain were left on the ground with their broken spears and weapons to mark the place of the fight. Mostly, however, the dead were taken away for proper disposal. Nevertheless, there were occasions when a dying person was left by a camp fire. He met death alone, and his people made no attempt to return to the spot. Island and sea-coast tribes occasionally placed the body in a small canoe and let it drift out to sea.

In the Kimberleys an unusual practice was observed with men who had been killed for trespass. A shallow hole was dug in a termite mound and the body left there. The termites repaired the breach quickly, and the body was so effectively concealed that a party bound on revenge was unable to find it.

Cannibalism was rare and confined to the ritual eating of a small portion of the flesh. It occurred in northern Queensland and north-eastern South Australia and was observed only by close relatives.

Such practices as tree disposal, mummification, exposure, and cannibalism were usually only part of the funerary rites. In parts of Central Australia, for instance, the body was placed on a tree platform until the flesh disappeared. The bones were removed, the skull broken, and with the exception of an arm bone which was given to the mother of the deceased if she were still alive, the skeleton was buried in a termite mound. The final ceremonies were then performed, the arm bone broken in two and buried in the ground. The double ceremony emphasised the grief of the relatives.

It was not unusual for the bones to be collected and carried about for some time, but finally they were disposed of in some convenient location. Where they were allowed to remain in the grave the site was covered with heavy logs. The final act, whether it was re-interment or disposal of the bones in a cave, totemic coffin, or hollow tree, was marked by a special mourning ceremony as a prelude to the dismissal of the deceased from the life and thought of the group.

In considering such elaborate procedures, however, it should be noted that these customs were as a rule reserved for elders or those who had held an important position in the tribe on account of their knowledge of sacred matters.

In spite of the fact that a man's name and personality seldom lived on in his group permanently, lavishly decorated grave posts were erected in some places, and provided suitable locations for the deceased person's mourning dances. They are found on Melville and Bathurst Islands, where earth burial itself was an elaborate rite. Months of hard work went into the making of these posts, which were made from the trunks of trees. Three or four were erected first, and more at the time of final interment. Tree trunks were carved beside the graves of notable men in eastern New South Wales.

No matter how much local customs differed, the intention always remained the same: the deceased person had rejected the companionship of the common life, and his spirit was hustled on its way to its next or final home, lest it remain or return to cause trouble for the living.

Cannibalism, Death, Inquest, Mourning, Possessions, Posts, Spirits, Spirit worlds.

BUSHCRAFT. To conceal his own tracks, to discern the tracks of other people, no matter how carefully they had been effaced, and to follow the spoor of animals, was part of the training of every Aboriginal boy. His powers of observation were highly developed. The habits and haunts of every animal, bird, and reptile were known. The safety of the group, his family and himself depended on this knowledge, together with: the ability to discern changes in the seasons where to look for food, whether it was digging for yams or spending days on the trail of a wallaby; and to know the exact location of every waterhole in the tribal territory. Although it was the product of years of training and experience, the Aboriginal's ability to go straight to a waterhole appeared uncanny to the early travellers. Women as well as men possessed this wonderful knowledge of their environment and its living creatures and plants.

Adaptation to a hostile environment over hundreds and thousands of years had brought the Aboriginal as close to Nature as any primitive race, and they turned their knowledge to practical use. Where others would have starved or died of thirst, the Aborigines supported life adequately by their knowledge of bushcraft, and adapted it to the type of country which was their spiritual as well as their material home. On stony deserts, in dense bush or heavy jungle, they moved with sureness and purpose.

Fishing, Food, Hunting, Tracking.

C

CAMPS. Regular camp sites existed in fertile, well-watered parts of the country, being revisited when the seasonal foods obtainable there became plentiful. Such camps were moved only in flood time, or when all the members of the group went to some other place where a seasonal supply of food was to be found in abundance. There were favoured places where geese, swans, or ducks congregated and eggs could be gathered by the thousand. On such occasions, the scattered clans and family groups came together and held sacred ceremonies as well as the social dances called corroborees.

In the desert, especially during long, dry seasons, conditions were very different. The groups were constantly on the move in search of water and fresh game. They remained in one place only until water or food ran short, and always shifted camp when a death occurred. In many cases only one night could be spent on a single location, so close were the people to death, but with senses sharpened by the battle against Nature, they went systematically and contentedly through the day's round.

Each morning the women rose at dawn, as soon as they could discern bushes and trees in the growing light, taking their coolamons to bring water to their husbands and children. "This," said Tindale and Lindsay, "is an aboriginal woman's hour of abject misery", and in the cold and cheerless dawn of winter it must surely have been a recurring trial. Life was dependent on water, but it was often a slow laborious process to secure even a few drops. Douglas Lockwood quotes an Aboriginal as saying: "When I was a boy our waterholes were so scarce that they were secret. We called them jilla, which means they gave us life."* In the western desert tribes the one word denoted "camp" and "water", and the only place to camp was at a water-hole.

After the day's travel, when the next waterhole had been reached and before darkness set in, the men set up the shelters and windbreaks while the women brought in the vegetables, grubs, and other food they had been gathering,

* *We, the Aborigines,* Cassell, page 185.

and began to prepare the evening meal. The shelters were set up in such a manner as to protect the sleepers against the wind. They were made of brushwood, about 2 or 3 feet in height, and arranged in the shape of a semi-circle.

If conditions were favourable for a reasonably long stay, bark lean-tos or huts might be erected when the weather was cold at night. Rock shelters and hollow trees were also used when they were available, but caves were avoided as sleeping places unless it was essential to find shelter from inclement weather. In the miniature, temporary "villages", there were strict rules for the siting of windbreaks and huts, even to the routes by which members of the group passed from one shelter to another.

Except during corroborees there were no communal fires. Each small family unit made its own fire. Sleeping pads of fern, grass, leaves, and twigs were placed on the ground in the shelter of the windbreak, or else the family lay naked on the bare earth. After the hot, sunny days the nights could be bitterly cold. Men and women could seldom hope for unbroken sleep. With a fire at their feet and another on either side during the coldest nights, and a pile of logs close at hand, the family settled down. The wood for the fires was shaped like a T with a short stem. The smaller log was replaced at frequent intervals throughout the night, as soon as a sleeper was wakened by the cold. Boughs were often arranged radially and pushed further inwards as the night progressed. This might happen several times in an hour.

When dingoes had been tamed for hunting purposes, they slept alongside their owners. Warm skin rugs such as were used in the more permanent camps in southern districts would have been welcome under these circumstances, but desert tribes on walkabout could not afford to carry any surplus weight.

Mothers and fathers, together with small children and girls, slept together, but after a certain age uninitiated boys and young men were required to sleep in a separate part of the encampment. Latrines were not used. When the environs of the camp became soiled the tribespeople knew that it was time to move on.

Huts, Rest, Sleeping, Walkabout, Water-holes.

CANNIBALISM. While the practice of cannibalism was reported from several regions, in every case it had some ritual significance, and was sparingly indulged in. It was part of burial custom, before or after the body had been exposed on a tree platform, or when the body was mummified. A small part of the flesh was eaten by close relatives in order to gain some part of the strength of the deceased person, and was a symbolic act. Pieces of the flesh were also carried about for a lengthy period if the dead relative had been a noted hunter. It has been reported that in the vicinity of Goulburn Island, and on the island itself, three holes were dug. Some of the organs were destroyed by fire before being buried, while others were interred at once. The third and largest hole was an oven. The body was placed in it and the flesh cooked and divided amongst the relatives. In no case was cannibalism indulged in to satisfy the appetite nor, so far as we can tell, for purposes of revenge.

It should be noted that Mrs Daisy Bates in *The Passing of the Aborigines* gives a number of examples of cannibalism, and states: "Cannibalism had its local name from Kimberley to Eucla, and through all the unoccupied country east of it, and there were many grisly rites attached thereto. Human meat had always been their favourite food, and there were many killing vendettas from time immemorial." This opinion has not been seriously recorded elsewhere. There had been considerable degeneration amongst the tribes to whom Mrs Bates ministered, owing to the disruption of their natural life by the white man. More factual information records that men killed in ritual battles at the conclusion of initiation ceremonies in the Blackall Ranges in Queensland during the bunya-bunya wet season were eaten by the participants. Flesh from the limbs, thighs, and stomach of the dead were eaten in south-eastern Australia. According to Spencer and Gillen, tribes on the southern coast of the Gulf of Carpentaria and inland ate the bodies of the dead as part of delayed disposal, the bones being placed in a paperbark parcel in a tree.

Burial customs.

DUGOUT CANOE

CANOES. By means of bark canoes for rivers and lakes and an occasional dugout canoe, and with log canoes (with or without outriggers) in coastal districts, the Aborigines were able to fish and to make journeys of some length between the mainland and the offshore islands. Bark canoes were seen by Captain Cook and others on the open sea off the coast of New South Wales. They were used for fishing in the swell around the rocky headlands at the entrance to Port Jackson.

Although rafts and dugouts must have been used to transport the first-comers to Australia from the northern island groups, the bark canoe seems to represent the first stage of development in many parts of the continent. Their frailty and short length of life were compensated for by the ease with which they were made and handled. It was usual to choose a straight stringybark tree and encircle it with two cuts about 10 feet apart. A vertical cut was made between the two rings and the sheet prised off with sticks. As a rule the rough outer bark was burnt off. Several feet at each end were scraped thinner to make the bark more pliable for shaping. In northern Australia the sheet of bark, up to 15 or more feet in length and perhaps 5 feet across, was held over a fire to soften it. It was then folded lengthways and the ends sewn together with cane or strong fibre. To give further strength the top edge was bound with vines and strengthened with light poles, and thwarts of cord or sticks were placed transversely to retain the shape. The canoe was light and strong enough for the work that was required of it.

Bark canoes were universal in eastern Australia and Arnhem Land, dugouts with one or two outriggers in Cape York. The south-east Australian bark canoe was folded and tied at the ends, the northern ones were sewn. The bark canoes of the Darling-Murray River systems were basin-like in shape and stopped with mud at one end.

Bark canoes were propelled by poles in the shallows, by wooden paddles in deeper water, or with pieces of bark. A carefully constructed bark canoe, well strengthened and bound with vines, could stand up to a certain amount of hard use, and lasted a long time when kept in quiet streams and lakes.

The simpler types of dugout canoe were made from light logs roughly hollowed out, with the ends trimmed to a sharp edge. Such canoes could be made in a few days when half a dozen people worked on them with stone axes or adzes. Except when equipped with an outrigger, the largest dugout canoes seldom exceeded 20 feet in length, carrying seven or eight people. On the northern coasts they were used for fishing, for turtle and dugong hunting, and for providing transport to nearby islands. Except when equipped with an outrigger they were rather unstable and unsuited to rough seas, but their instability was offset by the fact that they were unsinkable.

The Arnhem Land dugout was made from the trunk of a giant paperbark tree, which has a tough, hard, fine-grained wood. The making of these canoes involved much heavy labour. The Cape York dugouts were made of a lighter timber—probably one of the giant fig tree species. Both types were well made, the Cape York one having a harpooning platform at each end. The Arnhem Land dugout was very stable under sail in a swell and journeys of up to 20

miles or more to offshore islands were commonly made during the south-east trade winds. The north-west monsoon weather is too rough even for mission luggers, and could not be braved in dugout canoes.

It was in the north that the art of canoe-making reached its highest development. The canoes were well shaped, with ridges for seats (board seats in the dugouts), and sometimes equipped with stone anchors and sails woven from the leaves of the pandanus palm. The Macassan-type sails measured up to 15 by 10 feet. The bark canoe used on the rivers and lagoons had a knife-sharp prow which enabled it to force its way through water weeds.

On the northern coast, New Guinea and Indonesian influences were apparent. Many of the canoes on the eastern coast of Cape York Peninsula were equipped with outriggers and carried a crew of twenty or more, together with a load of supplies. Voyages were frequently made from Bathurst and Melville Islands to the mainland and back in simple dugout canoes, and in such cases well-made paddles were used.

Rafts.

CAPS, WIDOWS'. Amongst certain tribes in the Darling River to Cape Eyre region widows were forced to wear a heavy head-dress of clay during the period of mourning. It was finally placed in or on the grave of the deceased husband.

Mourning.

CARPENTARIANS. According to a new theory of Professor J. B. Birdsell and N. B. Tindale, the last of the migrations of three different peoples were the Carpentarians. The theory has not been generally accepted and scientists await the publication of evidence. The theory regards the Carpentarians as the late Australoids. They drove the preceding wave, the Murrayians, the early Australoids, southwards and occupied the greater part of the Northern Territory. They are described as tall and dark, with thin legs, and little hair on their faces and bodies. The Carpentarians came to Australia in the last wave of migration, many thousands of years ago. They were a more highly developed type than their predecessors, with superior weapons and implements.

Australoids, Origins, Tasmanians.

CARRYING. On walkabout the men carried only spears, boomerangs, and other hunting implements. It was essential that they should be free to pursue game the moment it was sighted. Their possessions varied in different parts of Australia. Fishermen carried their gear in canoes or on rafts. Hunters always carried several spears and a spear-thrower, and they might add a shield, club, or throwing-stick in their belts. On the march between camps a hafted chisel and axe would also be carried, and perhaps magic crystals, ornaments, gift exchange objects, ochres, and stone flakes in a small basket or bag. The desert men limited themselves to spears, a spear-thrower, throwing stick, and hafted chisel, and perhaps a boomerang.

The women carried all the family possessions. Few though they were, they were burdensome when children had to be managed as well but the toddlers soon learned to fend for themselves. The only "luggage" was the dilly bag and the coolamon where used, either or both of which were filled with smaller articles. Larger implements such as digging sticks and fire sticks were carried in the hand. Women became adept at carrying coolamons on their heads, and used a grass or hair ring pad to balance them. In some areas and on some occasions the women also carried grindstones, which normally were left at the regular camping places. Under these circumstances a woman might carry a load of up to 30 lb as well as a baby.

Babies were carried on the back, under the arm, or in the larger coolamons. In recent years it has been noticed that when not engaged in hunting, men helped their wives to carry the younger children. It can be assumed, therefore, that though it was accepted that women were the burden bearers, men had some concern for their womenfolk and were ready to lend a hand when necessary. Contact with Europeans may have affected their attitudes. In the Kimberleys supplies were rolled in bark and slung over the women's shoulders with cords.

Carrying cradles were made of paperbark with the ends closed, so that they looked like miniature canoes. The baby snuggled down into the carrier, which contained sand to act as a napkin, and could easily be renewed. In south-eastern Australia the baby was lodged inside a plaited rush mat tied on the mother's back.

When the baby was older the mother carried it on her hip, where it clung tightly to her, or across the small of her back. With the right arm round its neck and the left hooked under its knees, both mother and child were kept warm, and the hands were free. Pouches or bags of animal skin for the baby were slung by bands to the forehead, the child resting on its mother's back. Later still, the young boy or girl sat on the mother's shoulders, its fingers clutching her hair with a grip that could not be broken by any sudden movement.

Babies, Bowls, Walkabout.

CARVING, ROCK. Carvings in rock are found in caves and shelters, particularly in New South Wales in the Sydney-Hawkesbury galleries, where there were large areas of flat surface, and where the art was most highly developed. It has been estimated that there are about 4,000 figures of human beings, mythical figures, birds, animals, and other living creatures in the 400 to 500 galleries. The designs were not confined to the representations mentioned, but also included weapons, implements, and ornaments, and complete hunting and ceremonial scenes.

The techniques used in rock engraving included abraded and punctured grooves and outlines. This work is to be regarded as a form of religious art.

Specialists have investigated the various types of carving. F. D. McCarthy, late of the Australian Museum in Sydney, for instance, has studied the carvings over the continent from the north-west to New South Wales, and has identified four main types:

1. Abraded grooves.
2. Figures of men, women, animals, and inanimate objects carved in outline.
3. Pecked intaglios, as in 2.
4. Geometrical designs of rectilinear and curvilinear forms.

The same freedom and imagination shown in painting and drawing were displayed in this more difficult medium. Rock engraving galleries have also been found north of Broken Hill in New South Wales, and in the Port Hedland district, Western Australia, where the galleries are extensive.

Art, Caves.

CARVING, WOOD. Decoration of weapons and implements was practised in many parts of the continent. Some of the "best" art is in north-eastern Arnhem Land where evidence suggests not only recent influences, but also survivals of the very early Australian language. In the south and east, however, the art of dendroglyphs or tree carving was developed with geometrical and curvilinear patterns cut into the trunk and framed in an oval from which the bark had been stripped. These designs had totemic and mythical significance, for they surrounded the bora grounds in New South Wales where initiation ceremonies were held; they were also used as grave posts.

Since the coming of white men, most of the striking dendroglyphs have been destroyed by fire and by cultivation. The most beautiful designs have been preserved on boomerangs, spear-throwers, clubs, and tools, and here too they often had some esoteric meaning which was known only to initiates. The talent exhibited by the northern Arnhemlanders in making models in wax from bees' nests has in later years been diverted to the carving of representations of animals and men.

CAVE PAINTING. Caves provided ideal surfaces for rock painting and carving. Protected from the weather, magnificent examples of Aboriginal art have in this way been preserved for all time. Cave paintings are numerous in the north where the most colourful and intricate work is found, and to a lesser extent in the south, where the pictures are simpler in conception.

In the northern Kimberleys and in western Arnhem Land the art of cave painting flourished, and countless examples exist. In the Wondjina paintings in the Kimberleys and in the Oenpelli-Liverpool River area of the Northern Territory, the art reached its zenith. The colours remain vivid and breathtaking to the present day, yet the only materials used were variously coloured earths—red, white, brown, and yellow—and black and grey charcoal. The painting of the original picture released the spirits of growth and fertility, while subsequent retouching and freshening of the designs ensured the recurrence of good seasons and plentiful growth. F. D. McCarthy states that increase rites were carried out in northern and central Australia, but that the concept of fertility is equally or more important, and that the distinction is not yet clearly understood. In addition, he says, hunting and love magic, records of fishing, hunting, fighting, mortuary rites, corroborees, and various spirit scenes were also important motifs.

Yet the sacred significance of the paintings is rooted far more deeply than in pictorial homage to the spirits. Many of them represent mythological ancestors, spiritual beings, men and gods of the Dreamtime, the great creator spirits, the All-Father who made the world.

Even more, the original paintings were supposed to have been made by these supernatural beings and some were in physical, visual form, the very beings themselves. To touch them was to communicate with the spirit world, to enter into the never-dying stream of the Eternal Dreamtime, to become a part of the continuing process of creation and fructification which began with the cult-heroes, and which reveals and renews itself in each new manifestation of growth.

A wide range of human and animal motifs was painted in the caves. The spirit that pervaded them ensured the continuance of life, and that the spirit of man would remain part of the spirit of the ancestors, whether in their bright colours in the darkness of the cave, or in the totemic sites where they rested on their long journeys.

Art, Carving (rock), Painting, Tabus.

CAVES. The Aborigines were seldom troglodytes, but rock shelters, as distinct from caves, were used as a protection against winter storms. In fact radio carbon dates going back 16,000 years show that they were then being used for this purpose. Limestone caverns were occupied by the Aborigines in the Nullarbor Plain area. They were penetrated 300 feet or more to obtain water, flint for implements, and to decorate the walls. Deep caves were lived in only when the surrounding country was flooded. In such cases the walls and roof might become smoke-blackened, and the floor worn smooth. Whether they were inhabited temporarily or not, cave walls were frequently decorated with paintings.

CEREMONIES. It has often been said that there were two types of ceremony observed by the Aborigines: the religious; and the secular, pleasure, or "playabout". But it is not possible to divide the rites into watertight categories. There is no doubt that there was great enjoyment in participating in the ceremonies, but the pervading presence of the secret and sacred powers was always there, for the ritual that found expression in dance and chant was one of the means whereby belief was translated into reality and became alive. Professor Elkin regards ceremonies, i.e. ceremonial, as part of ritual, in fact almost the mechanics of ritual, while the corroboree is playabout. No ritual could ever be playabout.

The most sacred dances were held by the men alone, and it was death to any woman who observed the ritual. Sacred dances were often part of the increase rites, which had of necessity to be held every year if the tribe was to survive. Participation by the younger men led to a sharing of the knowledge preserved by the older people. The degree of relaxation of the strict rules of tabu varied with the importance of the ceremony. Many increase rituals lasted for days. As the fully grown men were occupied by them for so long, considerable responsibility fell on the young men in hunting, and on the women for food-gathering to provide enough for the whole tribe to eat.

There are several ways in which the ceremonies may be catalogued. Elkin has suggested the following divisions: historical rites; increase rites; and initiation rites. In greater detail the Berndts refer to three major divisions:*

1. The use of song and dance to re-enact myths and stories that have been inherited by the tribal group, corresponding with Elkin's historical rites.
2. Dances and songs which had no totemic significance but had a long history of traditional authority behind them.
3. Mime, song, and dance which were in-

* Ronald M. Berndt and Catherine Berndt, *The World of the First Australians*, Ure Smith, 1964, pages 325-6.

spired by "the contemporary events of everyday living". Such ceremonies, which were normally part of corroborees, were certainly more in the tradition of playabout, and were characterised by spontaneity and improvisation.

The non-totemic ceremonies had less relation to ritual than increase and initiation rites, which were predominantly sacred and to a large degree secret. These in turn might be subdivided into rites which were performed solely by men, from which women were excluded; those where men alone took part, frequently on the bora ground, but where women had a lesser part to play that was essential to the ritual but was required to be performed in a different place; those which were shared equally by men and women; and those with men excluded, it being held proper that women should reserve some sacred mysteries to themselves.

The Berndts explain that the dominance of men in the magico religious world was due to the fact that in their ceremonies they expressed symbolically the functions which were peculiar to women. Some deep-rooted jealousy seemed to be embodied in this attitude. The physiological functions are natural to the female sex, and as they are vital to fertility and fruition, they were emulated by men in the symbolic rites of blood-letting. In the initiation rites men took possession of these important faculties in this way.

The other important element in ritual was its link with the life and work of the ancestral spirits. This was the essential element in all fertility rites. The Aboriginal did not fight against natural processes. He made use of magic and ritual to ensure that the processes first brought into being by his ancestors were encouraged to continue as they had planned them.

Food supplies were the most vital of living things and were the focal point of fertility and increase rites, but there were other manifestations of Nature that were separate from but contributed to the same purpose. Rain was needed to make plants grow and to replenish the waterholes, calm weather was needed to make good fishing conditions. Strange as it may seem, there were rites to encourage the swarming of flies, but the logic was inescapable. Too many flies were a plague, but at least they would drive unwanted visitors away, and the meagre supply of food would be preserved for the local group.

Each clan or cult group had its own ceremonies which had been handed down from the Dreamtime. They might be shared by or known to other tribes, but could not be owned by them. The designs on sacred objects and the patterns painted on the bodies of the participants were all related to the secret lore of the group. A great proportion of the dances were pantomimic, relating part of the myth owned by the tribe or the clan. Those who took part were re-enacting the deeds of the totemic ancestors.

Corroborees, Engwura, Fertility, Increase rites, Initiation ceremonies, Totemism.

CHANTS. With its strong rhythm the chant was an aid to memory and an important feature in ceremonies of all kinds. Legends of the ancestors, myths, and tales that were the possession of a single tribe or clan, were preserved principally in this medium. The Aboriginal entered in mind, body, and spirit into the dancing and chanting; and so, instead of a spoken story, the chanting, accompanied by clapping-sticks, stamping feet, and heaving bodies, was the way in which the immemorial legends of the tribe were remembered. They were taught to initiates and passed unchanged from one generation to another until the meaning of many of the words and phrases was lost.

Corroborees, Songs.

CHARMS. Various forms of charms were the stock-in-trade of those who performed magical rites with evil intent. The principal object in the charm bag was the pointing bone, but there were frequently other tools of the craft—spirit bones of men, pieces of agate and stone, carved sticks, birds' claws, the eyes of crocodiles. The range of objects varied in different parts of Australia, but they were all designed for use in bringing supernatural forces into contact with the natural world. They were often used to bring sickness and death, but were equally efficacious when used by wirinuns in defeating the purposes of the malignant evil-worker. Charms of many kinds were worn by men and women to ward off sickness, by hunters as an aid to success, and by warriors to escape injury or death. Charms and sorcery objects were carried in string, fur, and paperbark rolls or bags.

Magic, Pointing bones.

CHEWING. The leaves of two plants known as pitcheri (pituri) and balandu were objects of trade over a large area of the interior of Australia. They were mixed with ash to form a wad or quid which was used as a kind of chewing gum. When not in use it was parked behind the ear. In tribes where adults were addicted to the habit a flat depression was formed behind the ear for holding the chew.

In Queensland the root or sucker of the pandanus palm was crushed and mixed with the contents of a honeycomb, which usually contained a liberal supply of dead bees and grubs. When the root was well impregnated the "chewing rope" was sucked with great enjoyment.

CHIEFS.
Leaders.

CHILDREN. Childhood was a happy period, free from restraint. Parents and older people were normally indulgent, and seldom meted out punishment except when some thoughtless or mischievous act imperilled the welfare of the group. It was as though mothers and fathers, aware of the trials of endurance that lay ahead, were anxious to spare their offspring until they faced the grim realities of the initiation rites and adulthood. But with all the licence that was permitted, punishment was severe when they exceeded the bounds of prudence.

The earliest years were spent in the mother's company, for weaning did not occur for two to four years, according to the seasons and the amount of food available, and the ability of a child to walk without undue fatigue. Apart from matters of ritual, nothing was hidden or secret in camp, and children soon became acquainted with the most intimate aspects of family life. In their games they imitated adults, gaining from observation and practical experience the knowledge that would be necessary to them when they were eventually adopted into the mature life of the group. When the clan was on walkabout, their environmental changes and range of experience were constantly enlarged.

Children played with each other, asked questions, copied older people, experimented singly and in company, learned what was good to eat and what should be avoided (sometimes through painful experience), how to follow the tracks of insects and small lizards, snakes, and animals, where the best vegetable food was to be found, and how it could be secured. Though not expected to contribute to the food supplies of the group they were proud to do so; they were well fed by their elders, but a supplementary diet secured by their own efforts was always welcomed by small boys and girls.

The girls accompanied the women on vegetable-gathering expeditions where they learnt how to search for grubs and dig for roots; the boys went out for the same purpose when they were young, but as they grew older they reserved their strength for the more manly pursuits of the chase. Their first lessons came from the women, who taught them much bush lore about animals and plants; later the elders took over this work, and many and painful were the lessons learned at their hands.

Games of various kinds helped in bushcraft, and boys graduated from the fussy care of women, until they came directly under their fathers' control at the age of about 12. Girls received training in basket-making and cooking as well as in food-gathering.

Because of the kinship rules, children were related to every member of the group, and their care was a communal as well as a parental responsibility. If a father died, another man took his place. At nights the older men sang chants which told something of the mythological journeys of the ancestors and without revealing the secrets that would come later at the time of initiation, the reason for the sacred and totemic sites was unfolded, and the children encouraged to emulate the qualities of their ancestors. The local myths were simplified, preparing them for the more involved revelations that would be made later in life. In some places songs were composed specially for children, providing pleasant and informative legends about animals, insects, birds, reptiles, and fish.

As they grew older children were required to accept responsibilities, such as the care of young children while the women were gathering food. An unusual practice was observed in Arnhem Land, where a mother might punish a child "in spirit" by beating its footprints without touching it.

Boys, Games, Girls, Spirits.

CHISELS. Fine woodwork required the use of small chisels and scrapers rather than large stone flake knives and axes. Delicate stone flakes half an inch in length and upwards were knapped, sharpened by grinding, set in wooden handles with gum, and used as chisels. The art of making them was an ancient one.

The smallest pre-historic chisels are known as microliths. In some tribes a row of microliths was embedded in gum on a wooden handle and used as a knife. Shells were also used as chisels.

CHURINGA.
Sacred objects.

CICATRICES.
Scars.

CIRCUMCISION. Circumcision was an important rite in initiation. There were large areas where it was not practised, notably in eastern and south-western Australia. Apparently the custom originated in the north-western region and spread east and south. It was observed from the Kimberleys to north-eastern Arnhem Land and down to Adelaide. The more painful custom of subincision was frequently observed as a final initiation rite in the Central Australian-Northern Territory region.

Initiation ceremonies, Scars.

CLAPPING-STICKS. Time-sticks or clapping-sticks were used to beat out a rhythmical accompaniment to songs and dances. In some places unornamented sticks were used; elsewhere boomerangs were used for the same purpose. In northern Arnhem Land the wood was carefully chosen for its resonant qualities. The sticks were painted or carved with incised designs in a variety of symbolical shapes, feathered ornaments sometimes being added. The lower piece was often a piece of hard, resounding wood, and the upper or striking piece of softer timber. A single pair might be operated by one performer, or a group might tap out the time in unison. Striking instruments such as these more closely approached the principle of the gong.

Musical time was kept amongst the desert and central tribes by striking the ground with a stick or with a special beater.
Gongs, Music and musical instruments.

CLAY. There were a number of uses for clay. It was smeared over the body to provide camouflage when a hunter needed to approach close to his prey, and to suppress body odour. Painting the body with white clay was a widespread custom during mourning. White clay often provided the base for painting and decorating the body with down and feathers. Widows' caps worn during the mourning period were made of clay. Clay was used to cover open wounds. Lumps of clay were employed as fireplaces in canoes. White pipeclay was universally used in all kinds of art—on rock, wood, body, ground, human hair, and bark surfaces.

It was also used as a beautifying agent. The hair was impregnated with wet clay which dried into solid wisps. Sometimes small clay balls (or seed pods) were attached in the same way, forming a fringe of bobbles.

Where large, raised welts on the back were regarded as aesthetic, the open wounds were filled with clay which prevented them from healing and so left prominent scars.
Food, Pigments.

CLEVER-MEN.
Medicine men.

CLIMBING. Where tall trees had to be climbed in order to gather honey, fruit, nuts, and birds' eggs, or when leafy branches were broken off for huts, a simple device was employed in eastern Australia. A strong vine was looped round the bole of the tree, the ends being held in the hands and twisted round the forearms in order to secure them. Leaning backwards so that the loop pressed against the tree trunk, the climber walked up it, jerking the loop upwards from time to time, and was quickly able to reach the branches.

Women as well as men were adept at climbing the bare trunk. Where the arms could embrace the tree trunk, men and women used a frog-like action in climbing. On tree trunks of large diameter shallow notches were cut in the bark on either side of the tree and, clinging tenaciously with the body pressed close to the trunk, the climbers were able to scramble up to the distant branches, and to slide down even more quickly.

Boys liked to climb the long lawyer vines of the rain forest until they were lost to sight in the tall trees. But climbing was not confined to young people. Women were ready at any time to follow a goanna up a tree and dislodge it, to raid a wild bees' nest, collect food, or hide from raiders.

CLOTHES.
Garments, Head ornaments.

CLUBS. Heavy wooden sticks used for throwing and for in-fighting, and as hunting weapons, were known as nulla nullas or waddies. The nulla nulla was mainly a fighting weapon, and was made in different shapes and sizes. The throwing-stick and club (used also in hand-to-hand fighting) was an interesting development

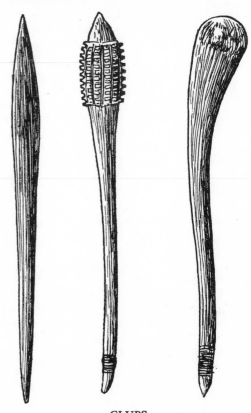

CLUBS

in Australia, where the only way to kill some of the fleet-footed animals was by means of the spear or throwing missile. The Western Australian throwing-stick was about an inch or so in diameter, up to a couple of feet in length, slightly curved. A knobbed end was added in south-eastern Australia and on Bathurst and Melville Islands. It was thrown with great accuracy at birds, lizards, bandicoots, and other animals.

In Victoria the leawill or leeangle was a large heavy club bent at the striking end. "It is of the shape of a pickaxe, with only one pick. Its name is derived from another native word, *liang*, signifying a tooth. It is a very formidable weapon, and used only in war."[*]

A wide range of clubs was used for fighting and hunting in eastern Australia, where there were varieties with disc, spherical, conical, curved, and bladed ends. Long pole and boomerang clubs were used in the Central Australian region. They were two-handed weapons used mainly in personal duels. The flat-bladed lil-lil of New South Wales and Victoria was a hand or throwing weapon, often neatly decorated.

Nulla nullas, Plongges, Waddies.

COFFINS.
Burial customs.

COLOURS. The principal colours used in art were red, white, black, and yellow. The red and yellow pigments varied in tone, several shades often being used in one cave or bark painting. Blue, purple, pink, and pale and deep brown have been recorded in limited localities.

Art, Painting, Pigments.

COMPETITIONS. The competitive element in games and sports was a welcome change from the daily search for food. It could occur only at times when food supplies were plentiful, in long occupied seasonal camps, and when separate clans gathered together for ceremonial purposes, or for communal activities such as egg-gathering, turtle-hunting, etc. In fact it was more the privilege of settled tribes in eastern and western Australia, and in Arnhem Land and other fertile areas, who were not condemned to constant travelling on account of the aridity of the land. Ball games, top-spinning in Queensland and the Lake Eyre region, and boomerang-throwing all featured in competitions. Dart-throwing, wrestling, and spear-throwing were also among competitive contests.

It was not unusual, for instance, for two tribes in the vicinity of Lake Alexandrina to challenge each other to a fishing contest. In spring or early summer they came from a distance of 100 miles or more, eager to show their superiority over their rivals. A great deal of preparation was entailed, the experts assembling a week or so before the contest began. Then the tribes assembled, a corroboree was held at night, and before sunrise the next day the canoes were carefully inspected and made ready for the day's fishing. It is probable that several other tribes had assembled to watch the contest, and that the lake shore would be lined with excited spectators. Expert judges and marshals took up strategic positions in canoes

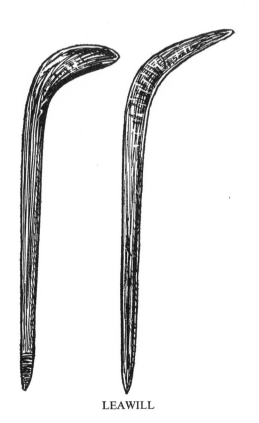

LEAWILL

* Charles Griffith, *Present State and Prospects of the Port Phillip District*, 1845.

to make sure that no offences were committed.

In many cases the competition extended over a period of days. On the first day the selected representatives paddled out to a proven fishing ground to spear fish. As soon as one of them succeeded he held it up for all to see. His fellow-tribesmen called out "Kai hai! Kai hai!" and jumped up and down with excitement. It was easy for the onlookers to follow the contest for the representatives of each tribe took up a position in turn for a given period. (This information was recorded by W. Ramsay Smith.)

As in all Aboriginal activities, certain tabus had to be observed. When the day's fishing was over the contestants returned to their wurleys without speaking to their wives and children, and took no part in the evening's feasting and dancing. They were not allowed to eat the fish they had speared, which were given to the elders. On the other hand the fishermen needed to be fed well, and were provided with fish by the tribal leaders. The fish were cooked by their wives and put in the branches of a tree to cool, because hot food was forbidden them.

In some places the restrictions were more severe. The competitors were required to live alone; no female was allowed to speak to them, to touch the canoes and fishing gear, or even to go near the path that led to their wurleys.

Mimic warfare was a favourite sport, and took many forms. When several tribes came together for trade or other peaceful purposes, it was an occasion for friendly rivalry. An exciting form of sport was noted by an early observer. A single visitor was adorned with feathers, and took up a position on a nearby hilltop. The several tribes assembled in groups. Someone shouted, "An emu is climbing the hill!"

It was a signal for the men of the local tribes to rush up the hillside and attempt to catch the emu intruder, who fled to the shelter of his own people. It was often an exciting chase, and the "emu" was frequently captured. If he succeeded in eluding his pursuers and escaping to his own people, they formed a ring round him. Their opponents tried to break through. If they got inside the ring they retired with the emu feathers as a token of victory. Intense excitement marked these and other contests.

Amongst children the competitive element was strong. Boys and girls challenged one another in tree-climbing, wrestling, tracking, swim-ming, fighting, spear-throwing, and memory contests, and in the endurance of pain.

Boomerangs, Fire-making, Games.

CONCEPTION. There was a widespread belief that the spirits of children occupied the branches of certain trees, and that women who ventured near them became the mothers of the spirit babies. The spirits of girl babies, said the Iuwalarai women, were made by the moon, assisted by Wahn the Crow; those of boys were made by the remote ancestors of the Dreamtime.

Other causes were ascribed to conception, among them dreams that became transformed into reality, the giving of a piece of roasted flesh by a husband to his wife, or simply by his telling her that she is to have a child. There were also beliefs such as that the spirit children came to the mother in the form of a curlew if they were girls, or as a snake if they were boys.

These were variants of the general belief in the pre-existence of spirits from the Dreamtime in water-places, and sometimes in branching trees. The father (or occasionally the mother) might see the spirit child in a vision. The spirit child might even enter a woman in the guise of food which had been given to her by her husband, or which she had plucked herself.

Babies, Birth, Pre-existence, Reincarnation.

COO-EE. The Aboriginal cry "Coo-ee" used to attract attention or to summon a friend from a distance was quickly adopted by white settlers because of its carrying quality. In a vocabulary from the Sydney area published in 1790 it appears as "Cow-ee—to come". J. West in his *History of Tasmania* published in 1852, wrote:

"Like the natives of New South Wales, they called to each other from a great distance by the *cooey*; a word meaning 'Come to me'. The Sydney blacks modulated this cry with successive inflections; the Tasmanians uttered it with less art. It is a sound of great compass. . . . The first syllable is prolonged; the second is raised to a higher key, and is short and abrupt."

A few years later W. Landsborough recorded in *Exploration of Australia*: "Coo-oo-oo-y is a shrill treble cry much used in the bush by persons wishful to find each other. On a still night it will travel a couple of miles."

COOKING. With an intimate knowledge of the source of food supplies, the Aboriginal was equally aware of the most serviceable methods of preparing food for consumption, whether cooked or uncooked. It was woman's work, though men were sometimes prepared to help by gathering supplies of wood for the fire. Generally speaking, however, man's work was confined to hunting game animals, birds, and fish, leaving the women to gather firewood, to secure the vegetable supplies, and prepare the meal. The men usually dug the oven pit, made the fire and baked the animal. Children often cooked their own food.

Large animals and birds such as kangaroos and emus were cooked in an earth oven, though perhaps the word "cooked" did not mean quite the same to the Aboriginal as to the white man. With hunger sharpened by the day's activities he was not prepared to wait for hours for his meal to be cooked. This was partly a matter of necessity, for when on walkabout camp was not made until the late afternoon, and the day might be well advanced before he succeeded in catching an animal and bringing home the meal. Apart from this, he preferred his meat underdone, sometimes with the fur and skin merely singed off and eaten practically raw. Occasionally a large animal or bird would be distributed amongst the various families, but normally it was cooked whole.

A shallow pit was dug in the sand or soft earth and a fire lit in it. When the earth was warm and the bottom covered with live embers, the fur of the animal was singed off, the sinews removed from the legs, and the animal dropped in the pit. Hot ashes and live coals were heaped round it. The skin protected the meat from burning (or at least from being charred to a cinder), and after a while the partly-burnt, partly-underdone meat was removed and eaten.

Procedures varied considerably. Quite frequently, and especially when time was not pressing, the method was rather more elaborate. When the coals had died down to a steady glow they were covered with fresh grass, leaves, and branches of shrubs. The whole animal was laid on this bed, covered with more green stuff and earth, and another fire lit on top of the mound. In this way the oven was made hot, the food cooking slowly and steadily until puffs of steam escaping from the ground showed that the meal was ready. In the case of large animals and birds the head and legs protruded from the oven, the legs providing handles with which to withdraw the cooked meat. Food prepared in this way took several hours to cook.

Another method, taking a couple of hours to complete, was used when time was available to cook it in big lumps. Once the fire had died down to dull embers they were raked out, the meat put in and covered with the hot ashes, paperbark, and then soil or sand to form a mound oven. When the food was ready the meat was removed, and distributed, the last piece being taken by the owner.

Smaller game such as ducks and swans were cut open, the intestines, gizzard, and heart removed, and cooked in the earth oven. The offal was regarded as the sweetest part of the bird. The intestines were cut through at the loops to provide tubes a few inches in length. The contents were squeezed out of the open ends and put with the gizzard, heart, and liver on rocks to dry in the sun. Whale and dugong were cut up for cooking; turtles were opened at the neck and hot stones inserted in the cavity. Fish were usually baked in the ashes or roasted on them, but in south-eastern Australia they were covered in clay before being baked in the ashes.

Yams were cooked, but the slicing, soaking and roasting was a lengthy process lasting two or three days. Most vegetable food was eaten raw, except for herbs which were wrapped round smaller portions of cooked meat and fish.

The native predecessor of damper or johnnycake was made of seeds—kuldoo, ega, or grass seed. It was gathered laboriously by the women who winnowed it in their shallow coolamons, crumbling the husks in the hand and letting them float away in the breeze as the seeds fell in the container. The seed was ground, sprinkled with water until it turned to a soft paste, which might be ground again on a flat stone, and moulded into oval cakes which were cooked in the hot ashes of a fire. Variety could sometimes be obtained by mixing more than one kind of seed together.

In parts of northern Australia the cycad

(*Macrozamia*) palm was plentiful and provided nuts which were shelled, the kernel being pounded, sliced, and soaked in water, preferably running, for several days to leach out a toxic acid. The cooked pieces were either eaten or fashioned into cakes which were wrapped in paperbark to prevent them from burning, and cooked on the embers.

Cycad bread could be kept for several days and proved a useful standby when tribes gathered for a corroboree.

Food, Meals, Ovens, Preservation of food.

CORD. There were many everyday uses for cord or string. Twine was used for making bags and nets, human hair twine for sacred objects, while cord (normally two-ply which usually had a diameter of a quarter to three-eighths of an inch) was used for the large emu and kangaroo nets, and for harpoon and sail lines in Arnhem Land and Cape York Peninsula. The harpoon rope was often made from hibiscus bark.

Nets, String.

CORROBOREES. The generally accepted spelling of the word corroboree has had many variants in the past, ranging from corrobbery to korobori. As a term for Aboriginal entertainment of several kinds, especially singing and dancing, it probably originated in the Botany Bay district where it was first recorded. It has been suggested that it was derived from korobra, to dance, and boroya or beria, to sing, from the Dharuk language inland from Botany Bay and Port Jackson. In view of the mimicry of animals and birds in this form of entertainment, there may be some truth in the theory that korobra was in turn derived from koro, a fairly common word for emu.

Writing in *Notes and Sketches of New South Wales* in 1844, Mrs Meredith gave the following impressions of a corroboree which she witnessed:

"Great preparations were made, as for a grand corrobory, or festival, the men divesting themselves of even the portions of clothing commonly worn, and painting their naked black bodies in a hideous manner with pipeclay. After dark, they lit their fires, which

CORROBOREE

are small, but kept blazing with constant additions of dry bark and leaves, and the sable gentry assembled by degrees as they completed their evening toilette, full dress being painted nudity. A few began dancing in different parties, preparatory to the grand display, and the women, squatting on the ground, commenced their strange monotonous chant, each beating accurate time with two boomerangs. Then began the grand corrobory, and all the men joined in the dance, leaping, jumping, bounding about in the most violent manner, but always in strict unison with each other, and keeping time with the chorus, accompanying their wild gesticulations with frightful yells, and noises. The whole 'tableau' is fearfully grand! The dark wild forest scenery around—the bright fire-light gleaming upon the savage and uncouth figures of the men, their natural dark hue being made absolutely horrible by the paintings bestowed on them, consisting of lines and other marks done in white and red pipe-clay, which gives them an indescribably

ghastly and fiendish aspect—their strange attitudes, and violent contortions and movements, and the unearthly sound of their yells,
mingled with the wild and monotonous wail-
like chant of the women, make altogether a
very near approach to the horribly sublime in
the estimation of most Europeans who have
witnessed an assembly of that kind."

A corroboree was a wild and uninhibited
spectacle for a European, but to the participants it was a joyful expression of emotion, a
relief from the tedium of daily tasks and at
times a prelude to an initiation, increase or
other ceremony, or even part of such sacred
rites. The entertainment was sometimes con-
cluded with the eerie voice of the bull-roarer,
which was a sign that the secret ceremonies
from which women were debarred were about
to commence.

The great rituals in which a number of tribes
participated were held at the beginning of
spring or at the end of the wet season in the
north. It was the most suitable time for increase rites when the dead world began to stir
into life, when the spirits of growth and fertility needed to be encouraged to pursue their
ever-recurring task.

Mrs Aeneas Gunn, author of *The Little
Black Princess*, has described how the entertainment on the Roper River begins with the
gathering round the camp fires, the men seated
in two large circles with clapping-sticks tapping
out the rhythm, the women and children beating time by slapping their hands against their
thighs. The fires die down in the first hush of
evening and a single voice rises high and piercing in a song. At once everyone joins in, the
men vigorously banging their sticks on the
ground, swaying their bodies to the compelling
rhythm, and joining loudly in the song. The
voices grow quieter as a group of men enters
the circle. Their bodies are painted in vividly
contrasting colours, and weird head-dresses rise
high above their heads. They carry in a long,
oval, wooden totem symbol and the sound
grows louder. The rhythm carries both men and
women to their feet and develops into an endless dance in which the actions of the bush
creatures are emulated, while the song embraces
the adventures of the ancestors of old in their
many animal forms.

This, however, was not the pattern of all
corroborees. In many areas women did not
sing at the camp dances. They beat time and
sometimes made quiet movements with hands
and feet, or danced quietly in the background
beside the fires or dancing area of the men.
The site was cleared of sticks and stones. Before long the spirit of the occasion began to
take charge. The sticks began to tap and when
the didgeridoo was used it was blown—and the
corroboree began in earnest.

Someone began the dance. Others, following behind, imitated him. Gradually the tempo
of the dancing and the pantomime increased,
and the song went on with minor variations.

Corroborees may be divided into two types:
sacred and religious, or profane and playabout.
The secular form that is described in this article
has been described as a primitive combination
of ballet, stage play, and opera, providing an
entertainment in which all could join, and which
preserved the traditions of the group. Although
the performance was often impromptu, providing a choreographical presentation of daily
life, events of recent history, and an opportunity to poke fun at those who had been detected in minor transgressions, it was often
planned well in advance. The corroboree
usually took place when hunting had been
good, bellies well filled, and liberal supplies of
water available.

Mime was an essential ingredient in the performance. The effect was heightened by the
representation of animals (frequently of totemic significance). Bunches of feathers were
attached to girdles, arms were extended to
imitate the necks of emus, and rolled up skins
took the place of tails. It was an imitative and
expressive art which had the effect of linking
human beings with the animal creation in a
cosmic brotherhood which emphasised the
essential unity of men, the animals who were
the culture heroes of the Dreamtime, and their
common descendants.

The performance continued for hours. It
has been said that frequently the performers
gave up only through exhaustion, but each
scene was short, and the performances were
rarely continued past 9 p.m. or thereabouts.
While the actors might become temporarily exhausted in long sacred rituals, they would
quickly recover in time for the next scene. One

by one they threw themselves on the ground and fell asleep, until only a few elders remained squatting by the fire, dreaming of the days of their youth.

Whatever the degree of participation, planned corroborees and ceremonies were devised and prepared by the older men on traditional lines, and directed by them in order that the ancient knowledge should be preserved.

A man who could compose corroborees was highly respected and would travel from camp to camp teaching the people his compositions. Groups learnt new ones on visits to other camps, especially at large gatherings for trade and ceremonies.

A spirited eyewitness account of a corroboree is given by Ion L. Idriess:

"These hissing, prancing, naked, heavily cicatrized, painted and befeathered bodies fitted in wonderfully with the primitive bush and starlit sky, the near-by trees throwing back the dancing flames, with beyond them the shadowed valleys, the hill-tops lit by the moon, great carpets of rosy light thrown far out on the swamp. Symbolic designs of totem and spirit and Ancestral Beings, of snake and animal and fish and bird in coloured ochres glistened on their skin; heads and arms and legs were banded with brilliant feathers, berries, shells, and dyed grasses. Here and there a swishing girdle of possum tails, a bunch of swaying emu feathers, strips of skin of the carpet-snake dangled weirdly from prancing limbs, with rattles of berries and shell tinkling in harmony with the short, metallic clacking of the kylies. Gummed to squads of hairy bodies by their own blood flashed symbolic and totemic designs of wild cotton or birds' down—yellow cockatoo crests, pink down of galahs, brilliant scarlets and greens of parrot plumage. Necklets of eagle claws, of shark and animal teeth, or tortoise-shell, swung below beards like those ancient Assyrian beards carved in stone, and shaggy heads of hair in waves and curls and towering topknots of stiff decoration interlaced with coloured feathers and berries and dyed twines of fibre barks.

"Ever and anon they would all fling up arms and body as one man, gazing skyward from gleaming eyes, then with one roar stamp down again and yet again, nearly lifting the roof off my head with a roar that fanned away out into the moonlit hills and went sweeping across the swamp. Then down would thunder the feet to a startling hiss, while their eyes seemed to leap from their heads. With that stamping I felt the very earth vibrating, and a queer, chilly feeling up my spine. . . . They were working up into a wild-eyed, shrieking, stamping, mass of smelly human frenzy, of primitive hysteria. As I gazed in a fascinated silence I thrilled to some deep feeling sweeping away back thousands and thousands of years ago, felt through these wildly leaping bodies, animal-like roars, screeching chant, and thundering vibrations, the blood of my own ancestors in such a dance far back in the mists of time."*

It is important to distinguish clearly between playabout corroboree and sacred ritual which was reserved to men alone.

Ceremonies, Competitions, Dances, Didgeridoos, Increase rites, Initiation ceremonies, Music and musical instruments, Songs.

COUNCILS. Much study is still being devoted to this difficult subject, and it is likely that further research will reveal more of the organisation of group activity. There was always a "power" behind the organisation and policy of tribal activity. It was usually unobtrusive, seldom formal, but always effective. Men, particularly the elders whose grey hairs entitled them to some degree of respect, medicine men, great hunters, and ceremonial leaders, gradually and apparently aimlessly drifted away from the camp and sat themselves on the ground in a clearing or some other convenient spot. Talk ranged over a variety of subjects. Much of it was local gossip. The events of camp life were examined, hunting activities discussed, and examples of defiance of age-old tradition spoken of disapprovingly.

The council was neither judge nor jury, yet partook of some of the functions of both. In most cases it did not need to organise punishment for wrong-doing because the established legal system of the Dreamtime heroes and kin-

* *Our Living Stone Age*, Angus and Robertson, 1963, page 64.

ship custom saw to this. Adultery and other transgressions of personal rights were dealt with by the individuals concerned. A war expedition might be planned by a council to avenge murder, the stealing of women, or trespass on hunting and fishing grounds. Emotions were roused at the time of death, and the men of the group were not slow to exact revenge. Nevertheless the "old men" saw all and knew all, and were the main element in enforcing compliance with tribal law, and in planning ritual performances by which knowledge was spread.

In the larger groups—tribal and linguistic units and hordes—the same principle was observed. The "councils" were held when the local groups met together for ceremonies, trade or gift exchange, and corroborees. Membership of these "councils", not strictly defined but nevertheless amicably and almost automatically decided, was confined to the tribes which shared a common set of myths, even though they each owned different parts of the set. The leader, who exercised no particular prerogatives and had no titular office, probably emerged naturally at the council meeting. Elders were not necessarily members of the council, which consisted of an informed and experienced hierarchy.

The larger meeting of this kind was useful in determining the timing of tribal rites, sharing secret ritual, enlarging the borders of their own knowledge, and in discussing action to be taken on matters that threatened the welfare of the whole society, such as infringement of territorial rights or of locally accepted tabus. The meetings were held at a distance from the main camp, or on the ritual ground. They enabled grievances to be aired and resolved amicably. No women ever attended, and by tacit agreement membership was confined to warriors who were also men of good reputation, elders, medicine men, and those who were regarded as heads of totemic groups.

The number of men in the informal councils varied a great deal according to the size of the group or tribe. In the larger ones there would be a dozen or more, not formally elected, but naturally taking their place by right because of acknowledged seniority, prowess, knowledge, and gifts of leadership.

Elders.

COUNTING. An early writer once said, "a blackfellow only counts up to two. His arithmetic is very simple, just One, Two, Little Mob, Big Mob."

It is true that many Aboriginal languages had only two numerals, one and two, and that three and four were designated by saying two one, and two two, or similar methods. The extended fingers were used to indicate five and, in a true digital sense, the fingers were employed for numbers up to 10, and in some cases to 20 by using the toes as well.

But as Elkin has pointed out, this is not counting but is simply a concrete method of indicating individual persons and objects. In his primitive life the Aboriginal had no need to be specific in counting. The things that interested him most became the objects of his attention only one at a time. If there was a number of them a "big mob" or a "little mob" was sufficient for his purpose.

Spengler remarked that all that happened was that they did not use our own system of counting, not through inability to count, but because the need did not exist. It is significant that Aboriginal children have no more difficulty than white children in learning to count when taught in school.

CREATION. Myths of creation were told in every part of Australia in remarkable complexity, showing a degree of imagination that surprised many Europeans when they gained some insight into Aboriginal thought. Because of the different journeys of totemic beings, or creative ancestors, each tribe knew only a little of the major myth, but many of them possessed ancestral knowledge of the fabulous and inspiring acts of the All-Father and other creative spirits at the creation of the world.

Spirit children from spirit centres in trees, rocks, and waterholes and descended from the original ancestor, entered into new-born babies, and after death departed or were reincarnated, and in dreams brought some understanding of the continuous creative urges and powers which manifested themselves each new spring. The "All-Father" cult was confined to south-eastern Australia. There were many diverse accounts of how man was created.

Ancestors, Babies, Dreams, Dreamtime, Gods, Spirits, Totemism.

CREMATION.
Burial.

CRYSTALS. Australia is noted for its minerals and precious stones. Apart from their use as playthings they attracted little attention from the Aborigines, who were not greatly addicted to ornament of this kind, and had no skill in lapidary work. Quartz crystals, however, were supremely important as "medicine", for they were obtained from the sky hero, the Rainbow Serpent, or some such source. Amongst some tribes they were carried in small bags fastened to the upper arm as a preventive of sickness and of evil influences. To the sorcerer and medicine man crystals were an essential tool of their profession. To take crystals from the body of a living man or to insert them was to have control over life and death. They were believed to have power to protect those who knew how to control them, and to injure and kill those who misused them. Quartz was equally important to ensure success in hunting.
Magic, Medicine men.

D

DANCES. There were many different kinds of dances, some of which were jealously guarded by their owners, others being spread further afield at corroborees and by way of "trade". No matter how greatly they differed in type, and whether they were secular or sacred, they were an expression of human emotions—humour, fear, ecstasy, escape from the dullness of daily life, and an effective method of realising the Dreamtime.

There were so many things to be imitated, so many experiences to be entered into. There was the emu dance, the dance of the frog, the lyre bird, the kangaroo, the wallaby, the crocodile, and the shark. One could be part of the long sea rollers, of a yam-stick digging into the earth, of bees buzzing, of the hunter pursuing game, and of the animal that fled from him.

Every part of the body entered into the rhythm and action of the dance. It might only be a swaying of the body with the feet perfectly still, it might be a graceful ballet dance controlled by the songman, in which every movement was planned in advance. There were "schools" of dancing, some vigorous, some graceful, some imitative. There was individual dancing in which a few gifted performers gained a great reputation, but essentially the dance was a group activity in which personality was repressed and absorbed into the spirit of the group.

Almost the sole relaxation of the Aborigines, impromptu song and dance were held on many nights, but there were other occasions when the elders spent much time in preparation for a corroboree in which an element of teaching was included in the performance. In addition to the rehearsal of steps, movements, songs, and music, the performers had to be properly dressed. The body was painted with coloured ochres, the eyes sometimes glaring from yellow circles, the feathered head-dresses placed carefully in position.

For the most important occasions it would take several people to prepare one of the dancers. Feathers were affixed in designs with blood, the face was thickly covered with down

DANCES

by the same means, a tall head-dress of emu feathers was fastened in place and then, with anklets of leaves, the dancer was ready for the maddening rhythm of the dance.

Songs and dances that were interpretative of ancient myth were often performed in a cycle occupying many nights. The words of the songs might alter but the dance was likely to be repetitive with only slight changes to vary the routine. Dr A. A. Capell has stated that "the Aboriginal ballet tradition is perhaps on a par with the folk ballets of Russia, South-East Asia, India and Indonesia. It is a priceless heritage for Australia with a strong claim for intensive study."

The secular dance of a normal evening's entertainment was primarily a form of recreation, with amusement as an ingredient in the activity. It might arise from the deliberate motions of the dancers, or from some inadvertent mistake.

There were dances for men, and others for women. When women danced alone the movements tended to be less energetic and more graceful. In the most sacred dances, which were part of ritual and not for entertainment, women's parts were taken by men. Similarly in women's own secret dances they took the parts of men.

Burial, Ceremonies, Corroborees, Head ornaments, Initiation ceremonies.

DEATH. Death was the end of life, a separation from the continuing life of the community, a severing of the link with the ancestral spirits. It might be feared, but was an expected contingency, and when the mourning period was over the departed one was expunged from memory. Except amongst the very young and the aged, where physical causes were apparent, death was supposed to be caused by evil magic and so contrary to Nature. Further, there was always the possibility that a dead person's spirit would linger around the camp, causing more misfortune to befall the group, therefore it was advisable to leave the place and seek a new camping ground. During the last hours of life relatives sometimes watched from a distance in order to escape injury from the spirit at the moment of death.

Death, so contradictory and inexplicable when it occurred to young and middle-aged people, must obviously have been caused by a malignant force which in turn must have been unleashed by an evilly disposed person. Who would be more likely than the sorcerer? The desire to injure and kill must have come from a man who wielded some power, such as ability to point the bone, or an enemy who had enlisted the aid of the sorcerer.

Neglecting the subject of superstitious beliefs for the moment, the Aboriginal lived a hazardous existence. There were few dangerous animals, but poisonous snakes were a hazard. Prolonged drought might account for death from thirst, although the Aboriginal had an uncanny ability in finding water. In the northern parts of the country floods and turbulent river crossings accounted for deaths by drowning. There were hunting accidents, fatal injuries when fighting, and various kinds of sickness which resulted in death—and the revenge expedition when someone was accused and

convicted of killing another by witchcraft.

Unless the cause of death was readily apparent, a great deal of trouble was taken to discover the culprit. Death affected everyone in the camp, directly or indirectly, and fear was abroad lest the inquest should reveal that the instigator should be found in the clan. This fear remained until the matter had been resolved, usually by fastening the blame on some person outside the social group, by choosing a victim from the group, or by allowing the problem to remain unsolved.

The emotions that were roused immediately after the death occurred needed release. They were exhibited in seemingly frenzied displays of wailing and mourning, blood-letting, throwing ashes over one's own body, and even by prostration on the corpse. For a while it led to intensification of feeling, rather than release, culminating in a demand for immediate revenge. Fortunately the restraining force of custom and ritual was applied at this point by the elders. Laceration of the body provided the members of the tribe with an outlet for emotion. The inquest was often postponed until the matter could be considered more calmly. At times it would be decided that the deceased had suffered death as the result of infringing tribal law, thus offending the ancestral spirits. When the apparent mass hysteria, which was a ritual performance, subsided, attention was given to the needs of the departed and the observance of ritual practices.

These usually took the form of disposing of the body and destroying everything that reminded the group of the one who had left them, but final burial might not occur for a year or more. Camp was shifted, and the departure concealed from the spirit by lighting smoky fires or by pursuing a tortuous path to the new encampment. Certain tabus were observed. Widows were separated, the dead man's name was no longer spoken, and if it were part of the common vocabulary the word was not used again, another being substituted for it. (It has been suggested that this was the reason for the word kangaroo being recorded by Captain Cook but not heard by later explorers until recorded by Dr W. E. Roth in the 1870s.)

Eventually widows and widowers remarried and the life of the group went back to normal.

Burial, Inquests, Magic, Medicine men, Mes-

sengers, Mourning, Names, Pointing bones, Sickness, Spirit worlds, Tabus.

DECORATION.
Art, Carving, Corroborees, Nose piercing, Ornaments, Painting (body), Scars.

DENDROGLYPHS.
Carving wood.

DESERTS. The curse of the desert wastes of Australia lay not in the complete absence of rainfall but in its unpredictability. Permanently sterile, waterless country would have supported neither human nor animal life. In most parts of the inhospitable regions there are usually 5 or less inches of rainfall annually, but there may be no rain at all in one year, or in a succession of years, and a deluge in another.

At such a time the desert blossoms into a garden of flowers almost overnight, waterholes are filled, and game becomes plentiful once more. The Aboriginal learned to adapt his life to these changing conditions. In fact it may be said that the conditions made him what he was. He was prepared to take advantage of the bounties so sparingly provided by the ancestral spirits; equally ready to trust them in the most trying conditions, for had they not already travelled the same country, made the hills and the waterholes, and spread the dusty scrub as cover for wild beasts and reptiles? He never panicked but went calmly through life, refusing to use nervous and muscular energy wastefully, but ready to spring into purposeful activity the moment opportunity came.

To ensure his survival, ritual, territorial rights, clan and totemic loyalties, family and kinship systems, and disciplines all had their purpose. They enabled him to live through months and years of privation, and made it all the more rewarding when rain came and the waiting yams, berries, grass seed, insect, reptile, animal, and vegetable life became plentiful again.

DESIGNS.
Art.

DIDGERIDOOS. The dronepipe or didgeridoo is the most interesting and "musical" of Aboriginal instruments. Spelt didgeridoo, didjeridoo, didgeridu, didgeredoo, and in several other ways. It is one of the most difficult instruments to play.

The didgeridoo was used only in the north of the Northern Territory and north-eastern Kimberley. The average length was from 4 to 6 feet. The larger varieties often as long as 15 feet required several men to carry them. The didgeridoo was made of hollowed timber or bamboo soaked in water. Ironbark or stringybark

DIDGERIDOO

timber was sometimes eaten out by termites to make a long, narrow tube. Some didgeridoos were of constant diameter, others were wider at the distal end than at the mouth end. The distal end was sometimes rested in a baler or other large shell which acted as a resonator. At the present day a tin or bucket serves the same purpose.

When employed in ritual ceremonies it had sacred significance. In north-eastern Arnhem Land, for instance, it symbolised the Julunggul

python, was decorated with a variety of ornaments and carved with representations of myth.
The didgeridoo was popular at corroborees
where it supplied the basic rhythm to the tapping of the drumsticks.

There were many men who were unable to
perform on the instrument. Apparently the art
came easily to some but not to others. The
greatest difficulty was to produce a sustained
note, or even a constant sound, for it was important that the drone of the pipe should not
falter. This was achieved by filling the cheeks
with air and continuing to blow while taking
short, quick breaths through the nostrils.

According to one description a didgeridoo
was about 5 feet long and 3 inches in diameter,
with a mouthpiece, and a larger orifice at the
other end. The sound carried a long distance.
It has been compared to the bass notes of a
pipe organ. Men have been known to practise
for months without succeeding in producing its
haunting note. Skilled performers, it is said,
were able to sound one-syllable words by the
medium of the dronepipe with the sound remaining unbroken; but the real art was to sit
down with the instrument resting on the foot,
supported and controlled by the big toe, and
to cause the droning to continue hour after
hour as an accompaniment to song and dance.

As in so many other matters, different practices were employed in different places. In some
regions a variety of sounds could be produced,
the performer singing several notes into the
mouthpiece in a nasal tone.

Occasionally a temporary instrument has
been made from the bark of the hibiscus stem,
but ordinarily the didgeridoo was a treasured
instrument, well cared for, with a long length
of life in spite of frequent use. In northern
regions the players took turns to keep the
dronepipe going all night long in order to soothe
the tribespeople to sleep.

Love magic.

DIGGING-STICKS. Also known as yam-
sticks, because they were used, amongst other
things, for digging up yams. The sticks were
fairly short and strong, some up to 4 or 5 feet
long. The stick was an all-purpose tool, handled
with delicacy and skill. It was essentially a
woman's instrument and weapon, and an inseparable companion. The stick was often made
of ironwood, pointed at both ends and hardened
by fire.

When searching for white wood grubs or
witchetty grubs, a woman would beat the
ground at the base of a mulga tree and begin
to dig to a depth of 1 or 2 feet. Stopping to
listen now and again, and with her fingers sen-
sitive to the feel of the stick as it probed further into the ground, at last she reached a root
of the tree. When the earth was cleared away
she was likely to find the grubs, which were
extracted and eaten raw. Tapping on the ground
could even tell the digger what type of yam
was growing there.

Prising honey ants from the nest, and killing
lizards and snakes were tasks that could be
performed with the digging-stick. Small girls
were provided with miniature sticks at an early
age so that they could help their mothers. They
soon learned to use them properly and to scoop
the dirt out of the holes with their tiny hands
when searching for bulbs and roots.

Fingers.

DILLY BAGS.
Bags.

DINGOES. The only domestic animal possessed
by the Aborigines was the dingo or wild dog.
It was not native to Australia. It was originally
brought from south-east Asia where, some
thousands of years ago, it was a small creature
inhabiting the upland regions. It is not certain
when early man brought it from the northern
countries in his canoes. The oldest skeleton
that has been found dates back about 3,000
years, so we can be sure it has been in Australia for at least this length of time. Archaeologists are still seeking further evidence.

Introduced into the northern part of the continent, the dingo spread to all parts except
Tasmania. The dogs that ran wild were hunted
for meat. Hunters often watched a dingo pack
killing a kangaroo or other large animal, and
then drove them off, but they left a portion of
the carcase as a reward for the four-footed
hunters. Dingo pups were regarded as most
appetising food. As there is only one litter a
year, it became a feature of some increase
rites to encourage the fertility of the female
dingoes.

DINGO

In camp dingoes were prized, not only because they helped the hunters, but because when domesticated they were warm and comfortable companions on cold nights. They were not highly trained hunting dogs.

DIVINATION.
Inquests, Magic, Medicine men.

DIVORCE. Not infrequently a young wife attempted to leave her elderly husband for the pleasures of life with a younger man. It was not unnatural for this to happen when her betrothal occurred at birth and her husband was a full generation older than she. Transfer of affections was a dangerous thing, both for the young man and the young woman. Bereaved husbands could be expected to take prompt revenge. This often resulted in a fight in which several people took part. Whether the deserted husband won or not, he relinquished his lawful wife only if he was well compensated with gifts. In some cases he would demand another wife to take the place of the one who had left him.

A further reason for elopement occurred when a husband became advanced in years. The wife knew that on his death she would be forced to marry his brother or some other man nominated by the elders, who might be repugnant to her. It was commonsense for her to take the initiative into her own hands.

It can be seen, therefore that the taking of a new husband was permissible under some circumstances. Nevertheless, in spite of the usual disparity in age between husband and wife, it can be said that the marriage system was reasonably successful.
Betrothal, Marriage.

DOLLS. It is not usual to think of such a sophisticated toy as a doll belonging to Aboriginal children, but the maternal instinct was as strong amongst the small girls of Australia as in any other part of the world. Dolls were not carried on walkabout because even the toddlers had to carry some item of utility at a time when all household goods and hunting gear had to be transported in bags, or carried in the hands. But what a joy it was to a girl to return "home" and find the carefully hidden twig or clay image that was her "baby".

Occasionally an older person would provide a twisted root or a rudely carved wooden figure for this purpose.

Like all dolls, they had to be dressed—but in this case the "dressing" consisted of painting them with stripes of red and white ochre in imitation of the older people when they took part in a corroboree.

DOWN. Down for decoration of the human body, sacred objects, and ground drawings came from two sources, vegetable and bird. Wild cotton and other plants were sometimes used, but the favourite material was down from eagle nestlings, or from ducks, geese, and other birds. Hunters who went to the mountains and found the nests of eagles killed the fledglings and plucked them, putting the down into bags. It was preserved until the time of festivities that was to be decorated, with blood. In some and then stuck to the body or to any object cases it was laid on in a pattern of narrow bands; elsewhere the head and body were completely smothered with a heavy coating, sometimes left white, or ornamented with patterns of red ochre and black charcoal.

DRAWINGS, GROUND. A particular development of art grew up, mainly in Central Australia, in the form of ground drawings which, in spite of the impermanence of the finished work, were made with careful attention to detail. This no doubt was on account of their sacred significance, and explains why the same methods were used in body painting. A suitable space was cleared of obstructions, sprinkled with water, trodden down firmly, and the surface carefully smoothed. An "undercoat" of powdered yellow, white, or red ochre was laid uniformly over the whole area, and the design built up with other colours. The designs or pictures were wiped out at the end of the performance; they were "tracing boards" for the contemplation and handing on of myths.

To the white man they might appear as a meaningless pattern of circles, dots, straight and zigzag lines, but clansmen who could read the mythological message were able to see the artist's purpose at a glance. Ground drawings were in fact charts with recognisable symbols. It did not matter if a line of footprints had a different number of toes in each impression; the important thing was that the footprints were recognisably the same to a hunter, and that the purpose of the track was apparent. The distinguishing mark or characteristic might not be recognised by a European, but the people who observed it knew. They were messages which Aborigines were able to recognise.

The message might be different to what we might expect. The drawing often contained a creative urge; it was a form of sympathetic magic portraying an historical event of the past in the lives of the totemic spirits of the clan, a constant reiteration of the link between man and his ancestors. The wandering trails of the ancestors brought a type of spiritual reincarnation; there were pictures of rainbow snakes, drawn to bring good seasons to the tribal area, and others designed to convey the urgent thought of fertility and reproduction to the ultimate benefit of the group. Maps and designs were drawn in the sand with a finger or stick to illustrate a legend. On the bora grounds of south-eastern Australia elaborate designs were engraved in sand and earth, and large figures of heroes and animals built up in high relief with earth over logs.

And there were childish drawings, and others made simply because it was good to make a picture that had been in the mind, and to share it with others. Permanent records were also actually engraved in rock faces.

Art.

DREAMS. An interesting folktale tells how dreams were made by birds. When the willy wagtail sees a bone being pointed, he tells the cockatoos, who make a dream and put it inside the victim, telling him who is pointing the bone so that he can take action against him.

With such a background it can be seen that dreams have some relation to magic and to the spirit world. It was in this "other world", which was part of the life of every man, woman, and child that they originated. Dreams were intimately connected with the Dreamtime. In every human being there was a spirit which was a form of reincarnation of the ancestral being who was past, present, and future; and it was in dreams that this mysterious presence manifested himself.

The personal or cult totems were the ones that manifested themselves most frequently during sleep. The dream was not an imaginary happening, a "might-have-been", but something that had actually happened to the dreamer, or to his spirit or familiar, in the past or in the future, or that was happening to him (or to it), at the present time, and of which he was unconscious during his waking hours. In Arnhem Land songs and bark painting designs were created in a dream by the men and became their personal property.

Dreamtime.

DREAMTIME. Other expressions used for the Dreamtime are Creative and Ancestral Times, implying that they were the days when creative acts were performed by the first ancestors of men, or by the spirits and heroes and heroines who established the pattern of Nature and Life and thereby created man's environment. "Dreaming" is a translation of the Aboriginal term commonly used, but a better form is Eternal Dreamtime. It had its beginning when the world was young and unformed, but it was a process as well as a period. It never ceased.

Time entered into the concept as well as space, not as a period or even a succession of periods, but as an ever-present "now" that eternally perpetuated the Dreamtime.

The ancestor who may have been a spirit, or a man, and who changed into an animal which became the totem of the clan or tribe (or of the individual) and who established laws and patterns of behaviour, is as alive today as when he performed his original enactments. The sacred past, the Dreamtime, is the sacred present, the Eternal Dreamtime.

The fact that heroes of old were alive in every generation, whether in their first or later forms, was a guarantee to men that they were following the precepts laid down at the beginning of time. Without the assurance, without the knowledge that the guardian spirits were part of their inmost being, life would have had no purpose for the Aborigines.

The belief explains many facets of Aboriginal life. In fact without this knowledge we cannot understand the Aboriginal at all. Song, dance, and ritual were the means whereby he kept within the territory of the Dreamtime. Sacred songs were Dreamtime songs. In ritual he was actually in the Dreamtime. The boundaries of his physical environment were defined by the extent of the journeys of the ancestor who was known to him. Every tree and hill and waterhole had its intimate contact with the ancestor who made it, or who performed some creative act at that particular place.

This close association of the tribal territory with the Dreamtime was another aspect of the reality of the spirit world. It was that which gave the Aboriginal the assurance that he would find waterholes in a featureless plain, because the ancestor of the Dreamtime had created it; the ancestor was still with him in spirit, so he and the ancestor were one.

Popularly, the Dreamtime was that period in the beginning of time when the ancestral heroes, the Old People, lived. It was the time of birth of the world, when man, animal, and spirit worked together and in harmony, and which was the subject of myth and legend. But it was certainly not a creative period that was a part of time that was past and half forgotten. The concept is one that has fascinated J. B. Priestley, whose Time Plays have been written round a similar theme. It is the recurring mystery that men have always experienced—the feeling of "having been here before". It was not a mystery to the Aboriginal. It was simply the Dreamtime, the sacred objects of which were symbols of the living presence that explained his totemic affiliations, and which he entered whenever he took part in increase and initiation ceremonies. The manhood rites were in turn symbolic of death and an entrance into the dream world, just as death itself was a final entrance into the Dreamtime.

"When the myths about the drama of the Dream Time are studied with care," wrote Dr W. E. H. Stanner, "it becomes clear that the Aborigines had taken, indeed, had gone far beyond, the longest and most difficult step toward the formation of a truly religious outlook. They had found in the world about them what they took to be signs of intent toward men, and they had transformed those signs into *assurances* of life under mystical nurture. Their symbolic observances toward the signs, in rites of several kinds, were in essence acts of faith toward the ground of that assurance."*

In modern times the Aborigines in country areas still go walkabout to renew their affinity with and to perpetuate their Dreamtime world.

Ancestors, Dreams, Religious beliefs.

DRINK. The common beverage everywhere was water, but there were several ways of flavouring or sweetening it. Honey, taken either from the nests of bees or from the bodies of honey ants, was used to sweeten the water. In many districts certain flowers such as wild honeysuckle were mixed with water. On the Daly River green ants were crushed and soaked in water. Pandanus fruit was also crushed and immersed in water, producing a mildly astringent beverage.

Beal (other spellings are bool and bull) was highly esteemed in the south-western district of Western Australia. In this case the sweet flowers of a dwarf species of Banksia were used. Lerp was an Aboriginal word meaning sweet. It was applied to a kind of manna secreted by insects on the leaves of mallee scrub. In *Australia Felix*, published in 1848, W. Westgarth wrote: "The natives of the Wimmera prepare a luscious drink from the Laap, a sweet exudation

* *Aboriginal Man in Australia*, page 215.

from the leaf of the mallee." In western Arnhem Land wallaby and kangaroo blood were
sometimes drunk.

Stimulants, Water.

DRUMS. Percussion sounds were usually made
by beating the open hand against the thigh, or
with the cupped hand on the opening between
the thighs. On Melville and Bathurst Islands
the buttocks were struck with the open hand
while dancing, and nearly everywhere clapping-
sticks, boomerangs, and lengths of wood were
tapped together or struck on the ground to provide a rhythmical accompaniment to song and
dance.

In a few places, however, some form of drum
was used to amplify the sound. In parts of
Queensland, South Australia, and New South
Wales an animal skin was rolled into a ball or
stretched across the thighs while the drummer
remained seated on the ground. Skin pads were
used on the Murray River, and in Queensland
a ball was stuffed with feathers and beaten
with the palm of the hand.

In north-eastern Arnhem Land a large ball
or pad of paperbark was treated in the same
way, and was regarded as a symbol of a fishlike
ancestor, the noise it made purporting to represent the sound emitted by a barramundi. Further west a hollow log with open ends was
struck during sacred rites, and this approached
more closely to the form of a drum. The
Papuan type of hand drum, the ends made of
goanna skin, was not evolved in Australia but
was introduced at some time to the Cape York
Peninsula.

In the Roper region a gong was used in the
Yabuduruwa sacred ritual. It was a piece of
hard, resilient wood held in one hand and hit
with another thin piece of wood, giving a metallic sound.

Clapping-sticks.

E

EGGS. The eggs of birds, turtles, and crocodiles were welcome articles of diet. Goose eggs were relished, and in places such as the Daly River and in regions with extensive lagoons, a large harvest could be gathered at the proper season. It provided an occasion for a number of tribes to gather together and indulge in corroborees, barter, and interchange of news. Certain rites and rules governed the procedure. When the first supply of eggs had been gathered, a small boy was given an egg yolk to eat, after which the eggs were piled round him in a heap until he was almost lost to sight. He then handed them out one by one. Boys were permitted to share in the egg feasts until the time of circumcision, after which they were forbidden to eat them until after the initiation ceremonies were completed.

The elders maintained a close watch over the gathering, and after a time forbade the collecting of further supplies. From then on only men of recognised standing and authority were permitted to eat them. This was no doubt an example of food conservation to ensure that plenty of young birds would be hatched, and that the supply of eggs in the following season would be adequate.

ELDERS. In any ordered, self-sufficient community there must be some body of responsible opinion, and a medium through which it is exercised, whether by democratic or dictatorial methods. The medium is the "government". In Aboriginal society, in small kinship and clan units and in the larger confederation of groups usually known as the tribe, custom and order were guarded by a group of elders who acted "in council".

The qualification of elder came not by election or appointment, but through experience, knowledge, and personality. Theoretically an elder was a man whose hair was turning grey; but as old age came early by European standards, years alone did not provide the necessary qualification. When a man was past his prime and unable to contribute effectively to the welfare of the group, either through failing skill or lack of purpose and decision, he was supported by his relatives. It was then that the system of early marriage of women to older men had its advantage, for they could be sure of a plentiful supply of food from their wives and younger relatives.

To be an elder, or perhaps more correctly, to be a "ruling elder", a man required to be in the full vigour of life, whether he were middle-aged or old. The council which, in a strangely informal fashion, made decisions that were binding on others, determined the course of action of their people, conducted inquests, and arranged expeditions of revenge, sanctioned punishments, and drew, taught, and explained totemic signs, was composed mainly of middle-aged elders. They had passed through the initiation ceremonies, were acquainted with ritual law and the mythology of the tribe, and were experienced in the varied fortunes and misfortunes that could befall their people. Knowledge, experience, and character were the three major characteristics of the elders who by acknowledged right sat in council meetings. Skill in hunting was not in itself sufficient, though an important attribute. The collective wisdom of the elders came from the ancestral spirits, and was an insurance against spiritual influences as well as against natural and physical dangers.

A young man who had sufficient knowledge of tribal lore might attend a meeting, but usually kept quiet and listened to his elders. It is probable that the right to speak came from recognised knowledge of sacred matters, but the man who had already shown himself prudent, bold, and resourceful would be a dominating influence. In the Arunta and related groups, provided that he had been conceived in the country of his father or his father's father, he could even rise to the position of totemic headman, with considerable authority in council decisions, but without the recognised status of chief.

There were no chiefs, in the sense that the title was used in Polynesia, Micronesia, and Melanesia. The heads of clans were the older men (excluding the very old), or those who had shown gifts of leadership, together with a full knowledge of totemic ritual. The larger tribal council meetings usually comprised the headmen of clans. The membership of this hierarchy was not strictly confined or controlled. In practice it appeared to settle itself naturally, and to work for the welfare of the tribe. The leader was usually middle-aged. The qualities of leadership in any society are such that no man can deny them, for they are of the mind rather than of the body.

Councils.

ELOPEMENT. For a number of reasons a man and woman might desert their group and travel long distances to escape revenge, but they were remorselessly tracked and hunted down. Punishment was death, or a severe beating, depending upon whether incest or kinship laws had been infringed.

ENGWURA. Amongst the Arunta, the engwura was a final phase in the series of initiation rituals which extended for several months. During the whole period of the engwura, rites were enacted daily. They began with a clan leader who, after consulting with elders of the totemic group, sent a messenger to kindred groups. He was called Ilchinkinja, a term meaning "beckoning hand". He bore a bull-roarer as symbol of his authority, and to show the purpose of his coming. The beckoning hand was obeyed, and before long the clans gathered together at the chosen ceremonial ground, bringing sacred objects carved or decorated with the local totemic symbols. It was a time of great importance and sanctity.

The sacred objects were disposed on two platforms, each representing the two moieties of the tribe. This important division was emphasised throughout the ceremonies. The young men were addressed by the elders and, to the accompaniment of the rubbing of the sacred objects with red ochre, the rites were explained, the meaning of the designs painted on the churinga and on their own bodies and on the ground expounded. The engwura was essentially a period of instruction in sacred lore, given to those who had passed all the tests and who were entitled to be admitted into the ranks of the men who were the recipients of sacred knowledge.

Ceremonies, Messengers.

EVIL. The Aborigines were conscious of evil as a malignant force, usually in spirit form, which worked against them; but such a statement may possibly be criticised on the ground that other concepts may be read into it. It was the opposite principle to that of beneficent ancestors, gods, and spirits which made the world ready for man in the Dreamtime, and continued to guard and protect them. The guardianship was necessary if life was to be preserved; and all ceremony, all belief in totemism, law, and order was designed to ensure that the Dreamtime continued to function efficiently.

Evil could be embodied in spirits of the dead, and burial ceremonies were designed to prevent a malevolent spirit from accompanying the group. The spirits which took control of animals, insects, birds, and reptiles were particularly difficult to destroy. They were liable to rise again, and to inspire dangerous thoughts and actions. An evil spirit of this kind was sometimes known in legend as the Evil One.

CROWS

Legends tell of his possession of human beings, and of how he could be driven from one material form to another. There is a culture hero story which tells how the Evil One inhabited the body of a wallaby. It was killed and thrown on a fire, but kept emerging in one form after another, each of which was burnt. Finally the fire died down and the ashes grew cold; and from them crept a tiny insect, which still sheltered the spirit of the Evil One.

Even in the time of creation Baiame had to fight against an evil spirit who sent clouds of insects to befoul the world that the Great Spirit had made. In a number of legends the crow is also the embodiment of evil.

Spirits.

F

FAMILIES. Tribal organisation included several types of group, such as linguistic groups, moieties, totem groups, clans, etc. The smallest of these was the family, which consisted of a man and his wife and children. It was usually larger than this, however, because of the plurality of wives, especially among older men. In very rare instances in Arnhem Land a man might have 15 to 20 wives, but as a rule there were only one or two. The family was frequently a self-contained, self-supporting unit.

The ties that bound husband and wife together were somewhat loose. Wives might be lent or exchanged, but the customs by which such arrangements were made were fairly rigid. For various reasons women might enter into successive marriages, and there were also valid reasons for divorce and remarriage on the part of men. Tribal, kinship, and totemic laws regulated marriage, and through them the structure and unity of the larger groupings were maintained. It was not unusual for several families to join together in hunting and food-gathering, and to shift from one camp to another in company.

Children absorbed the behaviour patterns inherent in kinship structure. They were part of their father's religious or totemic group, and of his social group, though in some regions the social group or totem was inherited from their mothers. The subject is a complex one, and is discussed further under the heading of Relationships.

Children, Divorce, Marriage, Relationships, Tribes.

FAT. Animal fat had many uses in camp. Rubbed on the body it gave strength and suppleness to the limbs, and also afforded protection against insects. If placed near streams, billabongs, and waterholes, it was believed to attract animals and birds to the spot (as it certainly would in a lean season), and fishes. Emu and goanna fat was usually employed to anoint the body and in some cases red ochre was smeared over it; in some areas its use was reserved for the old men.

The vitality and strength that came from fat may explain the importance which the sorcerer attached to kidney fat when encompassing the death of a person by extracting it from the victim. Eating the fat transferred the vitality of the dying man to the one who absorbed it. It has been stated that fat was the principal method of preserving implements and weapons, but F. D. McCarthy points out that few that he has handled in museums are so treated, and believes that constant daily handling ensured their preservation.

Magic, Pointing bones.

FEASTS. The scattered subdivisions of a tribe gathered together at certain times in the year when seasonal conditions made this possible. The only suitable occasions were when food supplies were abundant and sufficient in quantity to feed a large number of people. This occurred in coastal districts when fish and turtles were plentiful, or a whale became stranded, or in marshes and lagoons where wildfowl congregated and eggs could be obtained by the thousand; and, in south-eastern Queensland, when the bunya-bunya pines bore their large cones, the seeds of which were roasted in hot ashes, and also in the Snowy Mountains when the bogong moth emerged.

Hospitality sometimes extended beyond the tribal borders, cementing friendly alliances, and providing opportunities for corroborees, for adjusting differences of opinion by fighting as well as by discussion and peaceful settlement, and for arranging marriages.

Gifts.

FEATHERS. Feathers of many species of birds were used for decorative purposes in headbands, anklets, and other personal ornaments, as well as for bags, baskets, and other possessions. The soft down of birds was an important ingredient in decorating the body and making ground drawings. In a photograph in Mrs Aeneas Gunn's *The Little Black Princess*, the original caption describes the adornment as "scarves of red feathers to please Mr Thunder Debbil-debbil".

Bags, Baskets, Decorations.

FEET. There was a saying that "a friend would always leave a footprint", implying that an enemy would take care to disguise his tracks.

Generally speaking, the Aboriginal has small ankles and broad feet. Shoes of any kind were seldom worn (except for the kurdaitcha or emu shoes on special occasions), and the big toe was loosely jointed. Objects could be picked up from the ground almost as easily with the toes as with the fingers. After a lifetime of walking barefoot, men and women had a hard pad of leather-like flesh on the soles of the feet. The human foot track was a popular motif in rock engravings and paintings.

FERTILITY. The principle of fertility was all-important, especially in desert regions where existence depended so precariously on the ripening of a few nuts and berries, the supply of root vegetables, and the presence of game, which in its turn depended on a constant water supply. Fertility or increase rites were therefore closely associated with the cult of the Rainbow Serpent who was the giver of water. Even in well-watered, fertile areas, increase rites were observed with religious fervour to ensure a plentiful supply of food in the future. They were part of the general concept of fertility. The rites connected with them were, in some regions, associated with and performed separately either by men or women. Belief in the Fertility Mother was fairly widespread, but on the other hand the male principle was regarded as paramount in some areas. A large wooden pole was a phallic emblem among the Aranda and was the symbol of masculine creative power which in their belief formed the world and all living creatures.

Increase rites were totemic, the participants ensuring the perpetuation of animals and plants of their own totem by the exercise of the appropriate ritual.

In *The World of the First Australians*, R. M. and C. H. Berndt give detailed information about a fertility rite in Arnhem Land. The ubar gong sounded. It was the Mother calling men to the sacred grove. Singing and dancing began in the main camp among the women, accompanied by a didgeridoo. Gradually the tempo increased and a whistling sound was heard, a sign that the Rainbow Serpent was present, and that all would be well for the future.

Ceremonies, Gods, Increase rites, Rainbow Serpent.

FIGHTING. Belligerence was not a strong characteristic of the Aborigines, except when passions were roused during inquests, on the few occasions when territorial rights were invaded, personal insults given or personal rights infringed. Woman-stealing was also a frequent cause of aggression and retaliation. Inquests were held after the death of an adult when it had occurred from natural causes, for it was then assumed that the deceased person had been the victim of sorcery. When at last the medicine man pointed out the one who was supposed to have caused the death, there was a demand for revenge. As the perpetrator nearly always belonged to another group or tribe, a fighting party assembled to exact revenge.

In many cases the initial enthusiasm tended to evaporate before the expedition had proceeded far on its way. This was most likely when the warriors left their own territory and ventured into adjacent areas in which the totemic ancestors were unknown to them. This meant that they knew nothing about the local spirit centres, which could well prove inimical to them. But if their blood was still hot a fight would develop. On occasion it spread to other clans until finally there would be a miniature battle and the whole affair came to a conclusion. Relatively few casualties seemed to result from such fights.

The revenge party was protected by magic performed over the men and the weapons to ensure success and prevent injury. The party frequently awaited an opportunity to secure their victim by stealth, or walked into his camp and killed him in front of his group, who knew that death was the penalty and made no attempt to save him. They might even point out the man who was to be killed. This prevented the matter from spreading further.

The trial by ordeal among the Makarata of Arnhem Land was a form of fighting so regulated that it took the place of a formal trial. One account states that after the inquest had been held and the "guilty" party, who belonged to another tribe or clan, was named, representatives of the deceased's group and those of the supposed murderer stood in two lines facing one another. Some formalities were observed.

The attacking side advanced on the others and then retreated. The other party went through the same motions. After this the accused's people ran to and fro accompanied by several men who had no direct connection with the inquest. The attackers, who were the aggrieved party, hurled their spears at the darting, twisting figures, shouting insults. But the spearheads had been removed, and while the slender poles could inflict a painful blow, they were unlikely to cause severe wounds. Curses and threats, while wounding to the vanity, were soon forgotten. The victims were not permitted to return the spears, but had to endure them until the fusillade was exhausted. These actions continued for some time, but at length the accused person walked across the open space towards his accusers, and was ceremonially stabbed in the fleshy part of his thigh, and the conflict or trial was over. But it did not always end in such an amicable fashion. Sometimes a spearhead was not removed and the supposed killer was himself killed. This might then lead to further conflict. On the other hand if he escaped injury a further attack might be made at a later date.

As death was supposed to have been caused by sorcery, and the perpetrator discovered by magical means, it was only natural that a visit from another tribe or clan would be viewed with suspicion until their intentions were proclaimed. When a group of people were unable to decide whether their visitors came peaceably or with hostile intent, women would be sent to entertain them. If their overtures were accepted it usually meant peace, but if they were refused a fight was inevitable. Sometimes the gesture was made to probe the visitors' minds, but treachery was not unknown. Even though the warriors received the female visitors, they might make a surprise attack. Similarly the gift of attractive women might be designed to put them off their guard.

Except in parts of the Northern Territory where fighting was engaged in on a broader basis, leading at times to inter-tribal battles, it could seldom be described as warfare. The reasons for conflict were well defined and although injuries and death might occur and women might be stolen, the trouble was confined to small groups; even then, a token victory or show of force and the proclamation of

intention were frequently considered sufficient to wipe out insults and injuries. Tribal feuds and prolonged warfare were practically unknown amongst the Aborigines.

The weapons used included spears, clubs, throwing-sticks, boomerangs, and shields. In serious fighting women and children were sent away from the danger zone. Preparations were made well before the battle. A leader gave the call to rise and eat before sunrise, the warriors prepared their weapons and gathered their boomerangs and waddies ready for the fight. Each man was provided with a number of sharpened spears.

Games, Magic, Peacemaking, Weapons.

FINGERS. In some places it was not unusual for a mother to bite off the little finger of a girl baby in order to save the child from an ordeal which would be more painful if delayed for a few years when, not being a sacred rite, it would have to be performed in public. The child was then required to adopt the same stoical attitude shown by boys during the circumcision and initiation tests. The custom was not universal but was widely practised. It has been suggested that it had a practical purpose. A woman used her digging-stick to loosen the soil when probing for yams or grubs and then scooped out the soil with her bare hands. The absence of the little finger made the human trowel more slender and enabled her to dig the hole more quickly and effectively. Whether this is so or not, it was obviously a traditional rite among women.

A more usual method was to constrict the joint tightly by means of a tied sinew. As it dried it contracted until the finger finally dropped off. In the Northern Territory there was a spider's web which was so strong that it served the same purpose. To stop the bleeding the mother squirted milk on the stump and smeared gum or spider's web over it and anointed it with fat or oil.

FIRE STICKS. When moving from one camp to another, especially in cold or wet weather, the Aborigines carried a fire stick. It served a double purpose: to expedite the kindling of a fire for cooking or for warmth during the night at the new encampment, and to keep them warm when travelling. Timber of a suitable nature which kept smouldering for many hours was freshened up by knocking off the charred end and swinging it violently in the air. Fire sticks and leafy torches were also used for setting fire to grass and trees when burning off the land to drive out the animals.

There were occasions when the fire stick became symbolic of the permanent camp fire, and therefore of "home". In *Horne Expedition in Central Australia*,* F. J. Gillen wrote in 1896: "Carrying fire-sticks, they place rings, woven of fur and vegetable down, round a boy's neck and arms and sometimes over and under the shoulders; the fire-sticks are then handed to him, the lubras saying: 'Take care of the fire; keep to your own camp.'"
Fire-making, Fires.

FIRE-MAKING. The usual method of starting a fire was by the use of the fire-drill or fire-saw, but some tribes in Central Australia and eastern New South Wales struck pyrites against flint and ignited a fire from the sparks.

It was no trouble to light a fire in dry regions. When wood and grass were tinder-dry the fire could be started in less than a minute, but there were parts of the country where it was impossible to keep wood dry, so that if the fire was accidentally allowed to go out, it was difficult to rekindle. In such cases fire was sometimes procured from another group, the fire sticks being kept alight on the journey home.

The fire-drill was the most widespread type of equipment. A thin stick was placed vertically with its lower end resting in a hollow in a larger piece of timber. The drill-stick was twirled rapidly between the palms of the hands until the dust which collected through abrasion in the hole or groove began to smoulder. When it was hot enough the dust was folded into a heap of dry grass and blown vigorously until it burst into flame. Two sticks from 2 to 6 feet long from the grass tree were normally used. A light wood hearth stick and a harder twirling stick were also used.

In some regions the fire-saw was that ubiquitous implement, the woomera or spear-thrower. It was customary to select a split stick, or to split a dry branch and stuff the crack with dry grass or other inflammable material. The cleft

* *Anthropology*, Part 4, page 170.

stick was placed on the ground and often held steady by a woman or boy standing on it. The fire-maker rubbed the hard edge of his woomera backwards and forwards, pressing down on it until the hot powdered tinder fell on the grass and smoke poured out of it. More grass was placed on top and the material waved gently to and fro until it ignited. In Central Australia and the Northern Territory the saw was worked across the upturned side of a shield.

At tribal and inter-tribal corroborees contests were sometimes held between experts to see who could light a fire in the shortest time.
Fires, Fire sticks.

FIRES. Without fire the Aboriginal could not have survived under the conditions in which he lived. He used fire to keep himself warm at night, to cook his food, to burn off grass when hunting game, for illumination, and as a means of increasing the fertility of his tribal territory. In winter and rainy weather fires were kept going inside the huts.

In preparation for a cold night a fire was built in front of the hut. If the inflammable structure caught fire little harm was done for it could be rebuilt in an hour or so. In a temporary camp a fire was kept burning between each sleeper in the shelter of the windbreak. A pile of wood near the feet was used to replenish the fires during the night. There was no cheery blaze to illumine the general camp scene, however, for each camp fire consisted of three sticks the ends of which were pushed together to keep them alight, and replenished when they were consumed.

It was necessary to keep the fire alight continuously in wet weather. The responsibility was given to older women. They had many ways of preserving the fire—by keeping it in caves or rock shelters, inside hollow logs and trees, and by stoking it during the night. When no shelter was available the hot embers were buried in earth or sand, and could quickly be dug up and fanned to life as soon as the rain was over.

The flickering personal firelight at night was treasured for its feeble light as well as for the warmth it provided. When a corroboree was held or when sacred ritual dances took place at night, larger fires were necessary to light up the scene. Hollow logs were dragged on to the dancing enclosure and set upright round the circle. A hole was cut near the bottom of the log to create a draught. Dry kindling wood, sticks, and heavier branches were put into the shaft and lit at the bottom, turning the log into a fiery torch. Tussocks of porcupine grass and brushwood served the same purpose but burnt out more quickly.

As in other parts of the world, fire entered into religious ceremonies. In Australia it was used as part of the ordeals that the novices were required to endure at the time of initiation. The procedure varied among the different tribes. Sometimes the novices were required to sit close to the fire, staring at it with wide-open eyes until they fell unconscious to the ground. The elders watched closely to see that they did not shrink from the fierce heat and blazing light. As a purification ceremony the candidates were held over a smoky fire or laid on top of green branches and foliage placed on the fire. The practice of firewalking was observed by a few desert tribes, where fully initiated men walked on beds of living embers.

When hunting game grass fires were sometimes lit when the wind was in the right direction. The animals were speared or clubbed when driven out by the flames. In this way trees were killed but the grasslands became more fertile when enriched with the ashes. The new growth provided good pasture for animals and ensured a plentiful supply when the group returned the following year.

Camps, Fire-making, Fire sticks, Sleeping.

FIREWORKS. A "poolooloomee playabout" in the northern regions was an exciting occasion. Sheets of bark were peeled from white gum trees and cut with axes and knives into a shape something like a tennis racquet with a round head and short handle. When night fell the heads were put into a hot fire and as the bark was full of sap they did not burn but became red hot and luminous.

Meanwhile stout poles had been planted in the ground. When it was dark, to the accompaniment of singing and dancing the men took the poolooloomees from the fire, held them above their heads, and then struck them against the poles, breaking off the circular heads which spun off into the darkness, sometimes rising to a considerable height, whirling round

and round in fiery circles. Burning torches of wood, leafy branches or cord, illuminated rituals at night.

FISH TRAPS. In many parts of Australia fish traps were cleverly constructed with walls of stone, mud, wooden stakes, woven reeds, logs, brushwood, and grass. The fish swam or were driven into the traps but could not find their way out again, and were caught in the shallow water or, in tidal reaches, were stranded when the water receded. On the banks of the Katherine River there were permanent traps with stone walls. The blooming of the cotton tree was a sign that fish were plentiful; as soon as the yellow flowers appeared the tribes left their normal camping grounds and went down to the river to catch the fish they knew would be there.

FISHING. From an early age girls as well as boys who lived near lakes, rivers or the seashore were encouraged to recognise the different varieties of fish and to study their habits to prepare them for later life when they would be required to feed themselves and their families. In this way they soon became adept and knew the best methods to use under varying conditions. Fish-hooks made of wood, shell, or bone, gorges of bone and shell, spears, nets, and poison were all used, and harpoons for larger sea fish. One-piece hooks were used along the east coast, composite hooks of bone and wood or bone and shell in Cape York Peninsula and Arnhem Land. In the latter districts harpoons with detachable heads were used to catch dugongs and turtles.

Fresh-water fish were the easiest to catch. Of all the different varieties the Murray cod, where it was available, was the most highly esteemed. When the Murray was in flood it overflowed its banks in places, and the cod, perch, and bonefish swam in the shallow water. They were scooped up in nets or speared from canoes. Eventually the flood waters receded and it became the task of the men and women, helped by boys and girls, to wade through them and scoop the bewildered fish into baskets with a landing net. It provided a wonderful opportunity for boys to practice fish-spearing.

When the water was only a few inches deep the fish died if they had been unable to escape, because of rapid changes in temperature.

Turtles and small crayfish as well as fish attempted to get back to the river. The Aborigines knew when this was likely to happen and were ready for them. Floating downstream in their canoes they tied them up to the trees and waited for the ripples which denoted the presence of escaping fish. As soon as the water was disturbed they plunged their spears into it and whirled them round. The fish, turtles and yabbies, usually close to exhaustion, rose to the surface where they were caught by hand and thrown into the canoes.

Another method used in shallow water, especially on the coast, was for all the men to form a crescent and to wade ashore carrying spears to which leafy branches had been tied. When the shadow of the branches fell on the water the fish were frightened and fled towards the shore, where they were easily captured.

An ingenious method of catching fish with the aid of dolphins was developed by the Aborigines of Moreton Bay in Queensland and Proper Bay in South Australia. The friendly creatures were fed and petted. A watch was kept and when a shoal of fish was seen the fishermen ran to the shore and beat the water with their hands and pieces of wood. This was the normal method of calling the dolphins. They swam towards the shore driving the shoal of fish before them, where they were speared by the fishermen. It is said that the dolphins were suitably rewarded for their services with a meal of fish.

Fish traps were used extensively in many coastal areas and along the rivers. Bruised leaves and bark were used to poison the water in shallow ponds and billabongs. Night fishing with the aid of torches was another method used on the coasts and rivers, where nets and spears were also in use. Turtles and larger fish such as dugongs were caught with harpoons. A wooden float was attached to the line in case the quarry swam away after being struck.

Fish-spearing was the method most universally used by the men. There were several prongs at the end of the fish spear, used in many parts of the country, but the aim needed to be accurate, and years of practice were required to enable the fisherman to judge the speed and depth of the fish. When spearing fish near the shores of a lake a canoe was manoeuvred stealthily up to the edge of the reeds. The fisherman plunged his spear into the water to a depth of several feet. A bubble of air was carried down by the prongs, rose through the water and escaped with a distinct plop which alarmed the fish. Every nerve on the *qui vive*, the fisherman was alert to detect a stir and quivering in the reeds which indicated where the startled fish was to be found. As soon as he saw it his spear flashed downwards once more and impaled the fish on the prongs—if he were lucky and skilful enough. Even the most adept spearsman might have to strike several times before securing his fish.

In shallow water shellfish were found by wading. When they were felt by the bare feet they were thrown into a bag and carried back to the camp when the bag was full.

Competitions, Fish traps, Nets, Spears (fish).

FLINTS.
Knives.

FOLKLORE. By the telling of folktales, by chants, and by acting and various forms of ritual observance the elders of the tribe conveyed to a new generation the past accomplishments of their people, and of the cult-heroes and spirits who made their territory a sacred abiding place. Much supernatural lore was imparted in ritual songs and dances, but as with all primitive, Nature-loving, Nature-dependent people, local folklore emerged from their own living environment. The stories were full of adventure and an earthy humour, often stark and realistic, telling of life as they knew it, and giving ingenious reasons to explain the origin and purpose of natural phenomena.

In some tribes the spoken story was accompanied by drawings on sand or earth which illuminated the narrative, just as gesture was part of the story-teller's art. The drawings were obliterated with a flick of the hand and further actions delineated. The same principle was employed by the elders when giving preliminary instructions and revealing portions of sacred legend to initiates.

Legends are the unwritten history of a people. They will change according to the viewpoint of the observer, or of the group, and may be distorted, but in essence they are still history. Legend may often be truer to the spirit and temper of the original participants than the more formal histories of the western world, if one concedes that imagination and poetic licence can hold the kernel of ultimate truth.

Racial memories sometimes lingered in the simple tales. The original inhabitants who were the ancestors of the later people may have been larger or smaller than their descendants; in folklore they lived again. There are memories of a time when food was more abundant, and of seasons of great scarcity, which may preserve the recollection of climatic changes which occurred over a long period of time. The exploits of individual hunters and warriors were woven into legends of strange creatures and animals that became men, and of men who were really animals—an inextricable tangle of fact and history and religion which contained the living tradition and spirit of the people. There is a sense of timelessness in folklore, for a tale may have been composed about an event in living memory or may 1 ave passed through many generations of story-tellers.

The modernised version of legends bears little relationship to their original form. The following is an exact translation of the text of a folktale from the Katherine River district.

He-came came into-cave budidjmanaiwan (a kind of wallaby) that-one ? went Ganwulu. From-Ganwulu (to) Nganyordabmag from-there (to) Nganyoron. From-Nganyoron (to) Nganwaragbregbregmi. He-went-down into-cave at-Ninganda. To-the-cave (of) Ninganda not he-went-in. Children (and) women not-allowed. White-man (?ghost) cannot ?shut up, make play, (?blow). Not come-out cannot-go-out cannot-depart-altogether.

The brief story is paraphrased by Dr A. Capell who points out that Nganwaragbregbregmi was stated to mean "where the dingo broke his shoulder and cried out", but that the story of the giving of this name was not collected. "The sand-wallaby came and went into the cave. He went to Ganwulu, and from there to Nganyordabmag and thence to Nganyoron. From Nganyoron he went to Nganwaragbregbregmi. At Ninganda he went down to a cave. He did not go into the Ninganda cave. Children

and women are not allowed to go to that cave."[*]

A typical legend in its westernised form follows. It still contains the essential simplicity of the original story, but has a literary form and a rounding of the plot which makes it more acceptable to readers of the present day. It will be obvious that the sandpiper and the carpet snakes were totemic ancestors, and that the conclusion to the story is a westernised addition.

Pipipa the Sandpiper was making a spear. He had spent a long time trimming and polishing the shaft, chipping the head to a sharp edge, and binding it firmly to the shaft with gut. All that remained to be done was to coat the binding with melted gum.

He lit a fire and put a lump of red gum on a stone.

"As soon as I've finished I'll show it to my brothers the Carpet Snakes," he mused as he bent over the gum and poked it to see whether it was soft enough. A tongue of fire darted out and licked the gum. It burst into flame. Pieces of burning gum flew in all directions, some of them hitting Pipipa on the nose and legs and clinging there in spite of all his efforts to dislodge them.

"Help! Help!" he screamed.

Far away the Carpet Snakes heard him and turned to each other in alarm. "It is our brother Pipipa!" they exclaimed.

They raced towards his camp and saw him writhing in agony. "Look, he is covered with burning gum."

They tore it off. "What have you been doing? Your legs are burnt to thin sticks and your nose is not like any nose we have ever seen. It is a beak! You have turned yourself into a bird!"

"Don't be silly," Pipipa snapped. "How would I know that the gum would explode?"

He looked down at his thin legs and felt his sharp, protruding nose. "Don't you feel sorry for me, my brothers?"

The tears rolled down their cheeks. "We are truly sorry, Pipipa. Sorry because we laughed at you, but you did look funny and

* *Oceania*, Vol. 30, No. 3, page 218 by permission of Professor A. P. Elkin, Editor, and Dr A. Capell.

we couldn't help it. More sorry because you have hurt yourself and changed into a bird."

"I'm not a bird," Pipipa shouted angrily. He beat his arms against his body, but was dismayed to find that they looked like wings.

His brothers lifted him up and carried him down to the beach. He struggled and kept on shouting, "Not a bird! Not a bird!"

"Poor fellow," they said, wagging their heads. "We'll make a good camp for him. It will be like a swamp with plenty of water and with fish for him to catch."

They dug a wide hole. The tide crept up the beach and filled it, making a large lagoon. Carpet Snakes laid their brother beside it and went back to their own camp.

When they were out of sight Sandpiper staggered to his feet and bent over to look at his reflection in the swamp water. He sighed and whispered, "Not a bird!" but in his heart he knew he was indeed a bird destined to spend its life in the swamps and lagoons by the seashore.*

Mythology, Songs.

FOOD. Anything that was edible was eaten by the Aborigines. The supply and variety of food varied enormously according to the locality. In coastal areas where fish and shellfish were plentiful, around swamps and lagoons where wildfowl, eggs, fish, and waterlily roots could easily be taken, and in semi-jungle areas where fruit, nuts, and roots abounded, the gathering of food did not occupy all the time, and people had leisure to develop advanced art forms. In the fertile regions the Aborigines had a plentiful supply of food and a well-balanced diet of plant and animal foods, but those in the more arid areas were not so fortunate.

It is said that there were places where 200 square miles of territory were needed to support a single person throughout the year. But although food was scarce, wandering tribes knew how to make use of the harvest of the desert. R. M. and C. H. Berndt listed the varieties of indigenous foods obtained round the Ooldea Soak Mission Station and found that the Aborigines had taken 18 varieties of mam-

mals and marsupials, 19 birds, 11 reptiles, eight insects, six water roots, 17 varieties of seed, three vegetables, 10 fruits and berries, four other plants and fungi, and a variety of eggs.* It is true that in some cases the quantity was small and unsatisfying, and that a great deal of time and energy was spent in obtaining a meagre supply. Yet in good seasons a surprisingly large variety of vegetable food could be found in the western desert where the people lived on lizards, rats, bandicoots, yams, berries and seeds for most of the time. The banks of small creeks provided river yams; figs, fruit, and berries could be obtained in the hills; grass seed, quandongs, and edible roots from the plains. On flats in sandy districts the jala yam flourished, providing tubers ranging from a few ounces to 8 lb in weight.

When big game could not be found, vegetable food gathered by the women, and grubs, snakes, lizards, and small animals, provided a meal, even though it contained little sustenance. The art of digging for roots was well developed. Keen eyes searched for telltale cracks in the ground, and the tapping of the digging-stick told its owner whether yams were to be found there, and even the particular variety of root. An unexpected find such as a sandalwood bush with a good crop of nuts, a nest of emu eggs, or of dingo pups (a greatly relished meal) was always a welcome relief.

In the majority of languages there was a special term for vegetable food, as distinct from meat, the latter providing the staple diet in many areas. It was man's work to hunt and provide sustenance for himself and his family, though he would not disdain the help of his wife or wives. When large birds and animals such as emus and kangaroos were killed, the flesh was usually eaten before it had time to cook properly. Such food was shared by all members of the group, even though some of them were unable to contribute to the meal. A betrothed man had a responsibility to his future parents-in-law, and kinship obligations were recognised. Young men who had recently been initiated were also expected to provide some food for the men responsible for their education.

Criticism has been levelled at the Aborigines

* A. W. Reed, *Aboriginal Fables and Legendary Tales*, A. H. and A. W. Reed, 1965.

* *The World of the First Australians*, page 94.

ECHIDNA

the early hours of the morning or, more usually, late in the afternoon, especially when the group was on walkabout, for the daylight hours were devoted to hunting. When in permanent camp raw vegetable food was consumed at intervals from late in the morning until early afternoon.

Some food was forbidden to women, especially certain kinds of fish, while in some regions young men and women were prohibited from eating a number of delicacies such as fat turkeys and kangaroo tails. There were also short-term prohibitions imposed for different reasons, mainly at times of ritual observance.

The following brief list indicates the kinds of food available to the Aborigines. It should be remembered that this list, incomplete though it may be, represents the resources of a whole continent, and that tribes in one locality would have access to only a small portion of the food supplies mentioned.

Animals: The large animals, including kangaroos, wombats, wallabies, possums, and so

because they have been wasteful of their meagre supplies, devouring eggs and the young of animals without thought of their future needs, but this is far from the truth. The Aboriginal was in fact a conservationist, being careful to leave fruiting trees unharmed, and even in some cases to scatter seed on the ground to ensure a future harvest, to leave some yams untouched, and to abandon his fishing while there were still fish to be caught. His immediate need was to fill his belly, but he was familiar with the life cycle of plants and animals and knew where to look for them at the proper season in different parts of his territory, and always to think of the future. He collected enough food for one or two days because meat would not keep longer. Food-getting was therefore an almost daily task.

The gathering of food was a never-ending occupation. Even when the day's supply had been gathered the preparation was often long and tiresome. Animal food had to be eaten in

CARPET SNAKE

on, were the most highly prized. Smaller animals included rats, mice, dingoes, rabbits, echidnas, and flying foxes.

Birds: Emus were the most eagerly sought birds for the oven, but doubtless other birds proved a tasty meal.

Clay: Perhaps the strangest food of all was clay, though it has been known to be eaten in other parts of the world in times of great scarcity. In certain areas, however, white clay was regarded as a delicacy.

Eggs: Eggs of the emu, brush turkey, mallee hen and many other birds were taken. On the Daly River and at other places there was a season for the gathering of goose eggs, when the tribes gathered together and joined in games, entertainments, and tribal rituals.

Fish and shellfish: Salt-water and fresh-water fish were much esteemed. A stranded whale was a rare treat, and large fish such as dugongs provided a number of meals. All edible fish were eaten. Fish and shellfish recorded as food included Murray cod, bream, perch, Murray Mouth salmon, catfish, mudfish, silver bream, butterfish, sharks, stingrays, mussels, cockles, small crayfish found in water-holes, also larger coastal varieties, frogs, oysters, clams, limpets, mangrove worms, fresh-water tortoises and salt-water turtles, and crocodiles.

Fruit: Wild peaches (quandongs), cherries, plums, figs, tomatoes, berries, and pandanus nuts.

Honey was both a food and an ingredient in a refreshing drink.

Insects and grubs: The most popular was the witchetty grub, up to 5 inches in length, white and succulent, and eaten uncooked. Added to this was an endless variety of ants (eaten for the honey in their bodies), caterpillars, grubs, moths, and the larvae of wasps.

Lizards and snakes: Goannas, lizards, and snakes were all relished when game was scarce.

Vegetables: Seeds of nardoo, kuldoo, and many other grasses were winnowed and ground into flour for cake-making. Roots included yam, waterlily (also the pods), kuntyari, etc., sometimes eaten fresh, roasted, or dried and ground with grass-seed flour. In Queensland the seeds of the bunya-bunya pine were eaten.

G

GAMES. Like children throughout the world, Aboriginal youngsters enjoyed playing games and imitating older people. As soon as they could walk small boys picked up sticks and pretended that they were spears, thrusting at imaginary targets. When they were a little older their fathers made them miniature spear-throwers to enable them to send the "spears" a greater distance, and trained them in their use. (The spear-thrower was the only distinctive mechanical device developed by the Aborigines.) This was often the occasion which marked the beginning of the usefulness of boys round the camp.

Small girls were not supposed to play with such manly weapons, but were provided with a miniature reproduction of their mothers' digging-sticks. Stones were also made in the form of small replicas of grinding-stones, and tiny bark coolamons were used as cradles and vessels for holding seeds or water while helping mother. Most of the games of childhood were part of the training for life as an adult.

In regions where the boomerang was used, boys fashioned small boomerangs for themselves. Other weapons were also made and aimed at bark discs which were bowled along the ground. The boys stood in a row and threw their 5-foot spears at the disc as it rolled past them, preparing for the time when they would have to throw long spears at a swiftly moving animal. The next stage was that of make-believe combats in which the boys hurled the spears at each other, and avoided them by swiftness of foot or by parrying them with narrow shields. Life was becoming more real, and it was not unusual for boys to be injured at such sports.

Hide-and-seek and finding a hidden object had a serious purpose. The hidden object was almost microscopically small and was buried in the sand with the merest speck showing above ground. The children who looked for it were not permitted to disturb the surface. The game developed quickness of sight, a necessary qualification for boys when tracking game and for girls when looking for roots and other vegetable foods. Tracking was another game that de-veloped qualities that were essential to the full-grown man and woman, and was continued after they became adults. A man returning from the hunt hid his catch carefully and invited his friends and relatives to find it.

Children are the same the world over. Many of the games of Aboriginal children were designed not for training but simply for enjoyment. "Keeping house" in a primitive way, pretending to be mothers and fathers, were stimulating to the imagination and exciting in themselves. Then there were active games and sports: ball games, mud slides, chasing, swimming when they had the chance, tree-climbing, wrestling and racing.

From observations made as a young man, Ion L. Idriess has added to our knowledge of the games played by Aboriginal children. He has described them in an interesting chapter in *Our Living Stone Age*. He tells how they threw long leaves into a fire. They were borne upwards on the current of hot air. Two leaves were bound together in the form of a cross and revolved like a propeller as they were carried upwards. Other games included skimming flat stones from rock and water surfaces, playing with balls, hiding under the water and breathing through a hollow reed, making wheels of clay and throwing spears at them, playing with dolls, swinging from vines in the bush, climbing trees, sliding down mud banks (with a wary eye open for lurking crocodiles), making "skis" of bark for sliding over greasy, muddy swamps, diving and playing in the water, playing tipcat, cat's cradle, and other games known or unknown to white children. In the deserts and on walk-about many of these activities were restricted, but at heart the Aboriginal child was kin to other children, getting pleasure out of little things, one moment babyish by nature, the next a small and serious replica of mother or father.

Ball games, Boomerangs, Climbing, Competitions, Dolls, Sledges, String figures, Swings.

GARMENTS. In many parts of the country the natural state of the Aboriginal was complete nudity, but it is not possible to generalise for, as in so many other matters, customs varied. In the north and in the central districts it was usual for people to go naked, and in the south to wear kangaroo, possum, or wallaby skin rugs or cloaks in winter. Even in the southern regions a single skin was usually the only garment. In cold weather a larger skin would be chosen. It was worn fur side out, fastened with a wooden pin at the shoulder, leaving the other shoulder bare and the arm free.

"They were all muscular, active men," wrote E. M. Curr of the Murray district Aborigines he met in 1841, "two out of the three being about 5 feet 9 inches in height. Their dress consisted of an opossum skin cloak, which was fastened at the chest passing over the left and under the right shoulder. . . . The fur was worn next to the person, and the skin which was outside was painted in various carpet-like patterns with a sort of red clay which the Blacks burn and make use of for this and other purposes of ornamentation. . . . Around their necks they had necklaces of small reeds, cut into lengths of about an inch and a half and strung on twine made from wild flax. In a sort of rude kangaroo skin bag carried on the left shoulder, which opened out so as to be available for sitting or sleeping on, were conveyed their tomahawks, shields, waddies and other utensils; their spears and throwing sticks being carried in the hand. Their hair, which was straight and black, was confined around the forehead by a narrow net, through which were thrust the barbed switches with which they extracted the edible grubs from the trees; and around their arms near the shoulder were twisted strips of opossum skin with the fur on."*

The minimum amount of clothing was worn in all parts of the continent and at all times. In cold and wet weather a skin garment and even a rare head covering woven from leaves was sufficient protection against the elements. Men have been known to wear cloaks of rushes and twisted bark fibre woven into squares and sewn together.

While nudity seems to have been preferred,

* *Recollections of Squatting in Australia*, 1883, page 85.

there were a number of tribes where clothing provided a minimum degree of modesty. On Melville and Bathurst Islands and on Groote Eylandt women wore "more or less efficient aprons", or carried pieces of bark which they held in front of them when meeting men. In north-western Arnhem Land women had rough skirts of plaited pandanus leaves, and both men and women wore pubic aprons of possum fur twine.

It has been mentioned that no clothing was worn in the central districts, but men sometimes tied a slender belt of human hair or animal twine round their waists, or a few feathers or pieces of pearl shell inserted in the pubic hairs. Twine aprons were commonly worn by both sexes, some of them right across the thighs. Pearl shells were suspended from the belt in the Kimberleys and baler shell ovals on Cape York Peninsula. Elsewhere the shells were valued ornaments and articles of magic.

Apart from adornment the principal purpose of clothing was to indicate the onset of puberty, and full manhood and womanhood. Amongst some tribes a young woman was entitled to wear armbands, headband, waistband of hair, and a cord which passed round her neck and between and under her breasts when she had reached a marriageable age.

Thus it can be said that, apart from the fur coverings worn in colder climates, any form of clothing must be regarded as having been decorative, directed more especially to the recognition of manhood and womanhood, and to the initiation rites that followed.

Decorations, Ornaments.

GIFTS. The principle of reciprocity was part of the social life of most primitive people, but it is often difficult to distinguish between barter and trade on the one hand and gifts on the other. The principle in which the giver places the recipient under an obligation still applies amongst Polynesians and Melanesians at the present day. A gift is made, an obligation incurred, and the need for reciprocity arises. The same conditions were observed by the Aborigines. The rules by which giving was controlled were well defined, amongst both individuals and groups.

Kinship was a basis for the interchange of gifts on the individual level. Less frequently, in a society not noted for specialisation, gifts were made in return for services rendered or for objects of craftsmanship. Individuals and groups were frequently concerned with gifts made to settle feuds or to prevent reprisals for injuries. In this case the gifts might take the form of the loan of wives or even permanent marriage relationships. On the group level there were interchanges of gifts, which were simply a form of barter, but were not always apparent as such because the return gift was often made at a later date than the first presentation. Similarly inter-tribal trading on a wider scale, where the desirable goods might travel great distances and pass through many hands from one tribe to another, was still conducted on a "gift" basis. It became a matter of honour to ensure that no obligation was incurred by return gifts of inferior quality. The objects of trade included spears and other weapons, a few articles of clothing or adornment, bags, pearl shell, etc. Finally there was the ceremonial presentation of gifts, most frequently of food, made when a novice acknowledged the receipt of sacred knowledge from the elders.

There was a sacramental and legal significance in marriage gifts. It was customary for gifts to pass between a man and his wife's relatives, and also between the wife and her husband's relatives.

On the personal level the obligation to make gifts to certain relatives was binding, and in a definite order of precedence, such as to father, mother's brother, wife's parents. The obligation resulted from betrothal, marriage, and initiation, and ensured that men and women would be provided for in old age, and also that there would be a measure of security for girls and for the older men to whom they were betrothed.

Barter, Betrothal, Marriage.

GIRLS. A girl baby was as welcome in the family group as a boy, partly because she was regarded as a potential source of gifts of food. It was likely that she would be betrothed to a young man at birth, or at an early age, in which case the man would be expected to help to provide food for his future parents-in-law. In addition the girl was trained to gather vegetable food for her family as well as for her own needs. On the group level she might also be

YOUNG GIRL

valuable as a medium for confirming alliances through marriage.

Her first years were happy and carefree, the young girl imitating her mother and learning the skills she needed after she was married. A girl was under the direct control of her parents until puberty, when she would be married.

According to Mrs Aeneas Gunn, no girl might be spoken to by her "little-bit-father" or "little-bit-brother", but normally no restrictions of this kind were imposed during childhood. By the time she reached puberty, however, her new physical experiences were surrounded by ritual and formal instruction about the life that lay before her. The change from childhood to womanhood was sudden and dramatic. Initiation rites, of less severity than those of young men, had to be endured, and a great deal of formal instruction was imparted. After marriage she was exhorted not to smile or stare at other men but to prove faithful to her husband.

Girls were expected to endure painful tests to

prepare them for marriage, and to qualify them for their new status. In many regions they were required to submit to severing of the little finger, nose piercing, tooth evulsion, or the gashing of the back, belly, and buttocks by means of sharp flint knives or shells, in order to beautify them. The final initiation, far less sacred and comprehensive than that of young men, occurred prior to marriage, when the mother or some older woman took the girl into the bush to impart the lore that applied only to women. The training period was usually succeeded by a corroboree, after which the marriage was consummated.

Betrothal, Children, Games, Initiation, Marriage.

GODS. In many tribal areas, mainly in Queensland, New South Wales, and Victoria, there was widespread belief in a supreme being, the cult-hero, or the All-Father. Doubts have been expressed as to whether a sky cult-hero can be regarded as a god, but it may be conceded that such a powerful being has at least many of the attributes of gods of other cultures. Varying with the districts in eastern Australia, the supreme being was known by different names such as Baiame, Ngurunderi, Nepele, Bunjil, Mangan-ngana, Daramulun, Goin, or Beral. They were not different cult-heroes but the same sky cult-hero known by different names. With the singleness of purpose manifested by Jehovah in the Old Testament, Baiame (to give him one of his best-known names) created a world of light and life from dark, unformed chaos, separated day from night, gave sunshine and rain, running water, trees and grass and flowers, the glories of springtime and summer, and the living things that inhabited the world he had made, culminating in man himself. In one recorded series of legends, Baiame was assisted by Yhi the sun goddess and other beneficent beings.

Writing of Daramulun, the supreme being of the Yuin tribe, Howitt recorded that he lived on earth with his mother Ngalalbal. "There were no men or women, only animals, birds, and other creatures. He placed trees on the earth. Then Kaboka, Thrush, caused a flood which destroyed all but a few of the people Daramulun had made. They crawled out of the water on to Mount Dromedary. Daramulun

went into the sky, where he now lives, looking down upon the affairs of men."[*]

The Berndts are of the opinion that such a fragmentary outline could well have been influenced by alien contact. It is certain that the student who collects religious and mythological information after white contact has been established can never be certain what effect new concepts have had on indigenous belief. But it must be remembered that while religious development is a slow process, delayed by traditional beliefs that have become sacred and little subject to change, there is always a long-continuing evolution. It may be conjectured that the beliefs of the Aborigines during thousands of years of occupation differed from those of their remote ancestors who first came to the continent. Trade and culture contacts gradually introduced further modifications.

Religion was a living belief, hallowed by antiquity, but ever extending its frontiers. The god-like heroes were not dead. When the work of creation was over and they ascended into the sky, they not only watched over the affairs of men but also participated in daily life because of their contact with totemic centres of growth and fertility. Without them the initiation rites would have been meaningless; indeed they were responsible for the first rites celebrated amongst men.

The basic elements of the sky-father cult of eastern districts may have been of comparatively recent development, but it exercised a considerable influence over the tribes which believed in it. Apart from the creative acts at the beginning of time, the sky-father or his spirit attendants led each tribe to its own region and made the natural features of its home territory. The adventures that the god experienced were part of pantomime, dance, and song into which novices were introduced at the time of initiation.

Those who entered most fully into the sacred lore were the medicine men, who were credited with powers which enabled them to visit the Hero in the sky, thus proving his eternal nature, giving assurance to men and women that they were linked with the Eternal Dreamtime and would ultimately enter the land of continual life and rejoin their ancestor. This

[*] *The World of the First Australians*, page 202.

however was not held as a universal belief. Amongst a number of tribes reincarnation of the spirit in successive bodies with or without ultimate translation to a spirit world was a common belief.

The symbol of the All-Father was the bull-roarer. His laws were the authority for the full body of tribal custom, belief, and ritual. "Baiame say so" was the final authority in such matters.

In northern and Central Australia the belief in one creator god may have been held at one time, but if this was so it was abandoned in favour of clan totemic heroes whose spirits exercised the same functions as the All-Father. Everything was thus credited to the Dream-time, the Alcheringa. The sky culture heroes are there distinguished from clan totemic ancestors who in their continuing ministry must be regarded as spirits as well as ancestors. With divergent beliefs and half-understood accounts of bygone days, the distinction between god and ancestor is far from clear, but to Europeans there appears little doubt that in some places the ancestor was a god-like being, and reigned supreme. The one thing that all concepts have in common is the Alcheringa, the Eternal Dreamtime of yesterday, today, and all the days to come.

In Arnhem Land, the Mother Goddess cult served the same purpose. The Mother was a symbol of fertility and increase, her spirit children populating the earth and becoming ancestors of the tribes. There are certain distinctive differences between Motherhood and Fatherhood. For example, the symbol of her womb was a hollow log which was beaten during her cult and initiation rites, the sound of the drum being supposed to be her voice. She was also identified with the Rainbow Snake. It is interesting to note the belief in some tribes that women were the first to possess sacred powers and to have knowledge of sacred mysteries; and that these gifts were later transferred to men who stole them, women being subsequently excluded from participation.

The cult of the Old Woman (who had many names) was part of the Mother Goddess concept. This cult originated (or may have been brought from northern lands) in Arnhem Land and spread some distance east and west. She was accompanied by the Munga-Munga, a party of supernatural beings who were responsible for the birth of animals and human beings. Her coming was heralded by the Rainbow Snake, which also appeared as Yulunggul with the Wawalag sisters. As the Mother Goddess cult flourished in the tropical areas where rainfall was high, there is significance in the Mother as the origin and personification of fertility.

The following beliefs were held by some tribes in south-eastern Australia. Ngurunderi was the hero who instituted rites and ceremonies; the Wotjoballuk and the Kurnai believed in Bunjil as the Father, but the Kulim thought that he was a man who introduced the moiety system; amongst the Yuin, Daramulun lived in the sky and introduced the bull-roarer, his name being known only to those who were fully initiated; some of the Queensland tribes believed in a sky-god Kolim who wandered on earth and killed those who were guilty of transgressions against his law; to the Kabi and Wakka tribes, Biral, Jonjari, and Dhakkan were god-like heroes who lived in the vicinity of waterholes and could be identified with the Rainbow Snake; in Central Australia the Arunta had Dwanjirika who took boys at the time of initiation and through the medium of the medicine man renewed their internal organs; the same tribe believed in Oruncha, a mischievous spirit who did much harm; Atnatu of the Kaitish tribe fathered sons and daughters in the sky land but later grew angry with them and dropped them to earth where their descendants looked on him as their creator; the Binbinga were befriended by Ulurkura who opposed the evil spirits known as Mundagadji. Baiame was the Great Spirit of the great Kamalaroi and other tribes in New South Wales and was probably the most widely known.

Ancestors, Dreamtime, Rainbow Serpent, Religious beliefs, Spirits.

GONGS. In Arnhem Land hollow logs (the ubar or uwar) were beaten with sticks, and can be thought of as a primitive type of gong. Sometimes the log was wedged into a forked branch. It was a sacred instrument used in ceremonies and was elaborately painted with coloured ochres and decorated with feathered string. Solid logs up to 5 feet long were used in Roper River rituals in south-eastern Arnhem

STONE FOR GRINDING SEED

monial which occupied most of the time. It was customary for visitors to light a fire or to sit patiently at some distance until someone came out to invite them to the camp. This was an obvious safety precaution.

Kinship.

GRINDING STONES. Seeds of many different kinds were ground between oval stones. The lower stone was flat with a slight depression in the middle in which the seed was placed. The upper stone was oval or circular, with a flat or crown top and up to the size of the hand or slightly more. Water was sometimes added as the seed was ground, the resultant product then being a paste instead of flour. Stones used for this purpose were carefully chosen. They came from particular localities and were objects of trade over a wide area. McCarthy mentions that the millstones were large pebbles. The slabs were roughly flaked into an oval shape or beautifully pecked all over and pointed at one end. They were up to 3 feet in length but usually 1 to 2 feet. There were two kinds, one

Land. In the Roper River region a solid length of resonant timber was held shoulder high in one hand and struck with a stick about an inch in diameter, producing a gong-like sound which could be heard at a distance of half a mile.

GRAVES.
  Burial.

GREAT SPIRIT.
  Gods, Religious beliefs.

GREETINGS. When men from different clans met there was an accepted form of address. Each would first reveal his clan name, followed by his kinship appellation, e.g. son, father, mother's brother etc. A stranger might be introduced in the same way, thus proclaiming his relationship to everyone in the group, and defining the obligations that existed between them. On formal occasions the exchange of names was part of the song and dance cere-

WITCHETTY GRUB

with a large grinding depression, the other with two narrow parallel grooves.

Axes, Cooking, Seeds.

GROUND DRAWINGS.
Drawings (ground).

GRUBS. The witchetty or witjuti grub, which is the larva of a species of longicorn beetle, was one of the most eagerly sought after foods in the interior amongst the Aborigines. It is white and succulent, grows to a length of 5 inches, and was usually eaten uncooked. It was found over a large area, and dug from the earth and among the roots of the kurrajong and mulga trees by women and children. The grubs were also found in tree trunks, and were dug out by men with axes. Specially made hooked sticks were carried about to hook grubs from their hiding places in timber. Cobra, mangrove, and other large whitey-grey or black grubs were eaten elsewhere. Heaps of boughs and logs were put in rivers and creeks along the east coast for cobra grubs to infest, and were subsequently harvested.

GUM. Gum from trees had many uses. The resin of the pine, gum, bloodwood and other trees, spinifex grass gum, and other tree resins were used to make handles for stone knives, and to secure the blades of axes and chisels to their handles. Other uses were in making ornaments, repairing spear-throwers and coolamons, mounting spear-blades, and sealing canoes.

Axes.

GYPSUM.
Rain-making.

H

HAIR. Although varying a great deal in different parts of the continent, the hair of the Aborigines was usually abundant and glossy. This was not apparent in the early years of white settlement and even later in the desert areas where there was no opportunity for washing hair. The hair of the head became matted with dust, wax, and grease, and was often smeared with ochre. Hair and beards were the handtowels of the Aboriginal, and their natural beauty was hidden. Nevertheless the red and gold tints in the dark hair of some tribes were greatly admired.

Generally speaking the hair was long and curly, never woolly like a Negro's. It was dark brown or black, with some exceptions turning white with age. Men usually wore beards and moustaches, and facial hair also developed amongst some women.

In northern Queensland the straight hair of babies became a mass of curls some time after birth. In the Great Western Desert it was tawny even into early adolescence, but turned darker as the children grew older. In central districts it was dark brown and slightly wavy. In the lower Murray River district some of the children had fuzzy hair. As they grew older they had a tendency to become bald (this occurred infrequently). In some men the whole body was covered with a mass of fine white hair, and some of the women grew moustaches and beards.

Although it was the usual practice for both men and women to wear their hair short, men's hair was long in many tribes, e.g. northern Kimberley and the Western Desert. Nevertheless it was practical to keep the hair short, partly because it became matted when too long, and partly because of the necessity to keep it out of the eyes while working. Warriors with shaggy hair kept it off their foreheads with headbands, sometimes decorated with feathers. Unless it was tied back with a hair cord a gust of wind might blow it into the eyes at a crucial moment when a hunter was taking aim with his spear, or it would alarm an animal which had been patiently stalked for many hours. Hair was impregnated with clay, and decorated with seed pods or clay ornaments; or frequently greased and tied in a peak.

The practice of depilation was not uncommon, and was usually connected with the ritual of initiation, or with magic and the spirits of the dead. In the Great Victoria Desert, for instance, the hair of a dead man was cut off by his wife's brother and given to a particular woman to be made into a band that was believed to contain part of the dead man's spirit. A dead woman's hair would be cut off by her husband, and made into a band and in both cases the band was worn on the arm until the death was avenged.

Charms sometimes had to be made of human hair to be effective. The Berndts have told of an interesting practice on Bathurst Island where, as part of the increase rituals, the men plucked their beards and moustaches and soaked them overnight in water with sliced yams. It was a form of sympathetic magic, because yam roots are covered with fine hair-like roots.

Hair was taken from living persons and used for practical purposes. A woman's hair belonged to her husband, her daughter's husband, or other close relatives, who were permitted to cut it off so that it could be made into string. Human hair cord was strong and was employed in making girdles, dilly bags, and pads to be placed on the head by women to enable them to balance coolamons filled with water, as well as for other uses, especially ceremonial articles and symbols.

Belts, Head ornaments, Rope, String, Widows.

HAMMERS.
Axes.

HEAD ORNAMENTS. For ritual purposes elaborate headgear was constructed. It had great sacred significance. It was not unusual for large objects such as sacred boards and bull-roarers (churinga) to be built into the headgear. One form of high head-dress in the central regions was the conical type tipped with feathers in the construction known as wonigi or waninga. Two or more sticks were crossed (four to make a taller construction) and provided a foundation which was wound round with string and ornamented with down and grass. The hat was light in weight. It fitted right over the actor's head, the lower crossbar sometimes being held in the teeth to give stability.

The materials of which the head-dress was made varied from one locality to another. In some places the hats were made of paperbark wound round with fibre to form diamond-shaped patterns painted in different colours. The diamonds here represented the paperbark trees, the patches of red and yellow ochre the flames, and the black pigment the ashes of the fire.

The headgear or masks of Central Australia were usually revered as sacred objects, especially when churinga were incorporated in their construction, and might never be seen by women and young people, who were not permitted to watch or take part in the sacred rites of initiation.

Kimberley men wore facial and head ornaments of twine. Some of the most remarkable head ornaments were huge masks representing birds, fish, canoes, crocodiles, and other objects, which were worn in the Cape York area.

Headbands worn by men were often made of fine twine covered with a smooth layer of wax and painted white, or with a row of kangaroo incisor teeth set in gum. These headbands formed part of a set given to youths at certain stages of initiation.

There were many forms of head ornament— bones and shells were attached to the hair with gum, the nose-bone was widely used, and in the Cape York Peninsula round plugs of wood were worn in the lobe of the ear. The commonest head ornament was the plume of the white or black cockatoo, or grey brolga feathers set in gum on a wooden or bone peg.

Headbands were worn by both men and women as a sign that the wearer had reached maturity, and to keep the hair back. They were constructed of twine or netting. Women "sang" over headbands worn by their husbands in a type of love magic.

Art, Ornaments, Painting (body), Sacred objects, Widows.

HEADMEN.
Elders, Leaders.

HEADACHES.
Amongst some tribes it was believed that a man's headache could be cured by wearing his wife's girdle. One end of a length of twine was rubbed on the lips of the operator until they bled while the other end was tied around the sufferer's head; the evil causing the headache escaped or was drawn out along the twine.

Belts.

HONEY.
Honey was always a welcome addition to the diet. It came either from the bodies of honey ants or from the nests of wild bees. The flight of the bees was observed in order that they could be tracked back to their nests. Sometimes a bee was caught, a piece of down attached to its body to make it clearly visible, and the flying speck followed to its home in a hollow tree. Arriving at the tree the hunter had work to do, swarming up the branches and chopping out the honeycomb with his axe, or even cutting the tree down if the nest was inaccessible by climbing. The honey and comb were eaten complete with drowned insects and debris embedded in the comb, or used to sweeten water as a refreshing drink.

"Honey climbing" was arduous work, for the nests gave a small yield, a pint or quart as a rule, compared with those of present-day hives. In eastern regions, where the trees grew to a considerable height, the climb up to the nest would often have been hazardous to a European, but the nimble-footed Aborigines made light work of it, sometimes carrying a lighted torch in their teeth to smoke out the nest. They often had to chop the branch away, holding on to another with one hand as the stone blade cut into the timber. Honey was a prized commodity and worth all the hazards of honey climbing.

Drink.

HOSPITALITY.
Family groups and clans within a tribe were normally self-contained and self-supporting, but those who were on the sacred pathways of the great ancestors or culture heroes who had created their home territory were linked to each other by the myth of his journey like beads on a string. Because of

the common possession of the myth within the larger limits of the tribe there was some affinity between the groups who lived on the "track", which might extend from their own territory for a distance of hundreds of miles and cover the territorial possessions of many groups. Every man, woman, and child within the collection of clans which comprised a tribe were tied by bonds of faith and a personal sense of belonging to their two tribal territory, and especially to their own segment of it. They were never at ease when away from "home". It was this factor that prevented invasion from a distance, or ambitions of territorial aggrandisement. As a result of freedom from fear of conquest, groups of people were usually ready to welcome strangers.

Visitors were most likely to come from the track of the ancestor, and even though there was no direct relationship between them, they had religious and social affinities with the host group by virtue of the possession of another portion of the common myth. From this there arose an obligation to feed and entertain the visitors who might be suffering from drought conditions in their own territory, or might be refugees from avenging parties. At totemic centres the common owners of the mythological trail were welcomed at corroborees and bora ceremonies.

Hospitality went further than providing food and shelter. Wives were sometimes lent to visitors, but from an Aboriginal point of view there was no prostitution or offence provided that kinship rules were observed. It was an institution which ensured satisfaction for a man away from home, and involved the incurring of obligations and reciprocal payment.

HUNTING. Apart from participation in religious rites, man's primary function was to provide flesh or meat food for his family. He brought endurance, speed, and skill in the use of weapons to his task—and many other qualifications in which he was trained from an early age. He knew the habits of every animal, its cry, its tracks, how long it was since the animal had passed, and even its physical condition. He could deduce the animal's passage through the bush by the flight of birds and insects, and the pres ce of snakes by watching butcher-birds. He could follow the flight of an animal across stony ground by reading its

mind and anticipating its movements, picking up the trail on softer ground with uncanny accuracy. He could lure pelicans within reach by imitating the jumping of fish by splashing his hand in the water. In these and many other ways he could provide ample food for himself and his family in places where a European would have starved.

These were not inherited skills, but were learnt by observation, practice, and ingenuity, commencing at an early age. Speed and accuracy with spears and boomerangs were encouraged by playing games. Two boys would take up a position at a little distance from each other, and some 30 or 40 yards from a row of players who were armed with throwing weapons. The two boys bowled short oval, round, or cross-shaped pieces of wood or bark to each other. One arm was about 9 inches long and the other 3 or 4 inches in length, tied together in the shape of a cross. Owing to the difference in length of the two arms they bounced up and down as they were bowled along the ground, imitating the gait of a wallaby or kangaroo. The players attempted to hit them while they were moving; and in this and other boyish sports they developed accuracy of aim and powers of observation.

The hunter was adept at gauging the force and direction of the wind in order that he might creep close to his prey without disturbing it. Patience was required of the hunter in no small measure, and self-control to remain motionless in one position for a long time, or to stop suddenly while pursuing an animal and freeze in his tracks to avoid being seen, even standing on one foot and holding a branch of a tree to screen himself. When the animal's suspicions were lulled he had to take up the chase again, and to repeat the performance many times until he came close enough to throw his spear or boomerang.

The hunter's equipment was simple but effective. In his hand he carried several spears and the essential woomera or spear-thrower. In the colder southern regions in winter he might also wear a warm kangaroo or possum skin cloak, but in hotter climates the most he would possess in the way of clothing would be a hair or fur belt and pubic apron. This provided him with the means of carrying other weapons such as an axe, a boomerang or kylie, and perhaps a waddy or short, heavy stick for throwing. Nets were carried on wallaby hunts, spears and fishing-lines and hooks when fishing. For some purposes and in some regions the hunter was accompanied by native dogs to help him in the chase. His only other equipment was a stone knife or chisel. So far as possible he kept himself free of burdens because the chase was often long and arduous.

When the hunter set out in the morning he needed to be on the alert to discover the tracks of animals, no matter how indistinct they might be. He did not present an attractive figure as he smeared himself with mud and ochre to camouflage himself like a tree trunk, and perhaps to disguise the smell of sweat which might alarm the animals. Tirelessly following the tracks, interpreting them with the skill gained in many a chase, he would eventually come in sight of his prey. Approaching it from the leeward side, he might spend many patient hours of stalking before arriving within throwing distance of his spear or throwing-stick.

In large groups teamwork simplified the task. The young men went in front in a long line, spreading out as far as possible to increase the chances of discovering fresh tracks. As soon as the quarry was sighted in scrub country the hunters crouched down until their heads were level with the tops of the bushes. Kangaroos and emus were stalked in this manner, and there was little doubt of the outcome unless they were startled by some other cause. The advantage of co-operative effort in open country became apparent. One man hid behind a rock or bush while the others made a long circuit until they were behind the animal. When they showed themselves the quarry fled and was killed as it passed the place where the solitary hunter was hiding. Whenever possible the larger animals were killed close to the camp to avoid a long trek back home with a heavy load, or the quarry was cooked on the spot while a smoke signal summoned the rest of the group. Hunters often carried a kangaroo 60 to 90 lb in weight several miles back to camp.

The animals were divided amongst the members of the group, the apportioning usually being done by the elders or by the leading hunters, who were fully aware of a man's kinship obligations. These were more pronounced among men than among women. Wives and daughters usually gathered food only for their immediate families, but meat was the staple food of the Aboriginal. The welfare of the group or clan was paramount, and the division had to be made equitably—so much so that the hunter who had killed the animal might get little for himself.

The procedures described above applied mainly to the hunting of larger birds and animals. Considerable ingenuity was shown in the methods of catching a variety of game, varying with the terrain, the season of the year, the number of men available, and the plentifulness or scarcity of animals, birds, and fish. The following sections describe in more detail some of these methods.

Animals
Kangaroos were intelligent animals that challenged the ingenuity of the native hunter. Their habits were well known. During the heat of the day they rested in the shelter of bushes or trees and lay concealed from sight, keeping a care-

KANGAROOS

ful watch. Under these circumstances it was difficult to surprise them. The hunters seldom made any attempt to stalk them at this time but lay in wait for them at their feeding grounds in the late afternoon, when they themselves had the advantage of concealment. It was often a protracted vigil, while the animals browsed in the mallee scrub until at length one came within range of the hunter's boomerang or spear. When several animals were feeding together care was taken to make the kill when the kangaroo was in a stooping position. It then subsided on the ground without alarming its companions. In this way lone hunters were able to kill the animals; when the whole group joined together in a kangaroo hunt, different methods were employed. This usually occurred when weather or other circumstances were unfavourable for a single-handed kill. Women and children were then employed as beaters and the beasts were herded through the scrub towards a point where a number of hunters were standing. Seeing them, the kangaroos would rush past, their escape in other directions being barred by the beaters. As they bounded past, the hunters flung their spears or clubs at them, sometimes crushing their skulls with waddies.

Another method required a good deal of preparation. Pits some 5 or 6 feet deep and about 12 feet long were dug along the line of bush tracks and lightly covered with branches and earth. This usually required a number of men, some of whom drove the animals towards the tracks by circling round the herd and heading them in the required direction. Hunters were stationed on either side of the track to prevent them from escaping. As the animals were driven along the track they crashed into the pits, where they could be destroyed at leisure. Long brush fences also led emus and kangaroos into an open pit into which they fell when startled by the hunters.

Sometimes dogs helped to make the kill, especially when solitary hunters stalked the feeding animals. In the event of the hunter's missing his mark, or wounding the animal slightly, the dog would be sent to bring it down before it made its escape.

Possums were an easier prey. Their presence was revealed by scratches on the bark of trees, or by hairs on the rocks leading to their holes. The patient hunter was frequently able to take

POSSUM AND YOUNG

them unawares while they were still asleep. Those that took refuge in hollow trees were smoked out. A hungry and impatient hunter in pursuit of an alarmed possum that had hidden in the hollow limb of a tree had a harder task. To enable him to climb the tree he sometimes had to cut steps in the trunk and after climbing up them, to cut through the branch with his stone axe.

Wombats were lethargic animals, and it was practically impossible to prise them out of their burrows, though sometimes they were dug out. The hunter lay in wait during the afternoon when he knew that the animal would have to come out in search of food and water. When it had gone he blocked the hole with stones a couple of feet inside the entrance, and set out in pursuit. The frightened wombat hurried back to its refuge and while it was trying to break through the barricade the hunter exerted all his strength to pull it out by the hind legs and despatch it with his club.

Bandicoots, marsupial rats, and burrowing

WOMBAT AND YOUNG

Birds

Birds were an important food supply. The largest was the emu which was often hunted in the same way as the kangaroo by driving it into a pit. In spite of its speed it was a fairly easy prey. It has been said that a rather amusing but effective method was for the hunter to crouch motionless beside a track through the scrub, catch the emu by the leg as it went past, stand up and send the bird off balance, when it could be despatched by a blow from his club; but further confirmation of this practice is needed.

Emus are curious birds, always ready to investigate anything new or unusual. Taking advantage of this characteristic, hunters climbed trees near a waterhole and let their spears dangle from the branches. Feathers had been tied to the heads of the spears. When the emus came close the hunter clubbed them from above. In a similar fashion the hunter hid behind a low bush and raised a feather-decorated stick or spear above it. As soon as the emu

animals were agile beasts that were hard to catch, especially in loose, sandy soil. Women were enlisted to poke long, flexible roots down their burrows. By this means the men knew where the actual nests were located. They dug into them from above, using pointed sticks or wooden scoops and spades. Alternatively a fire was lit near the entrance to the burrow and the scoop used to fan the smoke into the hole, driving the animal out into the open where it could easily be killed.

In later days a rabbit hunt was an exciting operation. All entrances to the burrow except one were blocked up. The remaining hole was enlarged until it was wide enough to admit a small boy, who crawled in head first and caught the animals with his hands. Rabbit-hunting was pre-eminently an occupation for boys. When the animal was discovered in the shelter of a bush two or three boys would run round it at high speed. The rabbit became bewildered, thinking perhaps that it was completely surrounded. It cowered back into shelter and was dragged out and killed.

BANDICOOTS

came up to the bush to investigate the strange object the hunter slipped a noose over its head and tightened it round the bird's neck.

Large nets were employed when a kangaroo or emu drive was made. Constructed of thin rope the nets were about 5 feet high and several hundred yards in length. They were staked out in a large triangle or crescent with one end left open. A flock of birds was driven into the net, and when the ends were closed they were trapped and clubbed to death.

Every aspect of hunting revealed the knowledge and skill of hunters, who were familiar with the habits of their prey. In northern tro-

EMU AND CHICKS

pical Australia, at the same time each year, magpie geese flew along the same routes from one swamp or billabong to another, feeding on the roots of waterlilies as they went. When they were due to arrive men hid in the branches of paperbark trees, where they were concealed from view. As soon as the birds came in sight the men imitated their cry, and as the geese flew down in response to the call, they were

killed by sticks that were thrown at them.

The same intimate acquaintance with the habits of wildfowl generally was put to good use. In search of waterfowl the hunter crept up to the edge of a pool and made a shelter for himself by bending and tying the reeds together. Hidden from sight he waited until a duck or swan came near, submerged himself, seized it by the legs, broke its neck, and tucked the bird into his girdle. In this way he was able to kill a number of birds without being detected by the remainder of the flock. When he had collected as many as he could carry he swam quietly to the bank, put them in a safe place, and returned for more.

In taking other species, flowering reed tops were waved in the air while the hunter remained out of sight. The birds became curious and congregated together. When they were a few yards away the hunter suddenly stood up and the birds took to flight. Immediately this happened the rest of the men, who were hidden amongst the reeds, sprang out and hurled their weapons amongst the birds. Another method was to throw a returning boomerang above them. Its whirring flight resembled the sound of the wings of a hawk, and the birds were driven down to the level of the water, where several of them could be decapitated at once by a well-aimed boomerang.

Ducks were caught when flying from one feeding ground to another. The first flight or two was allowed to pass undisturbed, but as the birds gained confidence a boomerang was thrown and one of the fowlers imitated the cry of a hawk. The birds flew low to escape their supposed enemy and were caught in a net slung between two trees. A man at each end of the net was able to catch a large number of birds at one time in this manner.

Snares and nooses were used to take swans. Concealed amongst the reeds, the hunter flapped the wing of a swan as though a bird was in distress. When others came to see what was happening he captured them by means of a noose at the end of a stick, drawing them under water and wringing their necks. Another method was to make paths through the reeds wide enough to admit only one bird at a time. Setting two poles in the water on either side of the lane with a noose strung between them resulted in the capture of the swans, which were caught by the neck and were unable to free themselves.

Reptiles

Clumps of scrub and grass were set on fire to drive out small game such as snakes and lizards from the shelter of tussocks and bushes. They were sometimes hunted early in the morning when they were still sluggish from the cold. Larger reptiles such as goannas were discovered by studying their tracks and following them to their lairs before sunrise. Then came a patient wait until the sun warmed the rocks and the reptiles emerged, when they were speared or

GOANNA

killed by a blow on the head. Goannas are agile reptiles and often tried to escape by running up a tree, but were dislodged and brought down with stones.

From these examples it will be clear that the Aboriginal was a skilful hunter, and could support himself in the most unpromising circumstances. The same skill was shown in catching fish, in which he employed hooks made of shell or bone, and used spears, cages, nets, hollow

log traps, weirs, dams, and poison. Cord was even attached to the remora or sucker-fish, which fastened itself to a turtle or dugong and enabled the fisherman to drag the larger quarry ashore. Powers of observation were highly developed, and the tracks of every kind of animal, bird, or reptile, and the presence of fish, could quickly be seen and interpreted.

Boomerangs, Boys, Children, Clubs, Competitions, Dingoes, Drawings, Fish traps, Fishing, Games, Nets, Poison, Shoes, Tracking, Turtles.

HUTS. In the temperate and hot, dry inland regions the only shelter required by the Aborigines were a small windbreak and, in wet weather, a hut of branches, grass, or bark. As it rains very seldom in Central Australia there was little need for huts, but when required they could be built quickly. The doorway consisted of forked sticks erected in holes in the ground, with a number of other sticks or branches placed in a half-circle. The tips were bent over to the top of the entrance, thus providing a roof

WURLEY

BARK HUT

as well as walls. Round huts in the interior and northern areas were solidly constructed of boughs set in an oval or circle, secured at a peak, and covered with spinifex grass, paperbark, or leafy branches. They were used in hot summer weather and in rainy seasons. The huts had something of the appearance of an old-fashioned beehive. In very cold weather the hut was warmed by the embers of a fire, and in wet weather was sometimes plastered with mud or clay to keep out the rain. This was done only when the camp was semi-permanent.

In regions where rainfall was persistent a slightly more substantial structure was made from sheets of stringybark or paperbark. These huts took a number of forms, the simplest ones being a folded sheet of bark stood on end like a partly open book. More permanent structures consisted of a frame of saplings covered with overlapping sheets of bark. Round ridge-pole and rectangular huts were also built. In damp places the entrance was kept as small as possible, and a smouldering fire kept mosquitoes at bay. In the northern areas "mosquito huts"

were often built on stilts. With the incessant rain and smoky fires kept going continuously in an attempt to repel the insects, life was very unpleasant. Sometimes the doorway was closed completely, or a fire lit on the ground underneath the platform on which the hut was built.

Although they appeared so flimsy and were so quickly made, native huts were constructed on sound engineering principles. As the basic construction of many of them consisted of pliant saplings or branches with their butts placed in a circle and the tops bent over and thrust into the ground on the other side of the circle and tied together where they crossed, the beehive-like structures were able to withstand the fiercest whirlwind. The framework was thatched with brush, foliage, and grass, which kept out the rain, and a hole at the top served as an outlet for the smoke.

There are several widely-used names for huts—gunyahs, humpies, miamias, etc. Edward E. Morris has given the places of origin of names that have become everyday words in the language:*

Gunyah Goondie	New South Wales
Humpy (Oompi)	Queensland
Miamia	Victoria and Western Australia
Wurley (Oorla)	South Australia

The word goondie which, unlike the others, has not entered into European vocabulary, came from gundai in the Wiradhuri dialect. Wiltja was another name for hut. Gunyah was possibly the most widely used term, and gibber-gunyah was a cave or rock shelter used as a dwelling, usually only temporarily. Perhaps the earliest written record of the word gunyah was by D. Collins in 1798: "Go-nie—a hut."† In 1830 R. Dawson wrote of "a native encampment consisting of eight or 10 'gunyers'. This is the native term for small huts which are supported by three forked sticks (about 3 feet long) brought together at the top in a triangular form: the two sides towards the wind are covered by two long sheets of bark, the third is always left open to the wind."‡

Camps.

* *Austral English*, Macmillan, 1898, page 206.
† *An Account of the English Colony in New South Wales*, page 610.
‡ *The Present State of Australia*, page 171.

I

ILLNESS.
Medicine, Medicine men, Sickness.

IMAGES. Images of men and women and of mythological creatures were made mainly in Arnhem Land and in the Kimberleys, in connection with sacred ritual and black magic. The smallest ones were moulded in beeswax, sometimes painted with the victim's totemic signs, and covered with down or feathers. They were crude representations of the person who was to be cursed or "sung" to death, or of the ancestor from whom he was descended.

Larger figures were carved in wood or made from grass bound up in bundles, paperbark, or clay. In western Arnhem Land a paperbark figure which represented a person recently deceased was set up near the burial place with one arm pointing towards the grave and the other to the new camp of the clan, the old camping ground having been vacated at the time of death.

A wide range of clan totemic spirit figures in human and animal form were carved and painted in the Cape York Peninsula. High relief ground figures of soil heaped over logs were fashioned in the shape of heroes and heroines, kangaroos, emus, and other animals on the bora grounds of south-eastern Australia. In north-western districts flat board figures of spirits were made. Human and animal figures and heads, beautifully formed, were made in Arnhem Land.

When figures were carved or modelled for the purpose of killing an enemy it was not necessary to make a three-dimensional figure. A drawing or painting on a piece of bark served the same purpose. The usual black magic was employed—pointing at the image with a bone or thrashing it with a leafy branch while singing the death song and repeating the victim's name. Figures were also used in love magic as well as in sorcery, but the greatest use of carved figures, as of drawings, was in sacred ritual.
Dolls, Magic.

IMMORTALITY. Religious thought amongst the Aborigines had advanced to the point of acceptance of the doctrine of immortality. The spirit of man was indestructible, whether it lived again in a new incarnation, whether it retained its individuality in a spirit world, or whether it went eventually to the company of the culture heroes of a sky world to be merged into the infinity of the All-Father. It was vital that the rites connected with mourning and the disposal of the dead be carried out faithfully to ensure that the spirit would return to its spirit home, otherwise it would haunt the area and prove harmful to health, hunting, and fishing.

The underlying belief was universally held, but the fate of the soul or spirit had many different interpretations. Ghosts, which were the spirits of the newly dead, were inimical to mankind and greatly feared. The local group hastened from its camp and as soon as the memory of the deceased had been expunged from the minds of his associates, the fear of haunting by the spirit vanished.

Some of the concepts of the after-life and of the adventures of the soul in search of a permanent home were interesting and ingenious. In a number of native legends the crow, who was often depicted as the embodiment of evil, but who also brought good gifts to mankind, was credited with revealing the concept of immortality and rebirth to human beings.
Religious beliefs, Spirits, Spirit worlds.

IMPLEMENTS.
Digging-sticks, Tools.

INCREASE RITES. Natural increase of all species of fish, birds, and animals was essential to the economy of the Aborigines. It was recognised as a condition that must be assisted by appropriate ritual and not left to the blind chance of Nature. While the performance of such ritual encouragement was found in a number of places, it was naturally of greatest importance in the territories of desert tribes whose chances of survival were more precarious than those of tribes who occupied fertile country with abundant rainfall.

Fortunately for the peace of mind of desert

tribes the great ancestral spirits who left spirit centres in their tribal areas also left increase or fertility centres in recognised places. Here the spirit, or the essential element of plant and animal life, was conferred in the Dreamtime and remained there, quiescent, it may be supposed, until released by the appropriate ritual. This took many forms and required active participation by those who were anxious to release the spirit or power of increase. Elkin remarks that it was not sufficient to say, "Let there be plenty of kangaroo here and there," for that was simply to express a desire. The desire needed to be converted into action by blowing powder from the increase stones, scattering them, or taking earth or powdered stone mixed with blood from the increase centre and carrying it through the tribal hunting grounds. It is difficult to enter fully into the Aboriginal mind, but Elkin reveals something of Aboriginal mentality by explaining that by performing such actions they were distributing sacramental expressions of the conception of animals, and that by disseminating the life of the sacred stone they were in fact distributing it to the various species of animals, causing them to increase.

The first ancestors left the stones, both as symbols and as a means for the continuation of life. The expression of conception and increase was released by the performance of ritual and ceremony.

Blood, Ceremonies, Fertility, Paintings, Rainmaking.

INFANTICIDE.
Babies.

INITIATION CEREMONIES. Throughout the length and breadth of Australia no boy could attain to manhood, nor could a girl become married, until he or she had passed the initiation tests. The purpose of the rites takes us into the deepest mysteries of belief and religion. On the simplest level they represented an increase in status for the novitiate, and served to emphasise the line of demarcation between the sexes, and between childhood on the one hand and manhood or womanhood on the other. The deeper meaning was the symbolic pageantry of death and of rising into a fuller life of the spirit. The attributes of childhood were abandoned,

and the candidate began a period of trial and testing, mental as well as physical, which prepared him not only for the responsibilities of manhood but fitted him, through the regeneration of mind and body, to receive the secret teaching of his people, revealed only to men who had attained the full status of manhood. Similarly girls were required to undergo a disciplinary training period to equip them for the lesser mysteries of womanhood; the period and nature of the tests was much less severe than for boys, and the degree of admission into sacred lore of a much lower standard.

There was first a period of preparation, a time of testing, and finally the initiation into sacred lore, so that the rites included education as well as transition into a new life. Neither men nor women were permitted to marry until the rites were completed; for many young men there was still a waiting time of many years until the babies to whom they were betrothed grew up into womanhood.

Although there were pronounced differences in the types of ceremony and their duration amongst different tribes, there were practices that were common to all. The fundamental issues were that the tests should commence at the age of puberty; that women had an important part to play in the preparatory ceremonies, but that during the "secret" part of the rite they were rigidly excluded; that in the secret rites the bull-roarer had a peculiar significance; that severe tests involving pain and fear were imposed upon the candidate, culminating in a period of instruction of esoteric significance; that in the closing stages some further ordeal such as circumcision or subincision, tooth evulsion, or depilation was applied to signify that he had passed out of female control; and that, finally, though some of these procedures and ordeals had taken place at puberty, full admission and understanding were not achieved until the candidate had reached maturity. It should be noted, however, that where tooth evulsion was the only rite, as in eastern Australia, the operation was comparatively late, but where this and circumcision and subincision took place, the tooth evulsion and even circumcision occurred at an early age.

As with all deep-seated beliefs and practices, initiation rites can be traced back to the Dreamtime. There were a number of myths in south-eastern Australia which ascribed the first initiation ceremony to the acts of Baiame the Great Spirit. In a revealing account of the origin of the Pleiades, for instance, the stars were at one time a band of young women who demanded that they be put to the full series of tests which were imposed on young men in order that they might prove that women were equal to men in their readiness for marriage and motherhood. They were subjected to the most trying ordeals, which were passed successfully and, as a final reward, they were translated into a constellation of stars as an example for all time of the endurance of women. A legendary account of their ordeals is interesting in that it details the tests which young women were forced to endure:

For three years the girls were taken to a place where no one else was allowed to go. The elders gave them only a small portion of food at sunrise and another at sunset. Their bodies became lean and sinewy, until they felt that they had learnt to control their appetites.

"Now we are ready," they said.

"No," the elders replied. "For three years you have endured your training. Now the time for testing has come. It is but the first test, to see whether you have learned the first lesson."

They were taken on a long, difficult journey for three days. They went through dense bush where thorns and sharp stakes scratched and tore their flesh; they crossed burning plains and high mountains, and in all that time they were not permitted to touch food. On the morning of the fourth day the elders caught kangaroos and wallabies, and gave each girl a flint knife.

"It is to cut your food," they said. "Take as much as you want to satisfy your appetites."

To the relief of the elders the young women took only enough meat to satisfy their immediate hunger. If they had obeyed their instincts they would have taken the whole joint to distend their stomachs after the long fast, but they had learnt the lesson well.

They returned to camp and the second series of tests began.

"This is to see whether you have overcome pain," they were warned.

One by one they were made to lie flat on their backs on the bare ground. A wirinum took a pointed stick, thrust it between a girl's lips so that it rested on a front tooth, and hit the butt of the stick with repeated blows until the tooth was knocked out.

"Are you ready to lose another tooth?" she was asked.

"Yes."

A second tooth was knocked out, but the girl made no sound. The others submitted themselves to the ordeal without protest.

"Stand in a long line," the wirinum commanded. With a sharp flint he scored a heavy line across their breasts until the blood flowed down their stomachs and dropped on the ground. Ashes were rubbed into the wounds to increase the pain, but they endured the double agony without a murmur.

"You may lie down and go to sleep now," they were told.

They stretched out on the bare ground and sank into a sleep of exhaustion, forgetting for a little space their aching gums and the wounds in which the ashes stung, as well as healed, the jagged cuts. Hours later one of the girls woke and smothered a scream before it reached her lips. She felt something moving across her body. She tensed her body until the straining muscles were as hard as wood. Every part of her body was covered with crawling insects. They slithered across her lips, wormed their way into her nostrils and ears and over her eyelids, but she remained silent and motionless; and so with every girl until daylight came to release them.

The tests continued until it seemed that there was no end to them. There was the ordeal of the pierced nose, in which they were required to wear a stick, which kept the wound from healing, through the septum. Every time it was touched it was agony to the wearer as it tore further through the flesh. There was the ordeal of the bed of hot cinders, and others that degraded the body and could be overcome only by steadfastness of mind and spirit.

"It is over," the elders said at last. "You

have endured every ordeal, every test of pain, every torture with fortitude and cheerfulness. We, the elders of your tribe, are proud of you. There remains the last test, the conquering of fear. You have gone a long way towards it. Do you think you can survive this as well?"

"We can," the girls cried with a single voice.

The ordeal came at night. The old men went to the isolated camp where the girls were to sleep without the comfort of fire, where the wind moaned eerily in the trees, and the spirits of darkness and evil seemed to hide in every bush. The elders chanted spine-chilling tales of bunyips and maldarpes, of the Yara-ma-yha-who and the Keen Keeng, of monsters such as the Whowhie, Thardid Jimbo, and Cheeroonear, and of the Evil One himself. Then they stole away, and the girls were left alone.

Horrible cries came from the surrounding bush and continued all night, as though the encampment was surrounded by spirits and monsters. The old men enjoyed themselves as they endeavoured to fill the girls' hearts with fear; but the young women who had passed through pain to the ultimate test of womanhood were able to call on their reserves of courage and endurance.

Morning came. The whole tribe assembled to greet them and congratulate them on the triumph of mind over body. Even the gods and spirits of the high heaven were present that day. The girls, now entered into full womanhood, were snatched from the midst of their friends and taken up into the sky where, as the Seven Sisters of the constellation of the Pleiades, they shine serenely on the world, encouraging every successive generation to follow their example.*

We may note the three main disciplinary elements in the ordeals, designed to overcome appetite, fear, and pain.

For periods which might extend for months young men were required to support themselves by hunting and eating alone, culminat-

* A. W. Reed, *Myths and Legends of Australia*, A. H. and A. W. Reed, 1965, pages 83-7. (First recorded by W. Ramsay Smith.)

ing in a walk or a hunt lasting two or three days without food, and being brought unexpectedly to a place where a meal had been prepared. Here they were required to abstain from eating or to take only a small portion.

Pain had to be endured silently. Many of the ordeals were severe, involving physical injury. For men the ceremony of circumcision was included, and the act had overtones of esoteric meaning.

The conquest of fear was the final element. It was all the more terrifying because it was given at a time when deep mysteries were being revealed, to the accompaniment of the unearthly music of the bull-roarers, with darkness round about and unexpected flares of light revealing the grotesque features of masked and painted elders.

In the Central Australian Engwura pre-ordeal the women and girls threw fire sticks at the youths. When the bull-roarers began to whirr they would run back in alarm, leaving the boys to endure the eerie sound and to face the ghostly appearances of the night. For a period of several days the young men were forced to lie face downwards on the ground without looking up. When they were permitted to lift their heads the first sights that met their eyes were the painted bodies and fearsomely decorated conical masks or hats worn by the elders who were made up to represent mythological beings as a prelude to the imparting of secret lore.

While it is not possible to give a single comprehensive account of initiation rites which would apply to every tribe, the following descriptions are typical of the practices observed throughout the country, no matter how much they varied in detail.

When a tribal initiation ceremony was held, messages were sent out to the clans, and it might take several months before all the men gathered together. Sometimes the boys had their incisor teeth knocked out at this stage, but frequently it was left to the concluding part of the programme.

In the preliminary stages the boys who had reached puberty were driven out of the camp. The men took charge of them, painting their bodies and tossing them into the air. In Central Australia and the north-west there followed the rites of circumcision. At this stage the boys were shown the bull-roarer for the first time, and the programme of instruction in totemic history, ceremonies, laws, tabus, and food restrictions followed as the first step in a sequence that came to fulfilment only in the final rites. The sound of the bull-roarer was the signal for the women to keep well away from the bora ground. Implicit obedience was required of the boys and young men. Little food was provided and most of the ceremonies were held at night or at daybreak.

Variations in the procedures give further insight into the ceremonies. In the Aranda tribe the candidates were placed on vegetation laid on a fire. Although tooth evulsion was a fairly widespread practice, some of the tribes did not practise body mutilation at all, other than pulling out body hair. Other practices included purificatory bathing, tying cords round the arm in preparation for blood-letting, tearing off of fingernails, biting the scalp, gashing the hand, piercing the nose, and cicatrisation. The wounds mentioned here were symbolic practices that were sometimes applied to a corpse after death in order to free the spirit from the body and drive it away.

In the Roper River district the ban of silence must have been an especially trying ordeal. Between the candidate and certain relatives conversation was forbidden for two years. Although he was permitted to speak to other boys he had to keep silent in the presence of men, and could reply to women only by nodding his head. Sign language enabled him to make known his needs.

The tests endured by girls were less severe than those of men, and indeed had a lesser significance, being regarded as rites to celebrate puberty and in preparation for marriage rather than initiation into tribal and totemic mysteries. Nevertheless some of the ordeals they endured were of the same type, and included seclusion from the tribe for a period, the imposition of food tabus, instruction in the less esoteric aspects of tribal lore, advice on marital matters, and final purification. The young women were then decorated with coloured ochres and led back to camp. They had gone out as girls and returned as women, ready for marriage and motherhood.

In the eastern regions the presiding guardian of the ceremonies of the bora ground was Baiame, or the god who was recognised as the All-Father. Although it is impossible to trace all local variations, circumcision as a practice at the first initiation (culminating in subincision before manhood) was observed mainly in Central and Western Australia; the knocking out of teeth was practised more extensively in the eastern regions and to some extent in the south and west.

There were usually two or three initiation ceremonies for boys and young men, each of increasing importance and severity. In Central Australia the first included tossing in the air and knocking out the front teeth; the second, circumcision; the third, subincision and the imparting of the more advanced elements of sacred lore. The boy acquired a new status term after each stage. When the wound caused by subincision healed, a young man was in theory ready for marriage, but owing to the custom of betrothing girl babies to the men at this time he might have to wait for at least 12 years before marriage.

It will be apparent that the initiation rites were not only a test of endurance, but also the occasion of initiation into the mysteries of the tribe. The imparting of knowledge was a long process. The simplest form of instruction was given during the first rites when they were still boys, and continued through the second and third series until full manhood was attained. In fact the expanding horizons of sacred knowledge never ceased. The older men revealed ever deeper mysteries to young men, who in turn passed them on to others as they advanced in experience and status in the council of the elders, so that the full body of lore might be preserved to each successive generation.

It was the task of the elders to teach the young men, and also to provide them with weapons fitted to their new dignity as full-grown men; thus the young men became heavily indebted to the older ones, incurring obligations that could never be fully discharged until they in turn became old men. The first flush of so-called freedom on the completion of the ceremonies soon faded, for many a young man discovered that a great part of his life would be occupied in providing food for the elders to whom he was indebted, and to the parents of his future wife, for whom he might have to wait for many years.

Blood, Bull-roarers, Circumcision, Corroborees, Dreamtime, Eggs, Fire, Gifts, Hair, Marriage, Scars, Teeth, Totemism.

INQUESTS. Except in the case of babies and old men and women, and when warriors were killed fighting, some form of inquest was held to determine who was responsible for causing the death of a member of the group. Death had not come from the ancestor, therefore it must have been through the intervention of some evilly disposed person who had used sorcery. In consequence it was incumbent on the friends and relatives of the deceased to discover, punish, or eliminate those who were responsible.

On the occasion of a death in the clan, strong emotions were immediately engendered. Desire for identification of the culprit and for revenge were intermingled with fear of the presence of death and of the intervention of the newly released spirit in the affairs of the group. The latter state was avoided by shifting camp, the former was satisfied by seeking out the culprit.

An inquest was usually held while the body decomposed on a tree or on a platform some time after death occurred, for a very good reason. The elders realised that for some time the emotions were likely to get out of control. The period of mourning provided release, and strident demands for revenge often reached an hysterical pitch which, unless deferred, might result in widespread combat that would lead to serious consequences. When the leaders permitted investigations to take place, the delay enabled them to be conducted more dispassionately. It was still necessary for a scapegoat to be found, the method varying amongst the tribes, and even within the one tribe. The inquest was not always followed by an act of revenge, the very act of identification itself sometimes proving sufficient. The method of revenge is described under the appropriate heading. The following methods were employed at the time of the inquest, but varied in different regions.

Inquests were amongst the occasions when the medicine man was required to show his skill, and he never failed. When he was baffled (or perhaps when in his judgment it was best to let sleeping dogs lie), his fellow-tribesmen were usually content with a verdict of collective responsibility by a group. If feelings were running high, further investigations might be made in an attempt to identify a single murderer.

One of the first things the medicine man was careful to do during the mortuary ceremony was to observe the actions of those who were present. If anyone did not seem particularly distressed, or failed to gash himself as others were doing, or behaved in an indifferent fashion, suspicion was immediately engendered. The next step (coming some time later) was to take a bone from the corpse, grind it to powder, and administer it to the suspect without his being aware of it. If he choked there was no doubt that he was the guilty person.

Another method was to cut the right forefinger from the hand of the corpse and place it somewhere amongst the branches of a banyan tree. A close watch was kept on the suspect, and if the forefinger of his right hand had become stiff or twisted, guilt was established.

Sometimes the task of identification was made easier when the spirit of the murderer was seen hovering round the corpse as it was placed on a platform. In northern Kimberley the medicine man placed rows of sticks or stones under the body. Each represented one of the suspects (or possibly the whole group, or a neighbouring clan). If the body fluids dropped on a single stick or stone, or crept towards it, then the truth was revealed. When inquest stones were set round the grave, it was believed that drops of blood emanating from the body would appear on the stone that was emblematic of the murderer.

A method that demonstrated the power of magic was for the medicine man to ascend into the sky and come down behind the wind. In some strange way he rolled time backwards and was able to see the murder re-enacted.

There were many other ways of discovering the guilty party—pulling hairs from the head, or examining signs that seemed to have little connection with the affair.

The circumstances of the death of every person were not always examined with such care. Age and social status had a great effect on the feelings and actions of the group, the degree of hostility aroused against the unknown murderer, and the lengths to which the clan was prepared to go to seek revenge.

Revenge.

INSECTS. There were a few insects which were an important element in the food resources of the Aborigines. Honey ants and witchetty grubs were notable examples; also moths, white ants, honey ants, grubs, and worms were among insects eaten, but most insects were as much a plague to them as they are to white man.

K

KANGAROOS. Important as a food supply, the kangaroo with its peculiar gait proved an inspiration to dancers. There is a legend that tells how a kangaroo, watching the dancers during a corroboree from behind a tree, was so carried away by the rhythm that he joined in. After a few moments of stupefaction the performers entered into the spirit of the occasion, tied rolls of skin to their girdles in imitation of its tail, and hopped around in a circle with the kangaroo. So the Kangaroo Dance was born. But the kangaroo had entered into a semi-sacred mystery, and to regularise the situation the elders were forced to allow him to join the candidates at the initiation ceremonies. The tale is in some way connected with the totemic ancestry of the social group.

Kangaroo skin rugs were used in colder climates, and a bone from the animal was often an important part of the sorcerer's and medicine man's equipment.

It may be interesting to note that there is a considerable element of doubt regarding the origin of the name. It was first recorded in 1770 when the *Endeavour* was beached at Cooktown, and appeared in print in 1773. But by 1778 the Aborigines of Port Jackson believed it to be an English word! In 1818 it was not even known by the tribesmen in the vicinity of the Endeavour River. Several theories have been proferred, such as that "Kangaroo" was the answer to a question, and meant "I don't understand"; or that, if the name had been borne by a member of the tribe, it had been expunged from their vocabulary after his death. Later evidence shows that it was used in Western Australia, and that a number of years after Cook's visit it was again in use at the Endeavour River in the 1890s; but, once again, it is claimed that the Aborigines of that district had taken it over from Europeans who were using the word.

Cooking, Food, Hunting, Names.

KINSHIP.
Families, Relationships.

KNIVES. The first primitive knives were no doubt simply flakes of stone of an appropriate shape, used for cutting meat and for other purposes. As the various cultures developed, techniques of implement manufacture improved, and men learned not only to knap lumps and pebbles of stone, but also to strike from them the kinds of flakes they needed for knives, scrapers, and other tools. They skilfully chipped their edges and later learned to grind them to

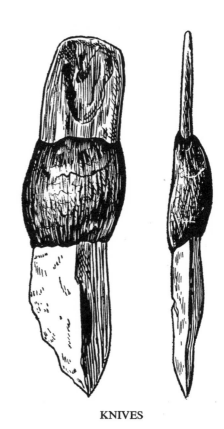

KNIVES

keep them sharp. Small and large knives were used, the outstanding type being a quartzite blade up to 8 or 9 inches in length. Smaller saw-edged flakes were in common use. In northern Queensland, sharks' teeth, and in south-western Australia small thin stone flakes, were set in a row on a wooden handle. Ground-

KURDAITCHA

edge knives and chisels were made in many parts of the country.

The knife was one of the few simple, essential tools of the Aboriginal, and was kept in a dilly bag or thrust through a man's girdle.

Chisels, Spears.

KURDAITCHA. An oval shoe made of emu feathers stuck together with human blood, forming a pad inside a twine or human hair net. These shoes were worn by a sorcerer and by the man for whom he was performing his magic when stalking a victim; also by the victim himself to confuse his pursuers.

Shoes.

L

LACERATION. The weals that covered the body of an Aboriginal were deliberately inflicted with stone or shell knives to mark the progressive stages of his initiatory rites and to demonstrate his conquest of fear and pain, as an act of mourning, or simply as an adornment. Women also adopted the fashion as an aid to beauty. The weals rose in pronounced ridges, vertically or horizontally, because ashes were rubbed into the wounds, partly as a healing agent but primarily to aggravate the condition. For the same reason clay was inserted into the wounds in some tribes, thus providing pronounced raised scars. The patterns of cicatrices vary in different parts of Australia, the commonest being up to four parallel scars across the chest and stomach.

Mourning, Scars.

LAND. Land was the most important possession of the Aboriginal, mainly because it included the abodes of the pre-existent spirits of the group. Even so, the land did not belong to him but to his group, clan, or tribe. The hills and valleys and plains, streams, waterholes, trees, animals, roots, birds, grubs, and ants were all the possession of many people who were tied together by the fact that they had inherited them from remote times, and shared them not only with their first ancestors but with all the people who preceded them and who would follow in the days to come.

This tribal ownership of land and its products was a perpetual inheritance. It was unthinkable that it could be sold, exchanged, or transferred. There would have been no point in such an exchange because the people belonged to the land just as much as the land belonged to them. Attacks on other groups were not made to take their land because it had no spiritual or totemic significance to the attacking group.

LANGUAGES. The latest estimate revealed that 633 dialects and languages were spoken throughout the continent. While the statement is substantially correct, it must be modified by appreciation of what constitutes a language, as distinct from a dialect. It is important to remember that there was no interchange of visits between distant tribes, and therefore what began as a common language could easily evolve into a series of dialects and then, as the need for special words arose in particular situations, the dialects would in turn begin to evolve into what appeared to be different languages. The linguistic unit common to a number of separate groups then became important as a means of classification. Sometimes a common language was the only unifying element in a tribe; even so, the grammatical structures differed among some tribes.

Until the 1930s no systematic study had been made, but many excellent studies of Aboriginal languages have been and are being made. Thus, even though many tribes have disappeared, and others who live on the fringe of white civilisation have lost their own culture to a marked degree, much is being preserved. Captain Cook was the first European to collect a local vocabulary on the Endeavour River. He was followed by early missionaries who made a number of such collections with great fidelity and also compiled grammatical studies. The first grammar and vocabulary of an Australian language, that of the Awabakal at Lake Macquarie, was compiled by the Rev. L. E. Threlkeld between 1821 and 1829. The list of words, published in books and such periodicals as *Science of Man*, together with unpublished lists compiled by private investigators, still remain as isolated collections.

Yet enough material has been collected for students to advance theories about the evolution of language throughout the continent. Authorities on this involved subject realise that in the 20,000 years or so during which the Aborigines have been in occupation, many changes can occur, as we know from what has happened to the English language in less than 2,000 years. One of the theories is that each tribal language has evolved from several common sources, the web being inextricably tangled during the passing of the centuries. In support it is said that, no matter how they differ in grammar and vocabulary, the phonetic values remain constant, except in some of the northern areas where Papuan influence has predominated. Dr A. Capell says that "the same common phonetic types of sound are found, and the same sounds are absent, over practically all the country."*

Such differences as arose (and it must be admitted that they are considerable, as we shall see later) could possibly have occurred because of the isolation which surrounded most of the groups, especially in the drier areas where it was vital that there should be no trespassing on neighbouring territories lest the scarce vegetation and animal life should be depleted. Even in more favourable areas wet seasons resulted in an equal degree of isolation, while occasions for corroborees when the tribes gathered together were few and far between.

Another theory is that of "Common Australian",† not necessarily originating with the first-comers, but with a later wave of migration which spread over the whole continent, displacing the earlier languages.

In 1946 two research workers, O'Grady and Capell, compiled a brief list of less than 50 words which were found spread throughout the continent. That is not to say that they were found in every language, but that they were widely distributed. It was not a lingua franca but a list that showed that, no matter how different the languages were, there were certain words which had the widest possible distribution.

In a communication to the editor of *Australian Aboriginal Studies* in 1962, Dr S. A. Wurm threw further light on the unsolved problems of Aboriginal languages, suggesting that there may have been only about 150 distinct languages. The note gives such a clear picture of the situation that laymen can readily appreciate the significance of his remarks:

"There are approximately 500 different forms of speech in Australia, that is, what linguists would refer to as 'communalects', not committing themselves to calling them either languages or dialects. Many of these are now extinct. Until very recently, it had been believed that between 300 and 400 of these communalects constituted different languages, and the remainder dialects. However, work at present undertaken by Hale in collaboration with O'Grady and Wurm in the field of the lexical comparison of Australian languages has shown that very great prevalence in Australia of what linguists call 'dialect chains': that is, out of communalects A, B, C, D, and E, A and B are mutually intelligible, and in consequence are only dialects of one language, and the same applies to B-C, C-D, and D-E. However, A and C are not mutually intelligible, and neither are A-D, A-E, B-D, B-E and C-E. In other words, a chain of mutual intelligibility runs step by step from A to E which would make them all dialects of one language, but if any of the non-adjacent links are compared with each other, they are not mutually intelligible, and therefore constitute different languages. In such dilemma situations linguists tend to regard the entire dialect chain as constituting a single language. The application of this principle of classification to the Australian communalects results in the number of distinct *languages* in Australia being only around 150."*

Examination of some of the languages, and of dialectal differences, will serve to show some of the problems, and perhaps give a clue to what has happened over the years. In Arnhem Land there were many "languages" in which the vocabulary differed to such an extent that one tribesman could not understand another who came from a different linguistic unit. But it was easy for him to learn the "foreign" language because its grammar and structure were similar to that of his own.

Even when the grammar was different there was still the common phonetic basis which was so widespread. The situation can be summed up, broadly speaking, by saying that there was a basic similarity of all the languages of Australia; they were *languages* of the same family, not dialects of the same language. Within these languages there were a number of dialects which often prevented communication between the tribes. Broad geographical differences were

* *Aboriginal Man in Australia*, page 116.
† The term was invented by Dr A. Capell.

* *Australian Aboriginal Studies*, page 130 f.n.

not sufficient to account for the divergences. "Although tribes might be separated only by a rock or by trees, yet they might be unable to hold converse except through an interpreter," wrote Sir W. Ramsay Smith in 1934.* It was the isolation of the self-supporting tribe, clan, or group that accounted for this phenomenon.

Five "groups" of languages with predominant affinities have been isolated: the Northern Australian Prefixing Group; the Barkly Tableland Group; the Western Desert Group; the Arandic Group of Central Australia; and the Victorian Group (the latter extending some distance into New South Wales). These broad divisions do not cover the full range of languages, but have been studied in sufficient detail to allow a further identification into subgroups. As the name implies, inflection is achieved by adding prefixes in northern Australia, elsewhere by suffixes. The unclassified languages are those of parts of Arnhem Land, Western Australia, Queensland, and New South Wales, where there was a profusion of tongues.

The following common elements are found in grammar—absence of relative pronouns, few conjunctions, similarity in the order of words, variety in the form of verbs, the use of the dual as well as the singular and plural. In the vocabularies there was a great contrast. The range and scope of Aboriginal languages are sometimes underestimated. Vocabularies of 10,000 or more words have been compiled in some Aboriginal languages. The Aboriginal, living close to Nature, needed and knew words for all natural phenomena and everything connected with his daily life, including his belief in and dependence on supernatural affairs and the Dreamtime that was part of his inner life; and he connected them with the essential framework of service words or constructions. It does not follow that his thought processes and his method of expressing them were the same as the white man's; in fact they were quite alien in many respects. In various parts of the country he needed different vocabularies, but though his verbal requirements differed, he was equipped with all he needed to translate thought and action into words.

* *Myths and Legends of the Australian Aborigines*, Harrap, 1934, page 332.

Professor Elkin admirably sums up the Aboriginal's use of language:

"We know that the general principles of these languages, in spite of their great variety, are basically the same, or of one stock, all over the continent. They are marked by precision, brevity of expression, an emphasis of concreteness and an endeavour to express in one word, or in as few as possible, a complete picture of the situation or desire; this is done by the inflexions of the word or words used. They are also related to the culture, and cannot be understood or satisfactorily mastered without a knowledge of tribal thought, belief and custom. . . . Finally, there is something about the form and sound of the words and sentences used all over the continent which suggests to a person working among the Aborigines that there is no fundamental difference between their languages. I found this in places so far apart as north-western Australia, Laverton District of Western Australia, western and north-eastern South Australia and the northeast of New South Wales."*

One of the regrettable features in such records as have been made is lack of uniformity. Most of the early vocabularies used a system based on Italian vowel sounds and English consonantal sounds, but as time went by they became contradictory and confusing. In modern times there have been attempts to standardise the spellings without using new characters.

Many attempts have been made at classification of the languages. There is more affinity between the northern languages as a group, less between the many languages of the south, where adjacent groups spoke their own language and knew something of that of their immediate neighbours, but found no common means of communication with anyone further away. In Tasmania the tribal languages were all related grammatically but varied in vocabulary.

In addition to the normal means of verbal communication, there were "secret" and esoteric languages, used by boys who were undergoing initiation tests, others for men who passed all

* *The Australian Aborigines*, pages 26-7.

the tests, and words—some of which were obsolete—used in sacred songs. Little is known of these languages. In addition there were specialised languages which were employed in conversing with certain relatives to avoid the tabus imposed on such relationships.

Sign language, Songs, Tribes.

LAWS. Law as understood by the white man did not exist in pre-historic Australia, but the principle of communal responsibility and regulation, and punishment for offences against them, certainly existed. As in most social and community practices, law was closely related to belief in the Dreamtime. The actions and practices of the first ancestors or totemic heroes became tribal custom. The tradition thus established was the law, developed through countless centuries to preserve the welfare of the group.

The offender who flouted any part of this body of tribal law was certain to be punished, either by the action of the social clan or local group, or by the more dreaded displeasure of the ancestral hero. The final authority in all matters of "law" was the group of elders. It should be noted, too, that the most stringent customs and regulations related to kinship in its many ramifications.

In *The Passing of the Aborigines*, page 236, Mrs Daisy Bates states that early in her work she had occasion to compare British justice with native law. "My first studies were, happily for me, conducted amongst the two most law-abiding people in Western Australia—the Bibbulmun of the South-west and the Broome groups of the North-west. From the remnants of these I learned the admirable native system, based wholly on legend and tradition, and implicitly obeyed without authority or overlord laws which made for morality and amity.

"A man who killed another gave himself up to the dead man's brothers to be killed. Breaches of the totemic and marriage laws among the law-abiding groups were capital crimes. Theft had been unknown, and there was never transgression of group borders."

Elders, Relationships.

LEADERS. There were no "chiefs" amongst the tribes; but in every society men who have the inborn qualities of leadership naturally exercise these attributes in times of need. People look to them instinctively, and so it was amongst the Aborigines. Each group had its informal council of elders which was recognised on account of age, experience, and knowledge of all things sacred and mundane. Amongst them the leader would emerge, usually middle-aged, yet in the full strength of manhood, so that he combined energy and determination with knowledge.

Occasionally he was a medicine man, or, to use the delightful expression that was commonly adopted, a "clever-man", with a profound knowledge of local lore. He was a psychological adept, credited with being able to feel danger before he could see it. Mostly, however, an acknowledged leader, although well schooled in secret matters, possessed no supernatural powers.

The leader's opinion carried a great deal of weight at meetings of men to discuss problems and plans. His task was to interpret the general view. The subjects that were discussed affected the local group in its movements, discipline, observance of custom, and ritual. A gathering of several groups was "governed" by the council.

The finest hunter in a group (who was the most skilful spearman) usually led hunters in a party of four or five; the greatest warrior took a leading part in warfare; the eldest active man in a clan or cult was the ceremonial leader in rituals; the finest dancer, actor, painter, singer became a leader in his own sphere. Leadership existed in many varieties of circumstances.

Councils, Elders, Tribes.

LEGENDS.
Folklore, Mythology.

LEPROSY. Some of the northern tribes were afflicted by this disease, probably brought in the first place by Malayan traders, and subsequently reintroduced by Chinese and European visitors.

LIL-LILS. Battle-axe shaped weapons made from one piece of wood. The head was not used as a cutting blade but as a club, the weight of the head giving force to the blow. They were also thrown. The blade and shaft were engraved with attractive linear designs. *Clubs.*

LOVE MAGIC. A number of forms of love magic were practised by both men and women, in isolation and secrecy, or as a community ceremony. In the latter case it took the form of a love song or dance which excited the listeners and performers.

There were several ways in which a woman could attract a man who had taken her fancy, some of them exhibiting a degree of symbolic ingenuity, such as winding a length of hair cord around a model of the one who was desired and drawing it close to her. The model did not need to be of human form, but frequently took the shape of an animal, and was probably of totemic significance, because the ancestors were as closely linked to courtship as to marriage and the rites of conjugal relationships. Other types of love magic were more uninhibited, and included performing ritual dances of sexual significance.

Men employed the same arts, but because they were more closely drawn into the Dreamtime through knowledge obtained during their initiation ceremonies, they had access to objects and practices of great sanctity. Totemic designs painted on bull-roarers had particular efficacy because the voice of the ancestor spoke through it, calling the young woman irresistibly to her lover. The didgeridoo served the same purpose when it was held over a fire and filled with smoke which the lover swallowed. When he sounded the dronepipe the young woman of his choice was supposed to be unable to resist. Women in Arnhem Land placed the string they used in string-figure making in a man's dilly bag to attract him. Men used pearl shell which was "sung" for love magic purposes.

However, in view of the system of marriage of young women to more mature men, it seems likely that the majority of love charms and devices were devoted to clandestine relationships. *Love songs.*

LOVE SONGS. Men as well as women joined in singing love songs in many parts of the continent. They were of a more personal nature, designed to attract a special member of the opposite sex, and were definitely magical in their intent. But apart from songs sung for special purposes, the singing of love songs was an outlet for emotion on the part of the whole community; they were related to what have been called "gossip songs", in which the news and scandal of the moment were re-enacted in the most fundamental of all the arts—poetry and song. Actual events, however, were not necessarily a part of love songs, which were sung to stimulate desire and intensify excitement. They were often quite uninhibited in their portrayal of the arts of love.
Love magic, Magic.

M

MAGIC. Every form of mishap and disaster known to the Aboriginal was not in his belief due to natural causes. Supernatural forces had been at work, usually through the medium of sorcery. The only cure for misfortune and misadventure was through magic and ritual.

Three main classifications have been generally accepted, although the terminology varies. They may be noted quite simply as productive, protective, and destructive magic. The two former categories were beneficent, and are known in some part of the world as "white" magic. The purpose and practices of productive magic are given in detail under such headings as Increase rites, Love magic, Rain-making, etc., and were normally inseparable from ritual observances. Protective magic was the responsibility of the medicine man, the detective who discovered the human sources of evil, and who frequently exercised a healing ministry in his own way. Destructive or "black" magic was the function of a medicine man appointed by a group to carry out black magic. Sorcerers were universally feared on account of their unearthly powers; but sorcery could be practised by anyone knowing the proper rites and chants.

The life of a sorcerer was a hazardous one, but no doubt it appealed to some men because of the power it enabled them to wield. There were some who would not admit that they possessed such gifts. When a man died suddenly his death was frequently ascribed to the work of a sorcerer who could not be found, or who, as so often happened, belonged to another tribe. Nevertheless such men did exist. They ran the risk of their evil magic turning on themselves if the victim became aware of what was happening and enlisted the support of a medicine man of superior powers. All the sorcerer's power availed him nothing against the armed force of angry and suspicious men bent on revenge.

The distinction between religion and magic was that the former benefited the tribe or group as a whole, whereas magic only partially did so. Black magic was directed personally to sorcery, to the death of individuals. An unexplained death was always attributed to the work of a sorcerer and so the belief that persons could exercise evil powers was fostered, even though no one could be found to admit responsibility.

Black magic was exhibited in three forms—contagious, imitative, and projective, the latter being the best known because it included the practice known as pointing the bone. In this performance an inimical object was projected into the victim. It should be noted, however, that the "projection" could be an immaterial object, as is shown by the equally potent form of singing magic. Unlike most procedures, this form of the art did not require a sorcerer-medium, and it was only the singing that was projected at the victim, who almost invariably had broken some part of the code of tribal behaviour which affected the whole group. The projection in that case was a group form of punishment, all the more effective because the recipient was aware of his misdeeds and of the inevitability of punishment.

The insertion of pointed bones or sticks was widely practised, but in different forms. In Queensland, for instance, the sorcerer, who might be many miles away from his victim, simply pointed the bone in his direction. A string passed from the bone to a container. Psychic influences caused the bone, or its spirit, to penetrate the body and draw blood, which was conveyed by the string to the receptacle. At the same time an evil force entered the flesh which had been punctured by the spirit bone. When the box and bone were burnt the victim died. Even to warm the implement of death caused great pain to the victim. Elsewhere the sorcerer approached his victim while he was asleep with the bone attached to a noose, and projected or pointed the bone at him. While the man remained unconscious the sorcerer cut open his right side below the ribs and extracted the kidney fat. Considerable importance was attached to this part of the operation. The fat was eaten, or smeared on weapons to give strength to them; without that essence of life the victim eventually died, and nothing that the medicine man could do would save him. It was believed that the sorcerer concealed his evil deed by biting the edges of the wound to close it without leaving a mark. The victim then recovered consciousness, and might go about the camp for several days, apparently well, but his vitality was gone, and the evil force working in his body made death inevitable within a few days. The essence of the operation was the insertion of the bone and the removal of the fat and the blood, and with them the vital spirit of the man.

The same principles were employed when punishing those who were guilty of violating established customs, against unfaithful wives, and for even comparatively trivial offences.

A curious belief was that a small piece of resin, with two teeth embedded in it, could be endowed with the power of extracting heat from the sun. By being sung, the heat entered the resin, and when this object, to which a cord had been attached, was placed in the victim's path, the burning heat ran from the object into his body.

Contagious magic made use of the universal principle that if one possessed something belonging to another, preferably some part of the body such as parings from fingernails, hair, or even personal possessions such as weapons, clothes, etc., it gave power over him. Conversely, it also conferred power on the possessor. This method was employed most effectively by sorcerers, but could be used by anyone who wished to harm another. It was a safer method of attack than by physical means—unless the perpetrator was discovered by a medicine man who could easily reverse the process.

Imitative magic consisted of fashioning an image of an enemy and subjecting it to the same treatment as the sorcerer wished to befall the victim. Burning the image, or attacking it with a sharp object, would have the same result in a more pronounced fashion on the victim's body.

The only drawback to these evil practices was that the perpetrator lived in fear of discovery and of having his own magic turn against him if he were discovered before the operation was complete. One of the first tasks to be performed when a man died unexpectedly was to smooth the ground near the body and examine the dust. The tracks of insects or small game would point in the direction of the culprit. With such clear evidence the sorcerer or murderer could hardly escape suspicion, certainly of guilt and, unless he was too powerful, punishment.

Art, Birth, Fertility, Images, Increase rites, Love magic, Medicine men, Names, Pointing bones, Rain-making, Revenge, Rope, Shoes, Sickness.

MANHOOD.
Initiation ceremonies.

MANNA. The name sometimes given to buumbuul (there were of course variants of the word amongst the many languages of Australia), a sugary substance obtained from gum trees, or deposited by cicadas, and used as food.

MARRIAGE. Marriage was a clearly recognised social institution throughout Australia, governed by strict rules of selection, but varying considerably in different regions. Generally speaking, women married outside their own social group. The state of marriage was an economic partnership in which husband and wife worked for the support of themselves and their family. There were few cases where they had freedom of choice in selecting a mate, but as a rule the results were effective and happy.

Over large areas a man's bride was chosen when he had passed his initiation tests, or shortly before, but the "bride" was still a baby and the actual marriage was deferred until after she had reached puberty. Betrothal arrangements were discussed freely by the relatives, who were fully aware of tabus and kinship obligations. The mother's brother (boy's uncle) was usually the most important person in these discussions.

It was usual for a girl's mother's brother (girl's uncle) to select a future husband for her at some tribal gathering. He discussed the matter with the parents, and might send a messenger to the family of the young man he had chosen. Not infrequently the boy's father would speak for the young man and convey his opinion of the proposed marriage. Regulations relating to degrees of consanguinity, and to the boundaries of social and totemic permissions are beyond the scope of the present work.

Although kinship restrictions were recognised, Elkin points out that "alternate" marriages were allowed, showing that the system was made for man, and not man for the system. He gives an example of marriage with a second cousin, the son's daughter of the mother's mother's brother, instead of with the latter's daughter's daughter. The significance of such a transaction lies in the realm of professional anthropology rather than of casual interest. It should be noted, however, that alternate marriages were still limited by tribal custom within strictly defined limits, and that nothing could ever be arranged which would be likely to result in incest.

The girl's mother gave her instructions about marriage when she was young, so that she was prepared for her new status at the time of puberty and initiation. Marriage usually occurred at a time when the people gathered together for ritual or social purposes. For some time the future bridegroom, unless he already had one or more wives, had probably been living in the unmarried youths' camp and had proved that he could support himself by hunting. During this period there had been some obligation to provide food for his bride's parents, thus establishing his right to marry their daughter. There was a "handing over" ceremony, extremely simple in character, but though the young woman might then go to live with her husband, she would not know when the marriage was to be consummated or recognised by the tribe. In fact in some areas it was apparently a casual affair that was not recognised until the birth of the first child.

It was sufficient for a man and woman to live together and share in providing for their mutual needs for everyone to recognise that they were married. There was no privacy in an Aboriginal camp. When a wedding ceremony was held it was of a simple nature. Fire was the element that symbolised marriage. In some tribes two fire sticks were tapped and placed beside the man. His bride came to him and together they kindled a fire. The fire stick and the grooved timber were the implements that symbolised the male and female elements in marriage. From that point onwards the girl had left the protection of her parents and had brought the spark of life to the union.

When the choice of a partner was left until the girl had reached marriageable age, the mother's brother was sometimes the intermediary. After consulting with the parents he took a spear in his right hand as a sign that he was ready to defend the decision at the cost of his life. If a combined meeting of families or clans was held to refuse or ratify the decision (elders having the right to speak on such occasions), a strong-minded man might stand with his spear ready to hurl it at an objector. When he travelled some distance to carry the invitation he made his coming known in advance by lighting fires and releasing smoke signals.

There were other types of marriage—by elopement without consent of the family (a dangerous procedure for the young people to take), by capture of a woman from another tribe (dangerous to the whole clan), or by the marriage of a deceased wife's sister, or a deceased husband's brother. In coastal New South Wales a bridegroom and some of his clansmen had to capture the promised bride from her group. The group would resist strongly in a mock but nevertheless serious struggle, to prove the bridegroom's fighting ability.

At marriage a man spoke with greater authority, and was usually admitted to the council of the elders; in old age he had a woman who was usually still young or middle-aged to look after him and his first wife. It would seem an arrangement that benefited the man more than the woman. Older wives were even known to encourage a man to take a second wife from among the younger women for the purpose of providing for their own old age.

Betrothal of an infant to a young man resulted in the marriage being deferred until middle age. This was a severe trial to young men, and resulted in clandestine relationships, elopements, and woman-hunting raids on other tribes. Young men who stole a woman from another group ran the risk of embroiling their group in a series of quarrels and even killings, which did not contribute to their popularity. In the case of an elopement both man and woman would be pursued by the bereft and irate husband and his companions relentlessly, with death at the end of the flight. Many young men passed through years of frustration when they saw young women of their own age being taken by older men as first, second, or third wives, living on their toil while they themselves were unsatisfied and, in addition, had the responsibility of feeding the parents of their promised bride. It has been suggested that such customs kept the population down to a level at which the tribe could be sure of sustenance. An uncontrolled birth rate resulting from the marriage of young people of the same age would have led to famine in less favourable areas, and to the eventual extermination of the tribe. Elkin, however, throws doubt on this theory, pointing out that there was much "mating" between single men and the wives of old men, and McCarthy reminds us that population was controlled by the inability of women to cope with more than one baby at a time.

The majority of marriages were monogamous, but for purposes of social prestige a man might take more than one wife. Two or three were not unusual. Sometimes this number was exceeded; but although the family's need for vegetable food was easily provided for by several women, the husband had a heavier task in providing meat for a larger number of people. A cause of strife arose when a man did not provide sufficient food for his family; if it was the woman who was lazy or unsuccessful, the husband could always adopt the remedy of taking another wife. Husbands and wives quarrelled, even fought out this problem—wives shamed a lazy or inefficient husband in public and even attacked him.

In the event of the death of either husband or wife, certain practices were again clearly defined. On the death of a man, the widow went into mourning for the period prescribed by custom, probably returning to her parents if they were still alive, after which she was free to marry again, probably to a brother of her late husband. In some tribes she even had the right of choice after consultation with her mother-in-law, and would indicate it by sitting for several nights in succession at the feet of the man she had selected. Similarly, when a wife died, the widower made a choice from his late wife's sisters. For a period the children had probably been cared for by their mother's family, but the new wife was expected to take over this responsibility.

Betrothal, Divorce, Gifts, Hospitality, Initiation ceremonies, Totemism, Women.

MASKS.
Head ornaments.

MATS. Round mats were made by twining pandanus fibres in Arnhem Land and Cape York, and by coiling rushes in south-eastern Australia. Paperbark sheets, pads of grass and fern, and skin rugs were used as mats.

MEALS. While practices varied according to circumstances, it was customary for the Aborigines to eat whatever was left over from the evening meal first thing in the morning. The women began their search for vegetable food when the children's needs had been attended to, the men after repairing or preparing their weapons. The wind had to be right for hunting.

Amongst some of the northern tribes a meal was eaten once or twice during the course of the day, as soon as sufficient food had been gathered, the food being cooked on a fire or in an earth oven. Normally, however, the second meal was eaten at the end of the day when the men returned from hunting. Animals and fish were eaten at once, and it was seldom that anyone waited until the meat was fully cooked.

When hunting, the men might cook a small animal such as a lizard or a fish to stave off the pangs of hunger. The women ate snacks of plant foods. Ripe berries and fruits were eaten by both sexes during the day. The main meal was in the evening when the men, women and children brought in the food collected during the day. They were really a two-meal people, with titbits eaten during the day when men and women were in different places.

When several groups gathered together for ritual purposes it was customary for the men to eat apart from the women, who had their share only when the men were finished. Then, while the men ate any vegetable food that was available, the women and children took the meat that was left, finishing the meal with scraps of vegetable food. In other cases, especially when roots and greenstuff were in short supply, women and children joined the men as soon as the flesh food was ready, and meals were eaten together in family groups. Strict rules were observed for groupings of families and orders of precedence.

Cooking, Food.

MEDICINE. It is always unlikely that a race of people which ascribes illness, disease, and death to supernatural causes will rely to any extent on herbal remedies, for the simple reason that supernatural visitations cannot be cured by physical means. Fortunately there were few diseases; the Aboriginal was more likely to fall victim to accident, or to injuries sustained in fighting. He had wonderful recuperative vitality, and for physical damage he developed commonsense treatments. In a few localities fractures were treated with wooden or bark splints bound with cord to set the limb; but normally a fractured leg meant death as there was no way to set it and the unfortunate person had to be killed, otherwise his immobility was too great a burden on the group. Snakebite was dealt with promptly by sucking the wound and binding the limb tightly. Lotions, resins, poultices, fomentations, and ashes were used for severe bruises, wounds, and cuts. In very few cases were potions swallowed. In these cases some element of magic or witchcraft may well have entered into the administration of the medicine. In Queensland persons who felt ill steamed themselves in hot sand or on a platform over a fire. An interesting treatment for a cramped leg was to allow ants to bite it.

Medicine men, Sickness.

MEDICINE MEN. A medicine man was not necessarily a sorcerer. There has been some confusion in the past because this distinction has not been clearly made. The sorcerer was the man who was a specialist in black magic directed towards other people. The medicine man was a doctor, medium, rain-maker, harmless magician, clever-man—there are a number of synonyms which served to define his functions. In central and northern New South Wales he was known in the native language as a wirinun. It required an exceptionally gifted person to qualify for the position, and a long period of training and initiation. Although a few women practitioners have been known, the long initiatory period and the knowledge of sacred lore that was confined to the male sex demanded men for this specialised trade or profession.

The functions of the medicine man have been defined as diagnosing and curing illness, holding seances, interpreting the omens for warfare, protecting warriors and giving deadly powers to their weapons; but these were not the whole task, nor did it indicate the wisdom and power of the specialists. The following schedule of duties and responsibilities of the munkumbole as recorded by W. Ramsay Smith[*] gives an insight into his work. He was a superior person, versed in the arts of the medicine man, with a knowledge of weather, climate, seasons, Nature in all aspects—astronomer, geographer, zoologist, learned in anatomy, orders of animals, spiritualism, clairvoyance, and telepathy. He was able to see what happened elsewhere, and in the past. He did not use his knowledge to do anyone an injury, but did good by relieving pain of body and mind. He took no part in tribal warfare, except to warn his tribe of the approaching enemy and their strength. In a vision he could see the progress of the battle, foretell the result, and sing a battle song for the protection of his own people. He was present at full-moon assemblies and gave advice when two or more tribes were gathered together. His purpose was to keep the clans and tribes together in harmony.

It does not follow that every medicine man was the Admirable Crichton portrayed by Ramsay Smith, but there is no doubt that they were men who received special training and had powers that were superior to those of common men; who claimed to heal the sick, make rain, interpret dreams, see spirits that were invisible to ordinary people, and to have the power to visit the home of the spirits in the sky. The supreme experience during initiation that qualified a medicine man was that of ritual death, followed by reincarnation as a new man with vastly heightened sensitivity to psychic influences.

Whatever place he took in the life of the tribe, his principal duties were to relieve pain and sickness, and to identify culprits who had been responsible for the death of others. The "medical" aspect varied a little in detail but was essentially the same everywhere. The patient lay on his back while the doctor projected magic crystals into his body. This was succeeded by sucking and massage, when the unseen poison bone which caused the trouble was withdrawn and the crystals retreated to their normal place in the medicine man's bag, or

[*] *Myths and Legends of the Australian Aborigines,* pages 201-2.

MEDICINE MAN

he was the most direct link between daily life and the Dreamtime. In his journeys to the spirit world he met the ancestral beings, the culture heroes of the sky, and brought back fresh evidence of the oneness of man with the personified forces of his all-embracing Dream World.

And though the clever-man was a man apart, sometimes feared, always venerated by his people, he was still one with his tribe. He did not work for material gain, though he might rightly expect some fringe benefits from his work, but he occupied an elevated position in the council of elders, and not infrequently received gifts from the grateful people he served. The important work that he undertook in inquests is described in the appropriate entry. For further information on this subject the student is recommended to read *Aboriginal Men of High Degree* by A. P. Elkin.

Crystals, Inquests, Magic, Pointing bones, Sickness.

MEN. From the time of his initiation a man accepted increasing responsibilities. Already he was trained as a hunter, for he had had to support himself by his own skill for considerable periods. At some later date he was free to marry the girl who had been chosen for him. She was responsible for supplying the vegetable food for her husband, herself, and her children, but the essential supply of fresh meat could come only from his spear and club.

As the years passed by, his knowledge of the secret lore of the tribe increased and, if he was judged worthy, he was probably admitted to the council of the elders, in which he slowly attained greater authority and prestige. In time it was possible that he might take a second wife to help in the gathering of food supplies. His family increased and with it his responsibilities —a growing clan of young people who would be expected to support him in his old age.

A trouble-maker, a man who did not conform to traditional behaviour, who was arrogant, rude to elders, or who seduced other men's wives, was usually disposed of by magic, or killed in a camp fight by men driven to desperation.

MESSAGE STICKS. Message sticks were a medium of communication between clans and tribes. The carved notches on their surface were

body. To see him at work was a study in faith. Sometimes the hands were moved slowly, as though physically drawing the pain and the evil away. At times he would send a lizard into the body for the same purpose; a string from his mouth provided a channel and the evil was spat out; or he would suck out a lizard, quartz crystal, bone, or other object which had been charmed and was the cause of the illness. In extreme cases, and with gifted doctors, the medicine man travelled up to the spirit land to capture a departed spirit and restore it to its owner. This was possible because the medicine man was the medium between the material and the spiritual worlds.

The insertion of a withdrawal medium was usually an essential part of the procedure, whether it was a snake or a lizard, or magic crystals, and was believed to be effective except when black magic had succeeded in removing the man's spirit.

The medicine man's extra-sensory skills were essential to the well-being of the tribe, because at one time thought to constitute a sign or hieroglyphic language, and to a very limited extent this was possibly so. In *The Little Black Princess*, Mrs Aeneas Gunn wrote that she had seen a "yabber-stick" with notches. It was an invitation to a corroboree, "and there were notches on it explaining what sort of corroboree it was, and saying that it was to be held at Duck Creek. There was some other news marked on it." This was a first-hand account, but it is easy to read more into it than is justified. While there may have been a few, simple, meaningful signs on message sticks, the fact is that the notches, dots, and bands were simply a mnemonic device, reminding the person who carried the stick what he was to say when he delivered the message. Each sign meant something to the messenger, but not to others, and enabled him to deliver the message accurately.

The sticks were also a guarantee of good faith, and proof that the words that were spoken were true, because they were confirmed by visual symbols. When carried for a distance through strange territories, usually in connection with trading activities, the stick not only provided a passport and guarantee of peaceful intentions, but also supplied a link with the safe totemic hunting grounds of the home of the messenger.

Pieces of bark were occasionally employed for this purpose, but the usual message stick was a piece of wood several inches in length. When used for ceremonial purposes, such as to announce a corroboree, a mortuary rite, notification of death, or any other ritual matter, the stick probably had sacred symbols carved on it, and was decorated with feathers to emphasise the importance of the occasion. It took several hours to carve a stick of this type.

MESSAGES. Besides message sticks that were carried from one place to another, information was sometimes given by those who were leaving camp to members of other clans who might follow them. In the Lake Eyre region the signs were called toa, which were carved and painted sticks. Unlike the message sticks, they conveyed definite information that could be "read" by others. Tindale and Lindsay provide an example in which a footprint pointing in a certain direction with three marks beside it and a small heap of stones would be interpreted as "We have gone three days walk in this direction and will camp by the rocky hill."[*]

It appears that the toa were sometimes elaborated to convey representations of the wanderings of the mythical ancestors, and may have constituted a claim to permanent territorial rights.

It was a common custom to leave a stick in the ground or at the fireplace pointing in the direction taken by the group who had departed, as a guide to others.

MESSENGERS. The death of a well-known person was an important and usually a tragic event, news of which was conveyed to other clans with whom he had totemic and family connections. The message was sent through the medium of a person carrying a message stick or, in such places as Arnhem Land, by emblems representative of the deceased person's totemic and clan affiliations. The emblems took different forms—carved sticks, feathered strings, or more elaborate three-dimensional representations. Arrived at a camp, the messenger did not enter but squatted on the outskirts and chanted a song without referring directly to the death, or to the one who had died. The sight of the symbols immediately conveyed the significance of the visit.

On more cheerful occasions messengers were sent out bearing summonses to corroborees and initiation rites, in order to prepare the clans for the coming celebrations, or to barter and exchange gifts.
Engwura.

MIAMIAS.
Huts.

MIGRATIONS.
Origins.

MOIETIES. A moiety is one part of anything that can be divided into two. As an anthropological term it refers to the two divisions or dual organisation of the tribe. The ceremonial significance of the moiety system was its most important aspect. In many tribes each moiety possessed some bird or animal for its totem and adopted its name. Eaglehawk and crow, for

[*] Norman B. Tindale and H. A. Lindsay, *Aboriginal Australians*, Jacaranda Press, 1963, page 122.

instance, were common in south-eastern Australia. Moieties were correlated with marriage rules, though not designed specifically for this purpose.

In different parts of the country the moieties were either patrilineal or matrilineal, and required men and women to marry outside their own group. There were many other groupings in a tribe, territorial, social, age, sex, totemic, etc., and the moieties themselves were sometimes correlated with sections or sub-sections. In the former the members of a tribe were classified into four groups of relations, and in the latter into eight groups.

The matter may be simplified (perhaps oversimplified) by emphasising the fact that moieties were not social groups, and were effective mainly in ceremonial matters. Initiation, totemic, and burial rites were the occasions when the duties, prohibitions, and privileges of the moiety system became most effective. Men of each moiety had specific duties in ceremonies and rituals.

Families, Social groupings.

MONSTERS.
Bunyips.

MOON. It was natural that the celestial bodies should enter into legend. Tales were told of Bahloo, the moon god, the maker of girl babies, who was usually represented as the reluctant lover or husband of the sun goddess. In other legends she was the Lady of the Night, wife of the morning star, and parent of the human race.

Sun and moon were represented by ovals of bark in the bora ceremonies of south-eastern Australia; and commonly in rock paintings and engravings, and in bark paintings.

MOTHERS-IN-LAW. It was an almost universal rule that once a man was betrothed he had no further converse with his wife's mother. The practice varied, of course. Amongst some tribes they were not permitted to speak to each other under any circumstances, but only through a third person. In other cases a special language or vocabulary was employed. In others sign language was used. It was customary for the woman to turn away when she saw her son-in-law or heard him speaking, and the tabu became absolute on ceremonial occasions. It has been suggested that the prohibition was designed to prevent competition between mother and daughter, especially when the younger woman was betrothed to her future husband at birth, and therefore the mother and son-in-law were closer in age than the husband and wife.

The tabu did not create ill-feeling between a man and his mother-in-law. When she was in need she looked to him for help, and usually found him ready to assist her, and even to devise ways of overcoming the barriers between them. While the man was betrothed, and even after his marriage, he was ready to make gifts of food, especially when his wife's parents were advanced in years and had difficulty in obtaining food supplies.

MOURNING. Death, which was an alarming interruption in the pattern of continuing life, brought a sense of insecurity. Pent-up feelings of fear and sorrow were released in violent acts that included wailing, laceration, prostration on the body of the deceased, and ritual chants. In some places the ritual was prolonged, involving a large number of people, and affecting the economic situation of the entire group; but whether the mourning period was long or short (and it must be remembered that most groups were anxious to separate themselves from the place and occasion of death as quickly as possible, and to expunge the name of the deceased from their minds), there was an immediate display of grief. It varied in intensity according to the degree of relationship. While there might be a display of simulated grief amongst those who were not closely connected with the dead person, death touched every member of the group. It was proof of the power of black magic, and no one was safe from its malignant influence.

When a death occurred, the whole group reacted immediately. The sound of wailing began, close relations and even those who were only remotely connected gashed their thighs, heads, and bodies with sharp stones, flints, splinters of bone, shells, or digging-sticks until the blood flowed freely. The members of different tribes lacerated themselves in different parts of their bodies. The widow threw herself on the body, begging her husband to return, while her friends worked themselves into a state of frenzy. Self-mutilation at the time of death, which was spontaneous and uncontrolled, was often succeeded by more deliberate acts.

Before the wounds were healed, probably when it was felt that the spirit of the departed was satisfied, hot ashes were rubbed in, which had the effect of healing the gashes more quickly, but raised heavy scars that became a permanent tribute to sorrow.

In Arnhem Land the art of composing and singing mourning songs had been highly developed. They were sung to the accompaniment of the mournful note of the didgeridoo, clapping of hands, and gashing of the head with sharp stones. The songs and chants provided an outlet for the emotions of women in other times of stress, such as the sickness of children, and even on happier occasions when close relatives returned after an absence. The songs were traditional but personal matters were woven into them to suit the needs of the occasion.

In many tribes a ban of silence was imposed upon close mourners. When they needed to speak to each other they used sign language. Above all else it was forbidden to speak the name of the deceased for a lengthy period. If his name was that of some common object that ordinarily entered into speech, another word had to be used in its place. It is possible that this fact accounted over a long period for changes in the vocabularies of the tribes. Food tabus also had to be observed, especially when a certain animal had been the personal totem of the one who had died.

Where mummification or delayed disposal was practised there was a second mourning period when the body was taken to its final resting place; elsewhere mourning ceremonies might continue until the inquest was held, revenge taken, or satisfaction obtained in some other way.

Various styles of mourning apparel were worn amongst a few tribes, notably mourning armbands in Arnhem Land, and widows' caps in western New South Wales.

Men observed a period of mourning for their wives, and then took another wife, usually a sister of the dead woman if available. The time of mourning for widows was prolonged, sometimes for a full year. For at least a month she probably wailed every morning and night, smearing herself with white clay from head to foot, and continuing to cut herself with sharp stones. In the western New South Wales-Lake Eyre region, the widow fashioned a cap of clay and wore this every day for many months, smearing her body continually with ashes and clay. When the period of mourning was over she put the cap on the grave, washed herself, and left the company of her parents to go to her husband's brothers, one of whom she would probably marry. Although the period of mourning was prolonged, the system ensured that a widow would eventually find security.

Burial, Death, Hair, Marriage, Widows.

MUD. In the wetter districts mud was used to protect adults and children from the bites of mosquitoes; and in many parts of the country mud and clay were smeared over the body by hunters as camouflage when they approached their prey in open country.

Clay.

MUSIC AND MUSICAL INSTRUMENTS. Aboriginal music was primarily vocal. Little instrumental music was performed without singing, for it was mainly an accompaniment to singing and dancing. Primarily it consisted of the tapping of clapping-sticks or boomerangs, clapping hands, and the slapping of hands on the thigh to beat out the rhythm for the dance. Rolls of skin were also beaten with the hand.

Apart from the didgeridoo, used only in the upper Northern Territory, all instruments were of the percussion type, and included skin drums (Cape York), clapping-sticks, gongs (Arnhem Land), rattles, rasps of notched wood scraped with a rubbing-stick, and dried leaves tied round the ankles or below the knees to make a rustling noise in time with the steps of the dancers. The bull-roarer was used in sacred ceremonies, but can hardly be classed as a musical instrument.

In spite of the paucity of woodwind, represented only by the didgeridoo with its extremely limited range, human emotions were expressed through music to such an extent that the Aborigines could be regarded as a musical race. It was in song and dance that music took shape. It was the vital, indeed the only source of entertainment and of sacred ritual. Each totemic clan had hundreds of songs about its totems, spirit ancestors, and ritual places. There was variety in tune and rhythm, not only in different areas, but between the different song cycles of a single tribe. Many of the tunes were simple, but they ranged up to complex forms that were limited only by the range of instruments available to them. Professor Elkin's definition of the component aural elements of a corroboree defines the range of music used in tunes for social enjoyment: ". . . a complex of singing, percussion sounds, didjeridoo notes where it is used, dancing and dancers' calls, shouts, sibilant and other sustained monotone notes".

It is beyond the purpose of the present work, and the compiler's capacity and knowledge, to attempt an analysis of Aboriginal music, but the following note in the monograph on the subject by Elkin and Jones in 1958 gives insight into the relatively complex music of Arnhem Land.

"In common with many other primitive styles, Arnhem Land songs use diatonic scales much more often than chromatic scales; their melodies observe the universal principle of downward motion, and tend to support the theory of dual origins in music; the rhythms used constantly employ syncopation and sequential repetition of motives; simple repetition is the normal method of building extended forms, which resemble those of nearly all primitive music.

"Important features that are rare or completely unknown elsewhere among primitive people include the strong preference for complete heptatonic scales and isometric structure, the advanced use of polyphony without resorting to parallelism, the use of instrumental interludes to build a rondo-like form in some secular music, and the construction of long song-cycles and corroborees by skilfully varying basic material, together with the constant employment of a quiet, unaccented style of performance, and a highly-developed professionalism in composition, singing and instrumental playing."*

Bull-roarers, Clapping-sticks, Corroborees, Didgeridoo, Drums, Gongs, Rattles, Songs.

* Quoted in *Australian Aboriginal Studies*, pages 287-8.

MYTHOLOGY. The mythology of any primitive race is normally a collection of narratives about supernatural beings and events which provide an explanation of the origin of natural phenomena, of the creation of the world, the advent of mankind, and of present-day behaviour and ritual. The mythology of the Australian Aboriginal was preserved in ritual, that is in song and dance and pantomime, and to a great extent in spoken narrative, and was at the heart of religion. The myth was not merely a conventional belief in creative deities, or a legendary tale of fabulous beasts and monsters, but the living reality of the Dreamtime, explaining how things came into being and continued to exist for the benefit of the tribe. It was intimate, and directly related to the needs of the people who preserved it. The myth, re-enacted in ritual, was life-giving. Without it mankind was lost; and in this intimate fashion it enabled each tribe and clan to become part of the very being of its own territory, made by the supernatural ancestor who first gave it to them and continued to manifest himself in the ritual performances that were the mainspring of community life. It is not an exaggeration to say that all sacred ceremonies were occasions when the myth was lived once more, keeping the tribal territory alive by the presence of the ancestor whose actions were being repeated.

Myths expressed the issues of life and death, the nature of man, the ultimate destiny of his soul, the mystery of fertility, and the relation of man to his environment. It was the cohesive force that explained and sustained. Without it the organisation of society would have collapsed. When a man left his own territory he was homeless and unprotected. He had lost his Dreaming and was not sure of himself until he came back to the familiar places where he knew he would be at home with his first ancestor. That this attitude was real can be proved by many examples. In her history of Echuca, Susan Priestley tells the story of an Aboriginal who was suspected of murdering another. The local tribe appealed to the white man's law: "Nevertheless the aborigine law retained its potency. Cocky escaped into New South Wales and when the troopers came upon him a week later he promptly expired 'of fright and exhaustion', probably more conscious of the terrors of having fled outside his own spirit country, than of the troopers pounding at his heels."*

No clan, group, or moiety owned the whole myth. The part that was known to it was its own personal property. The Dream track of the totemic ancestor might extend for hundreds of miles, particularly in the interior of Australia. The deeds that he performed in a certain territory were collectively the myth that belonged to the local group. It was jealously guarded, often not being revealed to women, or bearing certain meanings that became clear only when a man achieved full status and entered into the higher degrees of initiation into sacred mysteries. At times several clans joined together and in song and dance shared their departmentalised knowledge in order that they might attain greater insight and understand more clearly the purpose of the ancestral spirit.

The reality of the local myth, depending on places of totemic significance such as conception and increase sites, linked the smaller groups whose territory was defined by the portion of the myth that belonged to it, and explained why the tribal unit was so hard to define. The local group was usually an enlarged family unit with its hunting and food-gathering rites determined by its own section of the Dreamtime myth. This led to complete dependence on the ancestor rather than on the inherent power of an integrated tribe, and to the need to remain as a collection of isolated, self-

* Susan Priestley, *Echuca, a Centenary History*, Jacaranda Press, 1965, page 56.

supporting communities bound together by the proper observances which would keep the myth intact and the totemic ancestor alive within the groups.

Aboriginal religion, therefore, was not the worship of Nature and of natural objects; it was a direct link with the beings who represented life, and without whom life was meaningless. Religion was the sum total of the local myths, related to the continuing life and prosperity of the clan, and preserved by ritual practices. To this end the elders of the tribe devoted much of their time, ensuring that the source of life would not be lost by instructing younger generations in their own lore when they were judged fit to receive it.

It is difficult to distinguish between myth and legend, for there are features common to both. The story element in mythology was frequently broken down to child level, because it was important for children to learn the basic facts of their environment as a prelude to the larger understanding of later years. Legend, as distinct from myth, was full of amusing and instructive stories, sometimes allegorical, sometimes close to the borders of fact. They were related round the camp fire in addition to being part of dance, song, and acting.

Mythology was religion and life, expressed in song and story, and danced and acted in the territory of the local group to keep the gods, the spirits, the ancestors present among them.

Boundaries, Dreamtime, Folklore, Gods, Songs.

N

NAMES. Boys and girls were seldom given personal names. They were known by the degree of relationship. Older brothers and sisters called the younger ones "little sister", or "younger brother". Parents addressed them by terms such as "my child". By the time they had begun to display distinctive physical characteristics they were given what we would call nicknames, but which were really legitimate descriptive names. "Long neck", "Thick fingers", were sufficient identification until they had passed the initiation tests, during which the elders conferred adult names on the boys. Nevertheless the nickname was often used during the whole of a person's life. The new name was not at first revealed to the young man, who had to show his worthiness to bear it among adults. In certain tribes the name was never spoken aloud in company, nor were the owners addressed by it directly. Although the practice varied a great deal, it was not unusual for a man to possess a secret birth name, a nickname, a secret name of totemic significance, and a succession of names at different stages of his life.

The reason for name-giving during initiation ceremonies was that it had a sacred purpose, and was therefore part of the lore revealed only to those who were entering the esoteric mysteries of the clan.

As several names were sometimes given to one person, it also led to the sharing of a common name amongst several people. Possession of a common name then created a bond which brought with it some obligations, including the exchange of gifts and hospitality.

Names were seldom invented. They were taken from objects, certain localities within the tribal borders, or from ancestors, and were also frequently inherited, usually through the mother's side of the family. Reluctance to use a personal name led to the giving of nicknames or to the more general appellation of the clan or tribe. The fact that a person's name was that of a totemic ancestor was of great significance. It belonged to the secret life, to the Dreamtime, and therefore could not be used without proper precautions. Possession of the knowledge of the "real" name of a man or woman was likely to put the owner into the power of the sorcerer and was as dangerous as his possession of hair or other parts of the body. For this reason it was often used only in a whisper in the council of the elders.

After death a man's name could not be used for a long time, often for the term of a whole generation. It is possible that it might enter into a song cycle and emerge again as a new name at a later date when the original owner had been forgotten. If the name was the same as, or even resembled, a word in common use, that word was dropped from the vocabulary and replaced by another. "Where does that word come from, and what effect will it have on time-depth study?" asked Dr A. Capell. The question is a significant one, and has some bearing on the study of the many languages of Australia.

Identification of an individual with his tribe or clan was a feature of Aboriginal life. The identification was absolute, because he was part of the ethos of his people within the comforting assurance of the Dreamtime. For personal identification among his fellow-men and -women the definition of kinship or the use of a nickname was sufficient. Outside his own territory, or when speaking to a stranger he was not himself but part of his tribe or totemic group. But more frequently he would use the name of his local group.

Tribal names seem to vary according to the locality of the inquirer. Elkin gives an amusing example of compass directions as names. The Bemba in the north referred to their southern neighbours as Nyul-Nyul, the name meaning "south"; but to the people of the south the tribe was still known as Nyul-Nyul, in spite of the fact that the Nyul-Nyul lived to the north of them.

Elkin gives the meanings of several tribal names to illustrate the manner of their origin. Kamilaroi came from kamil, meaning "no"; Didjitara from didji, "a small child"; Tongaranka from "hillside", a local feature; and Koko-piddaji, meaning "speak-poor devils". From these, and from a name such as Nyul-

Nyul, it would seem that the tribal name was often conferred by others, not by the tribe itself. When the name contains a prefix such as Wong-, Koko-, or Nangi-, which mean "speech", it refers to a language rather than to a tribe.

Burial, Death, Greetings, Tabus, Totemism.

NATURE. Man's dependence on Nature in Aboriginal Australia was complete and absolute. Existence was precarious in the arid inland, because of prolonged droughts when shortage of water and food endangered life. Elsewhere the inhabitants encountered floods as well as droughts, gales that made fishing temporarily impossible, prolonged spells of rain that made food-collecting, hunting and fishing difficult; but apart from the rare floods life was not generally precarious in a land of plenty. The Aborigines derived a basic pattern of life from every kind of habitat in the continent.

With skill born of many generations of adaptation, the Aboriginal was confident that Nature would provide him with a subsistence. He did not regard Nature as a hostile force, because all natural phenomena had been created for his welfare by the ancestors. His task was to co-operate with this living force by means of ritual, to secure fertility of plant and animal life by means of increase ceremonies, and to observe the tribal lore which had been designed by the ancestors for the perfect ordering of natural forces.

Confident in the power of the totemic ancestors, even in times of drought and food shortage, and capable of sustaining themselves when men of other races would doubtless have perished, the tribesmen conserved their energy for the moment when it was needed, and were not normally worried or distressed. This mental attitude enabled them to survive the most trying experiences. Dr W. V. Macfarlane, physiologist, has suggested that further research is needed into the ability of the Aborigines to cope with thirst and heat, what sort of endocrine functions they displayed in this way of life, and what were the nutritional aspects of their storage and use of energy.

Ability to adapt to environment, emphasised by the climatic range varying from the aridity of the deserts to the luxuriant jungle of parts of Queensland and to the colder southern regions by the changing climate over a period of thousands of years, and by the migrations of the inhabitants from north to south, is a tribute to the Aboriginal people of Australia.

Fertility, Increase rites, Rest.

NECKLACES. Necklaces were one of the few ornaments favoured by both men and women. Necklaces were made of fur, seeds, shells, bones, and teeth. Grass and reeds cut into beads a quarter to half an inch long strung on twine, and lengths of red twine, formed necklaces that were widespread in use. In Carpentaria a flat disc of shell was hung round the neck or suspended from the waist. Among the more macabre pendants was the dried hand of a dead relative, used in eastern Victoria as an omen, a skull carried to give warning of danger, and the lower jaw suspended on twine in Queensland. In Arnhem Land men wore pendants of congealed blood in a small container suspended from the neck as a magical device to assist hunters.

NETS. There were many kinds of net used in northern and eastern Australia. They were made of bark fibre, twine, or rushes, with the familiar knotting technique. Oval and round nets suspended from a canoe were in common use. They ranged from 2 to 6 feet or more in length and were used by one or two men or women. A purse net was opened and then closed under water to catch fish. Seine nets were set in streams and tidal creeks, while cane traps were also in general use in these regions.

A long roll of reeds was sometimes pushed along a narrow shallow creek in the same manner as a net. There are no records of large seine nets being dragged in coastal waters, but fishermen formed a line and used the oval frame nets to catch or drive the fish ashore. Ducks were trapped in nets set across a creek and suspended on a tree at each end.

For emus, wallabies, and kangaroos, very substantial nets were needed. The hunters drove them into the enclosures and killed them with spears and clubs. These nets were made from bark fibre and were strong enough to withstand the plunging of the excited quarry. They were suspended from poles or trees in a crescent or semi-circle and were usually erected across the regular tracks of emus or kangaroos. They were 5 to 7 feet high, made of thick

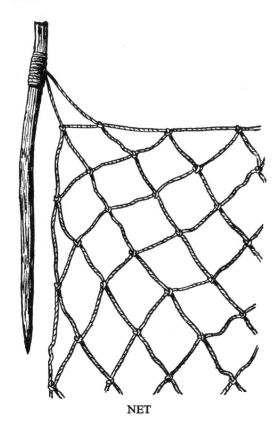

NET

sticks, or shells could be threaded through the hole. They were worn only on special occasions, because such decorations would have interfered with a woman's normal work. On the other hand, men and women throughout Australia wore a nose-bone or stick. Carved shell ornaments were worn in the Cape York district.

NULLA NULLAS. This name was given to a great variety of clubs used in southern Queensland, New South Wales, and Victoria. From 2 to 3 feet in length, with conical, round, pineapple, or thick curved heads, they were used mainly in hand-to-hand fighting. In other regions long sword- or boomerang-shaped clubs,

NULLA NULLA

cord, with a mesh of about 12 inches. A net of this kind was a group enterprise and a valuable possession. It was made in sections for easy transport. A smaller net was also suspended in one opening of a brush fence built round a waterhole. When the quarry entered, the hunter would appear suddenly at another opening and the startled animal would be caught in the net as it tried to escape.

NETTING.
Plaiting.

NOSE PIERCING. In a number of tribes there was a custom of piercing the septum of the nose of girls. It was a painful ordeal, performed in public. The flesh was pierced with a fine splinter of bone, and a smooth polished stick, greased with goanna fat, inserted. It was twisted round from time to time until the flesh was no longer tender. It was one of the ordeals in preparation for womanhood, and also a means of beautification, because feathers, painted

up to 8 feet in length, or straight round poles up to 6 feet, were used. Clubs were not common weapons in Arnhem Land and Western Australia.

NUMBERS.
Counting.

O

OCHRE. Red and yellow ochres were used on bark, body, and rock paintings, and in hair plaits. Red ochre sometimes took the place of blood in symbolic rites. Ochres were mixed by rubbing a lump in water on a stone. Many of the big traditional deposits were named, examples having been noted in Western Australia, in the Flinders Range, South Australia, and in Arnhem Land. These places were all centres of trade.

OLD AGE. Young people and those of middle age treated the older members of their group with tolerance and respect. Throughout his life a man entered progressively into the knowledge of the secret mysteries of his people, and his guidance was needed to impart knowledge to younger men. To a lesser extent this applied also to women. Even in extreme old age, when a man could do little or nothing towards the communal life of the clan, he was encouraged to tell others of his childhood memories, emphasising important matters that otherwise would be forgotten. The old men and women often followed their particular skills, the men in making weapons or stone implements, the women mats, baskets, and ornaments.

The strict rules of earlier life were relaxed, and for many old age was a pleasant time, with the comradeship of those of their own age, and respect shown by younger people. Married daughters and sons accepted the responsibility of providing them with food, and old women were sometimes allowed a measure of participation in the essentially masculine rites which would have been unthinkable when they were younger.

These were the advantages of old age; but in the desert areas where the group was constantly on the move the frailty of advancing years became a real problem. So long as the old men and women could keep up with the others they were assured of food and shelter; but there was no way of carrying them, and if they were unable to accompany their families they were left to die alone beside a fire or were mercifully clubbed to death by someone of the same family or totem. They might even be buried in an unconscious state before death finally overtook them. The practice was not dictated by cruelty, but by the unrelenting pressures of the nomadic life. To have attempted to care adequately for their needs would have imperilled the life of the whole group.

It must be admitted, however, that old women sometimes became quarrelsome and ill-tempered and interfered in the affairs of younger people, creating trouble by their malicious gossip. This was not a phenomenon confined to the Aborigines, but it brought severer penalties than in some societies. When such women lagged behind the others they were left to meet their death of thirst and starvation.

Elders, Marriage.

OMENS. Little has been recorded of omens, but it is probable that a body of superstition grew with each tribe. Two that were recorded in the Daly River area may be regarded as typical. Itching or any other peculiar sensation between the shoulder blades meant that a man would soon be speared in the back. If a woman had a burning pain in her stomach it was a sign that she would meet her brother. Each part of the body was connected with a particular class of relation.

ORIGINS. From the beginning of the twentieth century to the present day a number of theories have been advanced to account for the origin of the Australian Aborigines, ranging from the belief that they were all one people whose languages, customs, and physical characteristics were modified by the thousands of years spent in different local environments in Australia, to a theory that there were successive waves of migration of different but related peoples, mainly from south-east Asia, but also from the coastal areas of Melanesia. Although there is now less speculation and greater certainty than in the earlier years of the century, many of these matters are still in dispute, and further research will have to be undertaken and the results compared before the final answers can be given.

One theory is that the first arrivals were a Negrito people who spread throughout the continent, but who eventually left or were expelled from the mainland (except for a small pocket remaining in Queensland) to Kangaroo Island and Tasmania. The Tasmanians, now extinct, were, according to this theory, the Negritos who many thousands of years ago made their first landing on the northern shores of the continent; but there is also a belief that the Tasmanians came from New Caledonia and other Melanesian groups, or that they were composed of a fusion of these two separate races.

There is a good deal of evidence to support the Negrito-Murrayian-Carpentarian theory of Professor J. B. Birdsell, which is ably supported and explained by Norman B. Tindale and H. A. Lindsay,* but other opinions are held. The Murrayian-Carpentarian theory assumes that the former were dominant in the south and the latter in the north, together with a Negritic element. In the Centre there was an admixture of the two main elements. The student of this fascinating subject must be prepared to read widely in scientific papers.

There is much to be said for the widely held opinion that the Aborigines belonged to the Australoid division of the human race, which is also found in New Guinea and the Celebes and in one or two other places. The ancestors of the Australoids evidently developed as a separate division of mankind in the islands north of Australia, particularly in Java. From there they migrated north to Malaya and India, and south to New Guinea, and eventually to Australia. There were several sub-species, and one group, the Melanesians, spread south and east to Papua and the islands of Melanesia.

While the Australoids may possibly have been preceded by the Tasmanians (Negritos), it is held by most students that the Aborigines were essentially one people, though they arrived at the northern coast at different periods. This would not necessarily imply that there were no physical or typological differences between the arrivals who came at different periods, but that they were all of common Australoid stock.

Speaking of culture rather than of racial origins, when addressing the 1961 Research Conference of the Australian Institute of Abori-

ginal Studies, F. D. McCarthy summed up the present view when he said that his own study of pre-history in Indonesia and Malaya in 1937-8 demonstrated "that the sources of Australian Aboriginal culture lie ultimately in south-east Asia . . ., a theme that Tindale (1960) has more recently supported. Controversy exists, too, about the problem of whether separate migrations, or as Tindale (1960) puts it, frequent or infrequent injections of people, explain the differentiations of culture that exist in Australia, or whether they are best explained by the idea of constant injections or streams of culture traits through Cape York, Arnhem Land and the north-west coast; this is a problem for the archaeologist, ethnographer and physical anthropologist to consider, because evidence from all three disciplines will be necessary to decide the history of migrations of people and culture into Australia. Koppers (1955) drew attention to this problem when he said that material culture, social systems, and religious beliefs need not spread as one complex, and their distributions need not always coincide. He further pointed out that Australian culture history has a more or less common basis characterised by a hunters' and food gatherers' economy, enriched by a constant participation in the development of Melanesian culture. We have thus reached a point where inferential studies of Australian culture history have established the main framework of its reconstruction but further historical and archaeological sources have yet to be examined."*

In a further statement McCarthy writes: "The Aborigines belonged to the Australoid race, remnant strains of which are said to exist in New Guinea, Malay Peninsula, and India. Their place of origin is not known, but it is believed by most authorities to be in the south-east Asian region. A well supported theory is that they belong to a line of human evolution through ancient forms of man which include Peking man (*Sinanthropus*), Java man (*Pithecanthropus*), *Homo soloensis* (Java), and *Homo wadjakensis* or Wadjak man (Java). In ancient times the Asiatic continent covered the northern Indonesian islands and the Australian continent covered New Guinea and the southern Indonesian islands, and the place of origin

---

* *Aboriginal Australians*, Jacaranda Press, 1963.

* *Australian Aboriginal Studies*, page 182.

was in a relatively large region of south-east Asia."

The long period that the Aborigines have been in Australia would have been sufficient for pronounced changes to occur in physical development, language, and customs. Archaeological research, including carbon dating and other modern methods, has shown that the antiquity of man in Australia extends over a much greater period than was realised at first. The first arrivals came over 18,000 years ago. Some of the dates that have been advanced are even earlier than this, but it will be a long time before definite pronouncements can be made. We can be certain, however, that migrations from islands to the north were made about the close of the Ice Age.

In the Pleistocene period, which ended about 10,000 years ago, the sea was nearly 300 feet lower than at present, reducing the distance between islands and providing land bridges between New Guinea and Cape York Peninsula and other parts of the northern coast. The stretches of open water could easily be crossed by primitive canoes or rafts in favourable weather. It seems reasonably certain that the first-comers entered the continent during the last glaciation when the level of the ocean was lower, and at a time when the central regions were well watered and plant and animal food were to be found in abundance.

However primitive man came to Australia, and whatever the period covered by his migrations, we can be certain that the spread of the Australoids from the northern islands was governed by population pressures and the desire to find new hunting grounds and food supplies. In these migrations many tribes crossed the straits and spread throughout the island continent thousands of years ago.

Aborigines, Australoids, Carpentarians, Migrations, Tasmanians.

ORNAMENTS. The art of body decoration, apart from painting, was not as highly developed in Australia as in many other countries. Objects suited to the purpose were scarce in many parts of the continent, and clothing in the desert regions reached an absolute minimum. Nevertheless desire to ornament and beautify themselves is a universal trait amongst men and women. Some of the objects used provided a medium of trade over a wide area; others were made from materials which were readily available.

Young women rubbed their bodies with a mixture of fat and red ochre, and impregnated their hair with it. There are widely diversified standards of beauty throughout the world. To western eyes lank, greasy locks are the antithesis of beauty, which is discovered only when the hair is washed and brushed, bringing out hidden lights and revealing its natural beauty, but to the Aboriginal fat and ochre were necessary if a girl was to be in the height of fashion.

Necklaces and armbands were made of cane, plant fibres, and fur plaited or twisted into cord, coloured with red ochre. Shells, kangaroo teeth, feathers, tufted sticks, etc. were attached to them.

To a large degree ornament signified the status of the individual. Special kinds of ornaments were used for children, girls and women, boys and men, on everyday and ritual occasions, mourning, and warfare, and by messengers. They were worn in the hair, on the forehead and arms, round the neck, waist, and ankles. The men's corroboree and ritual ornaments were most elaborate in Arnhem Land, Bathurst and Melville Islands, Central Australia and Northern Territory.

Seeds, shells, feathers, teeth, animal-tail tassels, leaves, claws, and bones were used in headbands, necklets, armlets, body bindings, girdles, and pubic aprons. The use of red string and of human hair twine was widespread. Pearl shells were favoured in the Kimberleys, and feathered string in Arnhem Land. A broad, painted bark belt was worn by western Arnhem Land men in rituals, and neatly-shaped sections of pearl shell as forehead bands and necklets in the Cape York Peninsula. Throughout the country tufts of feathers set in gum were worn in the hair and on the arms by men.

Tassels were worn round the neck, waist, or arms, and were made of fur, bark, hair, grass, feathers, or seeds; women sometimes wore chaplets woven from human hair, and balls or pendants of feathers were held in the teeth whilst dancing.

Piercing of the nasal septum in order that sticks, feathers, and other decorative objects could be thrust through the nose was performed in many tribes, sometimes as part of the rites of womanhood, but in other cases purely for decorative purposes. In this connection it may be mentioned that certain adornments were really a sign of puberty, of having reached the age of marriage, or of actually attaining that stage of life. In fact the putting on and taking off of headbands, armlets, and other decorations marked successive stages in a woman's life.

The ornamental scars on the body must not be overlooked. The wounds were made at the time of initiation, mourning, and as the result of fights. Ashes were rubbed in, healing the wounds quickly and raising body scars which were universally admired.

Belts, Bracelets, Dances, Garments, Head ornaments, Necklaces, Painting (body), Scars, Shells.

OVENS. The making of earth ovens was a fairly standard procedure. A hole was dug in the earth and a fire lit at the bottom. When it burnt down to the embers leaves were placed on top, the body of the animal laid on the leaves, covered with more branches or vegetation, and a final covering of earth or sand. The entrails were taken out of kangaroos, emus, and turtles, and cooked separately as a quick snack. Hot stones or lumps of clay were put into the body cavity and over the carcase. In northern Australia sheets of paperbark were placed over the mound oven and covered with sand or soil to ensure a good seal.

The bodies of kangaroos and emus were rather large for an ordinary earth oven, but the legs of the kangaroo were allowed to protrude, and sometimes the head and neck of the emu. When steam came out of the bird's beak it was ready to be eaten.

Food cooked in this manner was seldom allowed to steam until the flesh was tender, but was taken out when it was half cooked, and eaten with relish; but when time allowed food might be cooked for a longer period.

Cooking, Food, Meals.

P

PAINTING. Aboriginal paintings are world famous. In recent years the designs, some geometrical, others conventional, others again of an imaginative type, have been recognised as distinctive art forms that must be preserved as a cultural heritage. They were achieved with the minimum variety of colour, red, white, and black being the principal ingredients, with the addition of yellow in certain areas. There were four main types of painting—on rock, ground, bark, and on the human body.

Rock painting

The cave and rock shelter paintings of the central and southern coastal districts of New South Wales have been classified by F. D. McCarthy into four main types:

1. Stencil, outline, and silhouette drawings.
2. Animal and human subjects, together with weapons and tools used by men and women, all painted either in red or black, or in both colours.
3. The same as 2 above, painted in black, or white, or in both colours.
4. The more liberal use of colour, and the portrayal of the cultural heroes of the Dreamtime.

Other sequences of change in colours, motifs, and style have been observed in Arnhem Land and Queensland. In the northern regions the colour range varied from red ochre to bright orange-red, while changes in style reflected the slow evolution of material culture.

The art of rock painting goes back several thousands of years, changing gradually in its use of colour, style, and subject.

Although some painting may have been purely for pleasure, the deeper significance of this type of art cannot be overemphasised. Not only was it part of ritual, it was frequently the whole ritual. In his article on "Art and Life" in *Australian Aboriginal Art*,* Elkin refers to the Wandjina paintings in the rock galleries of the King Leopold and Drysdale River areas, and points out that when the heroes of the Dreamtime died long ago they became paint-

* Page 15.

ings. Successive generations of Aborigines painted or retouched the original figures of birds, animals, and plants when they desired the enduring spirit forces to increase the supplies of these species. The operation of repairing or retouching was sacramental and ritualistic, and a form of sympathetic magic. It also had a practical aspect in their daily lives. "A man sees a fine fish in the river," Elkin wrote. "He paints it on the gallery, and then he is sure he will see it again and spear it. So I was told by a native when visiting a gallery in Arnhem Land." It was the very act of painting that was important, not the contemplation of the finished picture.

Bark painting

Arnhem Land is still the most productive area for painting on bark, but it was formerly practised in south-eastern Australia and Tasmania. There are considerable local variations in style in the different parts of Arnhem Land. Rectangular sheets of bark are taken from the stringybark tree, heated over a fire, and straightened by placing heavy stones on them. The inner surface is scraped clean and used as a canvas.

The pigments are red and yellow ochres, white pipeclay, and charcoal mixed with water on stones. A juice is used to harden the ground colour of red, black or yellow upon which the design is painted. Brushes are made from bamboo shoots or sticks, the ends of which are frayed by chewing, or from a feather tied on a stick.

The sheets of bark were placed flat on the ground or on the artist's knees, and in painting them he either walked round them, or turned them round on his knees. In order to appreciate the painting it is necessary to adopt the same procedure. Bark paintings were never intended to be hung in a gallery! There is a proper way to view a bark painting even though its explanation may begin at the middle or at the top or bottom.

It has been suggested that the first bark paintings were of a secular type, being the sheets of bark covering huts. Special sheets were painted in some rituals but these were left to decay and were not preserved. "Rangga" were hardwood objects painted each time they were used.

Differences in the style of drawings were most pronounced between the inland and coastal districts. Generally speaking, bark paintings of Arnhem Land were distinguished by the lively, imaginative portrayals of scenery, human beings, and animals in a natural manner, though action was seldom attempted. The bark paintings of Bathurst and Melville Islands were conventionalised designs of masses of colour. There was a paucity of geometrical designs, the artists preferring curves to straight lines, and concentrating on the principal subject rather than on the background. Even so, the lesser details were full of meaning. Hunting scenes, and others portraying love and magic, composite figures of animals and human beings, and mythological creatures were all popular. Bark paintings were also made by sorcerers as part of the magic used to kill their victims.

Body painting

Although thousands of examples of rock paintings are still in a good state of preservation, and bark painting has been continued as an occupation amongst northern tribes, the universal form of ephemeral art was the painting and decorating of the human body. A vast amount of time was spent in painting the dancers before a corroboree, participants in initiation rites, and young boys in preparation for circumcision, for it might take hours of work to complete the design on a single person.

The usual practice was to wash the body and coat the skin with a mixture of red ochre as a base for the actual design, which varied amongst different tribes, ranging from simple bands of colour over a limited area to complex designs covering the whole body. It was most usual to paint the face, chest, shoulders, back, and thighs; not infrequently the design was continued over the face, and surmounted by a tall head-dress.

Feather down, cotton, or kapok was used, especially in central and northern areas, fixed to the skin with blood. It had symbolic significance and was used in totemic rites, the whole design being emblematic of the heroes of the Dreamtime. Body painting was not confined to sacred usages, but was a joyous expression of vitality and life at dances and corroborees, nor to men alone, though women's designs were less elaborate.

Art, Cave painting, Pigments, Ground drawings.

PEACEMAKING. If it had not been for "peacemaking", fights, feuds, quarrels, expeditions of revenge, and retaliatory battles might have continued endlessly. In any intertribal or interclan dispute there came a time when the elders realised that the original cause was almost forgotten, and that hostilities must be ended. Douglas Lockwood says that in north-eastern Arnhem Land the rite was known as magarada, giving rise to the phrase "ad magaradum", meaning, "You do it to me and I'll do it to you." This was the elaborate makarata peacemaking ceremony.

Another ceremony called banburr was almost indistinguishable from a real conflict. It was an occasion to pay off old scores, to let hot blood, and to work off feelings of hatred and resentment. Sometimes it began at a corroboree, and for a considerable period, lasting perhaps for several days with rests for eating and sleeping, the banburr ground became an arena in which limbs and heads were broken and blood was spilt. Gradually the excitement died down, the women usually being the last to desist. It was an occasion to settle old scores, and peace was eventually restored. It was held before a ritual. To interrupt a sacred rite or ceremony by quarrelling and fighting was a major crime punishable by death.

A little ceremony observed by some northern tribes was simple and effective. The group seeking peace advanced without weapons, holding up green bushes as a flag of truce, and presented a message stick which conveyed an invitation to parley. If it was received, then a meeting was held, differences were resolved (though possibly also bringing further causes for fighting), and the past was forgotten.

After expeditions of revenge, honour was soon satisfied, often without fighting, sometimes by the lending or giving of wives, or by the peaceful ceremonial presentation of gifts.

PERSONIFICATIONS. The ancestral beings of the Dreamtime were not in the strictest sense of the word gods, but men and animals endued with supernatural powers, or spirits with animal and human characteristics, or people who turned into totem animals. It is important to make this distinction. Even the sky-heroes were in many cases supernatural men who lived on earth and finally went to the abodes of the sky at the end of the earth-period of their immortal life. Some were teachers and messengers of the "gods". The totemic ancestors, in whatever shape they appeared, were personifications in the sense that they still spoke and thought as men, though partaking of other characteristics.

The belief is significant because man's relationship with the Dreamtime was an intensely personal one; spirits he could conceive only in terms of his own experience. By ritual act and the attaining of secret lore the Aboriginal could link himself with these personifications of living creatures and ensure a continuation of the species they personified.

Ancestors.

PHYSICAL CHARACTERISTICS. Although there were many variations of physical types, affected by environment and probably by successive migrations, there were features that were common to all Aborigines. Because they were all of the Australoid division of mankind they were unmistakable as a race, and pronouncedly different even from the Melanesians. The greatest variations in height and facial features may occur, or often does, in one local group or community.

The following generalisations have been collected from the records of a number of observers. The upper part of the body was usually well developed, but the legs and arms were proportionately longer than those of Europeans. They were thin and wiry, especially those who lived in the desert, but in coastal districts where the struggle for survival was not so severe, there was a tendency for both men and women to be bigger-boned and heavier, though there were few cases of excessive growth or girth.

Pigmentation varied from very light-coloured skins that took on a deeper shade some time after birth, to dark chocolate-brown and almost black; meagre supplies of water and lack of facilities for washing often obscured the true colouring.

The hair was wavy, sometimes curly, and amongst men luxuriant in growth. In the south some women became heavily bearded after middle age. The eyes were brown. The forehead was low and retreating, the brow sometimes strongly ridged with eyes set deeply beneath it. The nose was straight and broad, and the nostrils wide. Arms and legs were thin and muscular, wrists and hands finely formed, and the hands usually small and narrow. The jaw was prominent at the mouth but often retreated at the chin. The skull was exceptionally thick and capable of withstanding heavy blows. The buttocks were slender, the carriage upright and, due to strenuous exercise and the feats of endurance that both men and women were called on to perform, the body remained in a state of physical fitness until old age.

Australoids, Feet, Hair, Skin, Teeth.

PIGMENTS. Four main pigments were used in painting—red, yellow, black, and white. From these few colours came nearly all the wealth of Aboriginal art. Over the greater part of the continent the palette of the artist consisted of red and white. Yellow and black were also used everywhere but not so commonly as red and white.

For black, charcoal was used, the finest velvety black being obtained by burning thick pieces of the bark of the corkwood or honeysuckle tree. Wad, a form of manganese oxide, was also used.

Clay, gypsum, or lime were used as a white pigment, mixed with water to make a creamy paste.

Reds and yellows were produced from ochres. Iron oxide provided a red pigment, limonites and nickel ores the yellow. The ochres were not obtainable everywhere and so became highly prized articles of trade. As red ochre was used wherever paintings were made, it was always in demand. There were occasions when the yellow hydrated oxide of iron was heated to drive off the water, thus producing red ochre. Blood was sometimes used as a reg pigment.

The pigments were rubbed in water on stones, or mixed with some liquid which acted as a fixative. On Melville Island the ochres were more friable and were crushed in large cockle shells. When bird or vegetable down, used for body or earth paintings, needed to be coloured, it was placed on a flat rock, the pigment

sprinkled over it, and rolled with the fingers until it was thoroughly impregnated.
Art.

PITS.
Hunting.

PLAITING. The anthropologist makes a clear distinction between the different forms of garment making and the uses of cord. In Australia knotting, simple loop, loop and twist, and hour-glass netting techniques were in common use, together with twining and coiling basket techniques. Plaiting, as such, was not important. The term is used here in a non-technical sense. From a very early age a small girl began to plait small ornaments for herself—grass headbands, anklets, and a broad forehead band to hold back her hair. This was usually done in well-watered country, and was in preparation for the time when she would be taught to plait fish traps from vines and reeds, and to help with rope and string, making fish nets and string bags and the big bird and animal nets that were used by hunters. String was twisted and rolled on the thigh, but plaiting was required to give strength and resilience to the larger nets. In addition to a knowledge of the operation of plaiting, it required experience to choose the best reeds or grasses, the season for gathering them, the manner of extracting the fibre, and ways to make bark pliant by soaking in water and pounding.
Bags, Baskets, Nets, Sewing, String.

PLAYABOUT. A word sometimes given to drawings and paintings produced, not for sacred purposes, but for pleasure and aesthetic satisfaction. The term is also applied to songs and dances as a form of entertainment as distinct from religious ceremonies.

PLONGGES. Weapons used in some regions, about 18 inches in length with a knob at one end. The plongge was employed for inflicting punishment on those who had offended against tribal laws. When the crime was a severe one death might eventually ensue. This particular weapon inflicted a lingering death which gave the evil-doer time to reflect on his misdeeds.

POETRY. T. G. H. Strehlow says that "per-haps the most common sacred verses in the whole of Central Australia were the two ubiquitous couplets referring to the totem-pole. They occurred in the songs of most Aranda and Unmatjera centres, and also at many Loritja sites. These were the couplets:

> *Lo, the tnatantja pole,*
> *Covered with rings and stripes!*

> *Lo, the kauaua pole,*
> *Covered with rings and stripes!"*[*]

Many of the legends, folktales, and songs of the Aborigines were couched in a highly-imaginative, poetic style.
Songs.

POINTING BONES. The most dreaded form of magic that could be used against another person was the pointing or singing bone. It was given these names because, to be effective, it was pointed at the victim, usually to the accompaniment of potent song charms. The pointing bone was used by sorcerers or initiated men (its effectiveness depending on their degree of knowledge), and occasionally by women.

As with most customs, different practices were observed amongst the tribes, but the principle was the same everywhere. Powers of evil hidden in the bone were projected into the body of a victim when the bone was pointed at him. A bone taken from the body of a dead man had death latent within it, but kangaroo or emu bones could also be used, and even short lengths of stick. The "bone" was but the instrument; death itself lay in the evil force that was projected from it.

The instrument often consisted of the bone itself, pointed at one end, with a string tied to the other, and a charm bag made of paperbark or other suitable material in which it was kept. When the bone was pointed at a victim the string was stretched in a straight line to improve the aim of the force (the invisible spirit of the bone itself, or a pebble or crystal of magical power) which entered the body of the unfortunate man. Procedures varied, but there was a general belief that in addition to causing the evil force to enter the body, the bone withdrew the vital essence of the victim, which

* *Australian Aboriginal Studies*, page 53.

THE POINTING BONE

Break him out heart, break him out heart;
Kill him deadfellow, kill him deadfellow;
S'pose him eat fish, poison him with it;
S'pose him eat bird, poison him with it.*

The ritual singing was necessary to make the bone effective, and was often performed by itself. When several men joined together the deed was done in complete secrecy, for if it were known who was responsible, retaliatory measures could be taken. Everything was shrouded in secrecy, and danger lurked behind every bush. If the sorcerer was observed by a willy wagtail, for instance, it would tell the cockatoos who would make a dream about it and give it to the man who had been bewitched, who would then know what was happening, and would promptly seek the assistance of a medicine man. The operation was therefore performed at night to keep it secret from the birds. It was not unusual for the pointing to be done in some hidden spot at midday.

For the magic to become effective it might be necessary for the victim to be made aware that the bone had been pointed without incriminating the perpetrator. The usual plan was to leave it at some place where the victim would be sure of finding it. An Aboriginal who believed implicitly in the death-dealing properties of the bone, and who came upon such evidence, would know that he was doomed. He would quickly become ill, waste away, and die in a short space of time.

There were many bone-pointing procedures. When bone pointing and magic crystals failed, certain South Australian tribes then resorted to the ngathungi. As the principle of projection of the ngathungi was the same as that of bone pointing, it may be taken as a description of all such ceremonies. Flesh and pieces of bone left over from a meal were carefully preserved and tied with kangaroo sinew to a pointed stick, about 4 inches in length, and covered with gum. The object was then placed in a secret place until it was required. In performing the operation the ngathungi was held in the left hand and spoken to with words of hate chanted softly in a ritual that could not be overheard. This was a necessary part of the operation requiring much concentration, and would have to

flowed back into the bone. From there it continued along the string which was attached to the bone and caused an internal fire which destroyed the body. It was also the aim of the sorcerer to extract the spirit of his victim. It was drawn along the human hair string and captured in a lump of gum at one end of the pointing bone. Many bones had no string attached, but simply a lump of gum at the end of the bone.

Such a potent instrument had to be handled with care lest the magic should be reversed and affect the sorcerer. This might happen if the sun or moon happened to be behind him, or if there should be a waterhole between him and his victim. The sorcerer pointed and jerked the bone in the right direction, adopting a correct attitude and singing the charm that would make the instrument effective. Mrs Aeneas Gunn freely translated a specimen chant:

Kill Goggle Eye, kill Goggle Eye, make him
   deadfellow;
Pull away his fat, make his bonefellow;
Shut him up throat, shut him up throat;

* *The Little Black Princess*, page 99.

be repeated many times until the "bone" was sufficiently charged with power. The worker of evil magic then crept close to his victim's wurley, pointing the ngathungi at him. He carried a bunch of emu feathers that had previously been placed under the arms of a decomposing body. By this time the magic had had its effect and the victim was unconscious. The sorcerer rubbed the feathers over his head so that when the victim awoke he would know by the smell what had happened to him.

A more elaborate procedure was adopted in northern South Australia with the kundela, a piece of wood about 9 inches long. Special training in its use involved the removal by the kundela of a piece of bone from the nose, and the piercing of the upper arms, palms of the hands, and the chest. After this the user had to practise throwing the instrument at a tree until he could hit it from a considerable distance. When he was sufficiently adept he was ready to use the kundela as an invisible spear. It was not actually thrown, but the user was required to prove his skill in a material sense before he was permitted to engage in the non-material projection of the kundela.

The wirrie was another kind of pointing bone which, amongst some tribes, was inserted into the body of a corpse, remaining there until the flesh had decomposed. After it had absorbed poison from the body it was wrapped in emu feathers and rolled in a kangaroo or wallaby skin. Piercing the body with a wirrie caused death, and the invisible projection of the instrument had the same result.

If the pointer of the bone was discovered in time, a medicine man with sufficient power could cure the bewitched person by extracting the poison or the crystals that were causing his death, and project them against the perpetrator; but the evil deed was done in such secrecy that it was seldom that this could happen. Belief in bone pointing was so universal that the majority of deaths, apart from accidents and fighting, were thought to have occurred in this fashion. The identification of the culprit was the work of the medicine man.

Crystals, Inquests, Magic, Medicine men, Rope, Shoes.

POISONS. The Aborigines were well aware of the danger of eating certain poisonous fish and plants, and in some cases were able to prepare them in such a manner as to nullify the effects of the poison. One of the earliest lessons taught to children by their mothers was to recognise and avoid poisonous plants. A root called "cheeky yam" could be rendered suitable for eating by soaking, preferably in running water. Some varieties needed further preparation. They were sliced and spread out to dry, and then soaked again before eating. On Cape York Peninsula flour was made from the yellow nuts of the zamia palm after treating to get rid of the poison. This palm tree (*Macrozamia*), the cycad of the north, yields a great crop of seeds, the fleshy part of which is treated in this way.

The principal use of poison was as a means of catching fish. Towards the end of summer certain leaves, seed pods, tubers, and roots of creepers and trees were crushed with stones and thrown into small billabongs, stupefying the fish and causing them to float to the surface. The fish were edible, but the water was not drunk until the next rainy season. It has been said that the fishermen took care not to handle the more poisonous plants directly, and wrapped paperbark round their hands before pulling them out of the ground. Acacia, derris, eucalyptus, polygonum and other plants were used for poisoning fish. The leaves, bark, and fruit frequently required several days to stupefy the fish and force them to the surface.

The same method was used to poison waterholes frequented by emus. The pitjuri or pitcheri plant was used for this purpose. The poisoned water stupefied the birds, which could be caught without difficulty when they were in this state.

POLES.
Posts.

POLYGAMY.
Marriage.

POPULATION. As a result of careful research, which includes the examination of many genealogies, it has been estimated that the total Aboriginal population when white settlement began was approximately 300,000. It is possible that this figure may be too high. Owing to the absence of adequate statistics, and the many people of mixed descent, it is not possible to record the present-day figure. One estimate made in 1957 was that there were 74,000 full-blooded Aborigines and persons of predominantly Aboriginal descent; another in 1959 that there were about 38,000 full-blooded Aborigines and a further 53,000 part-Aborigines.

POSSESSIONS. The extent and variety of personal possession of the Aborigines were probably less than those of any other people. As a nomadic or semi-nomadic race they could not afford to be burdened with the objects that are so often proof of wealth and status. Even in the more fertile regions the camps were temporary and flimsy, and in the north bark huts were built to last out the wet season. Without domestic animals or agricultural pursuits there was little need for the accumulation of implements, or provision for the storage of food.

The hunter carried his weapons, and was not burdened with further impedimenta. The burdens of women were limited to a few simple domestic implements, and to the food they gathered during the day for the evening and morning meals.

Travel in the arid desert regions was the sternest discipline of all. In such places a man's possessions were confined to several spears, a spear-thrower, a throwing-stick or boomerang, club, stone axe, and stone knives and chisels. The woomera or spear-thrower had several uses. The edge was used for making fire, and a flake of sharp stone fitted into the end of the woomera acted as a chisel. A shield was sometimes necessary. The essential equipment of a woman comprised a digging-stick, coolamon, a few magical objects, and possibly stones for grinding grass seed.

Where conditions were more settled, huts were erected, bark paintings preserved, sacred objects kept in storehouses, and baskets and other containers used. In such cases many of the objects were cherished and much time was spent in carving and decorating them, but when on walkabout the essential requirement was that equipment should be light in weight and easily carried. Sacred objects were hidden at sacred places—totem and historical sites or the spirit ancestors' routes.

The following lists of personal possessions cover most of what could be owned by men and women, but it was seldom that all would be owned by a single family.

Women: Digging-sticks, coolamons, baskets, grinding stones, fire sticks, waistbands and headbands made of hair, ornaments, knives, grease or fat, cloaks, sinews, gum, bone needles, pipeclay, ochre, and small objects which could be carried in a dilly bag.

Men: Spears, spear-throwers, clubs, throwing-sticks, axes, boomerangs, shields, stone knives, chisels, gum, bones, quartz, nets, and materials for painting.

Group: While some objects were owned by individuals there were others that were possessed by the group as a whole. These included sacred boards and other objects such as bull-roarers and feathered string ropes. Some were personal property, but the most sacred objects belonged to the group or tribe, such as deposits of red and yellow ochre and stone quarries from which the best grinding stones were obtained.

Many articles which were objects of trade were kept in the temporary care of individuals, but a man's most personal possessions were often interred with him after death, or buried in his hut. Possessions could be borrowed occasionally within a certain range of kinship, but the rights of ownership were jealously guarded. Infringement of property rights was speedily avenged. The concept of public property was also well developed. On the few occasions when a man went outside the territory of his own clan, he needed to be entirely self-supporting, especially in the more infertile areas, and would not dare to cut a sapling on the property of another tribe in order to make a spear for himself without seeking permission.

Barter, Carrying, Dingoes, Gifts, Land, Women.

POSTS. The erection of poles and posts was a feature of Aboriginal life in Arnhem Land, where they took the place of the flat boards and objects known in Central Australia as churinga. The visual arts were well developed in this area, and many of the sacred posts were ornately carved and painted and decorated with feathered strings and tassels. They varied a great deal in size, from a few feet long to some that were firmly planted in the ground and towered to a height of more than 20 feet. Some were trees shorn of their branches. The posts provided a base for the creative art of the people of Arnhem Land. In carving and in painting they rendered naturalistic as well as conventionalised designs and human figures. Most of them were connected with sacred rites and mortuary ceremonies, the latter being termed grave posts. Others were used for more light-hearted purposes and were in evidence during feasts and corroborees. Burial grounds on Bathurst and Melville Islands were surrounded by painted grave posts that were regarded more as gifts to the dead than as memorials. In New South Wales carved tree trunks marked the graves of important men.

From personal observation R. M. and Catherine Berndt have recorded a wealth of information about the posts and poles of Arnhem Land and the northern coast, some of which appears in their monumental work *The World of the First Australians*.* The djanda pole of the Djanggawul, for instance, is about 5 feet in length and carved to represent the backbone of a goanna. The design, painted in yellow and white ochre on a red background, represents the tracks made by the goanna. Other poles symbolise legends of fire, flowers, water, fishes, etc., or are totemic representations of natural species. One, described in detail, is the Diving Duck totem, with a carved head at the top. Pictures on the trunk show a billabong and splashing water, the tree on which the duck perches, water shaken from its feathers, and seaweed falling from its beak.

Julunggul the Rainbow Snake was portrayed on larger posts called jelmajandi, which reached a height of 23 feet. These were sacred objects, made by covering a sapling with a thick wad of grass enclosed in bark on which the tufts of feather down or wild cotton were stuck with gum or blood. The snake was represented in red down.

In Arnhem Land forked trees or poles were used as perches which men climbed to chant incantations during religious rites. In this locality the rangga took the place of the churinga. They were carved in the form of totem animals or as poles. The poles or posts used in rituals

were equivalent to those covered with feather down used in Central Australia and Northern Territory rituals.

Images, Sacred objects.

PRE-EXISTENCE. The doctrine of pre-existence was one of the most important elements in religious belief. Briefly, the doctrine was simply that spirit children were created in the Dreamtime by the totemic ancestors who also created spirit centres for them, or which resulted from their continuing activities. The spirits remained in these sites until incarnation. "While Aborigines may not believe that sexual intercourse is the cause of conception," writes Professor Elkin, "yet the father is necessary so that the pre-existent spirit of the child may be 'found', and the mother is essential in order that it may be incarnated."* After death the spirit returned to the spirit centre, either to await reincarnation or to go to a permanent spirit world. Thus it can be seen that the spirits of men and women existed before incarnation.

In the greater part of the continent the father dreamed of the spirit, so "finding" it—though it might also be the subject of a dream of the mother. In the central districts the mother's part was more important, for there it was realised that the baby was dependent on her for its physical being, but the father was still responsible for the child's participation in religious life. In all cases intercourse was a necessary part of the preparation for childbirth.

An understanding of the reality of pre-existence in the mind of the Aboriginal enables us to make a distinction between territorial and social clans. Because the spirit in the centre established by the cult-hero was "found" by the father, the person who was incarnated there belonged to the territorial clan. In places where the social clans were matrilineal, loyalties would be shared between the territorial group and the groups which constituted the social clan.

Ancestors, Reincarnation, Religious beliefs, Social groupings, Spirits.

PRESERVATION OF FOOD. The absence of agriculture and of hoarding of food supplies did not indicate improvidence. There were few native foods which would keep for any length

* Ure Smith, 1964.

* *The Australian Aborigines*, 4th edn, page 116.

of time, while the nomadic habits of many of the tribes prevented them from storing supplies for future use. The austere conditions of desert life provided sufficient food only for their immediate needs, but efforts were made to ensure a continuing supply for the future, not only by leaving sufficient fruit and grass for another season, but also by observing increase and fertility rites.

It was in the more settled, fertile regions that a certain amount of food was preserved. Supplies of eggs were stored for future use, for the Aboriginal had no aversion to a well-matured egg. Wild plums and peaches (quandongs) were dehydrated in the sun and, when covered with red ochre, could be kept for a long time. When required they were pounded and soaked in water. Crushed kangaroo meat and bone was sometimes added to the mixture. Dried fruit and nuts (particularly *Macrozamia*), were preserved by being buried in sand, and in some places fish were smoked and dried. In the Daly River region shark flesh was kept for a short while by placing it in leaf and paper-bark containers and squeezing it to express the surplus moisture. Other examples of food preservation included pulped turtle and birds' eggs, dried fish and kangaroo flesh, bogong moth cakes, and dried kangaroo flesh in strips.

PUNISHMENT. Violation of tribal rules brought swift punishment to the offender. In serious cases the result of breaking the law was a lingering death at the hands of fellow-tribesmen. Erring women might even be killed, but were usually chastised; fancy-free young men often bore scars on their chests, shoulders, and backs from the wounds sustained at the hands of injured husbands. Children were allowed a great deal of latitude. Punishment, when it came, was sudden and severe.

Inquests, Revenge.

Q

QUARRELS.
Marriage, Peacemaking, Revenge.

QUARRIES. Outcrops of suitable stone such as chert, quartzite, basalt, diabase, diorite and others, were quarried by men to obtain stone for implements and weapons. Quarries for axes, spearpoints, chisels and other implements are known in many parts of Australia. Flint, for example, was mined 200 feet below ground in limestone caverns, while some of the red ochre quarries are remarkable for the extent to which ochre was extracted from rock formations.

QUARTZ. Quartz crystals were a magical substance inserted in the bodies of people against whom sorcerers had evil designs in order to put them to death. It was the task of the medicine man to find the crystals and remove them. Unless he was successful the patient would die. Quartz and other crystals were used as charms against danger, illness, weapons, for success in fishing, hunting, and rain-making. They were obtained by the medicine men from the Rainbow Serpent or the ancestral spirits.
Magic, Medicine men, Pointing bones.

R

RAFTS. The first-comers to Australia probably used rafts and canoes when island-hopping on their southward migrations. Subsequently the Aborigines made use of rafts of bark, bamboo, mangrove logs, and tree trunks to cross rivers and inlets, or to navigate swamps and lakes at times of flood. There were no canoes in Western Australia but single-log swimming rafts were used in many localities. Multi-pole rafts were used in north-eastern Queensland and at Wellesley Island, Gulf of Carpentaria. Along the northern coast of Western Australia they consisted of two platforms. On the rivers and lagoons of Arnhem Land paperbark was lashed to pole frames, and sheets of paperbark used as rafts to hold the corms, sedge, and waterlilies as they were collected.

RAINBOW SERPENT. Belief in the Rainbow Serpent, which goes under many different names, was spread over a wide area. There are myths which show the snake's attraction to blood, and others in which it is the spirit of water, rain, and flood. At certain periods women were required to keep close to a fire, and this applied to mothers immediately after childbirth. As the essential spirit of water, the Rainbow Serpent would not go near the fire. An important function of this great spirit creature was to excavate the beds of the rivers as he travelled about.

The extent to which the Rainbow Serpent entered into fertility rites is indicated by the frequency of his appearance in sacred designs and drawings. Water was the life-giving element; similarly the serpent which brought rain was the life-giving force in religious rites. This vast serpent reached down from the sky to the waterholes and pools, bringing water to the earth. Medicine men whom he killed and brought to life again were able to conjure up the rain clouds by appealing to him when performing the necessary rites.

Elkin observes that the Rainbow Serpent

was associated with the Arnhem Land concept of the Fertility Mother, and the Wondjina rain ritual of the northern Kimberleys. It did not exist as a separate cult. The snake was sometimes regarded as male and sometimes as female. Kunapipi, the aged woman who made a long journey across country in the Dreamtime, was preceded by the Rainbow Serpent who cleared the way for her by uprooting trees and causing rivers to flow towards the sea. In this myth the serpent symbolised the floods and storms that caused the rivers to rise. By the name of Wonambi it lived in pools and lagoons and had an important function in the training of medicine men, while in Arnhem Land it protected sacred lore by sending floods to drown people who offended against it. In this area, so rich in art forms, it was called Julunggul or Yurlunggul. In the Kimberleys it was associated with the birth of spirit children.

Everywhere it was symbolic of rain, water, the products of rain, and the fertility of growing things. In Arnhem Land where the Fertility Mother cult was observed, it occupied an important place in the annual rites that took place before the wet season. A whistling sound was heard preceding its coming. It was the noise of the storm whistling through its horns. As the dances and songs began the Rainbow Serpent was seen to arch its body upwards to the sky.

In the beliefs of many Aboriginal tribes the rains would dry up, the earth would become parched, and life would cease to exist if it were not for the Rainbow Serpent.

Gods, Rain-making.

RAIN-MAKING. In the desert areas of Australia, where rain seldom falls, life depended on this vital element. The Aborigines had an uncanny knowledge of the presence of water even in the most minute quantities, and for this reason some early explorers held them captive until they revealed their nearest water supply. After a prolonged drought the most experienced Aborigines came to a point where they would perish unless rain fell, or would invade another group's territory to get water. Rain-magic singing was a combined attempt to encourage the totemic spirits to send water. The songs expressed their needs and longings. They referred to the blackness of thunder clouds,

the cold wind that comes before a storm, the sound of running water, the gurgle as it sinks into a waterhole, and the dripping of water over stones.

There were experts who were gifted in conjuring up the spirits of the rain. Usually they were medicine men, but there were others who possessed the gift of releasing the elements. They combined practical wisdom with a reputation for persuading the ancestral spirits to undertake their work. The expert waited until he could see that the weather signs were propitious. Although the sky might be clear he could detect the signs of a coming storm. He spent some time chanting incantations. When the rain clouds spread over the sky he leapt out of his hut, shouting and singing. His fellow-tribesmen were careful not to offend him, and flattered him and offered gifts when his efforts were successful.

The rain-making expert had a small bag containing the magic articles of his trade, sometimes tied to his beard. These included pearl shell, quartz crystals and other objects. He spread them on the ground, singing over them and chanting invocations to the spirits and to the Rainbow Serpent, the great provider of water. Pearl shell, a favourite article of trade often associated with the Rainbow Serpent, was frequently employed in the simple rites. Pearl shell was used in a vast area of Australia, being traded over great distances along traditional trunk routes.* In eastern Australia quartz, calcite, and gypsum crystals were commonly used. Sometimes the rain-maker scraped the shell, obtaining powder which he mixed with grass and put into a waterhole to attract rain. Blood-letting was also symbolic of the flow of rain, and feather down was thrown into the air to represent clouds. Water was thrown from a coolamon into the air to represent rain as it fell. This procedure was an example of sympathetic magic in which many people could share. Spitting was a symbolic gesture believed to be effective when combined with the proper ritual. The Lake Dieri tribes appealed to their Mura Mura spirits, the Aranda of Central Australia to their water clan's totemic spirits.

One of the most potent methods was the use of gypsum which was found in the form of

* See McCarthy, *Oceania*, IX-X.

stones or powder in some of the more arid regions. The rain-maker cunningly made use of a natural phenomenon without being aware of its scientific explanation. Gypsum has the property of absorbing moisture from the air, causing it to swell and become damp. When the atmosphere is dry the stone or powder shrinks, but as soon as a moisture-laden wind blows on it, it quickly takes up the moisture. Observing this phenomenon, the rain-maker knew that the Rainbow Serpent was regarding his people favourably. He mixed the powder with blood or fat and placed it in the water-hole, achieving much public esteem when the rain began to fall.

In wetter climates the rain-maker had an equally important task to ensure that fine weather would prevail after prolonged floods. His magic, which everyone believed in implicitly, was a compound of supernatural forces and skilled observation of the reactions of insects, animals, birds, and plants to the effects of cloud, wind, and moisture. To these he often added a form of sympathetic magic, enlisting the people in his group to take the parts of sun, moon, clouds, etc., in pantomime.

Art, Rainbow Serpent, Water.

RATTLES. Amongst the few Aboriginal musical instruments may be included rattles, which were confined mainly to the Kimberleys. Large baobab nuts were dried, decorated with incised designs, and painted in a manner which accentuated the grooves. The dried seeds were rattled inside the nuts, producing an accompaniment to song and dance. On the northern coasts a similar instrument was made by placing a pebble inside a large shell, or threading a number of shells loosely on a string.

Music and musical instruments.

REEDS. Boys took many years to pass through initiation, and it was too late for them to begin using spears when they reached manhood. As initiation began at an early age, from six to 12 years of age, they used reeds, grass, stems, grass-tree stems, etc., to practise with. They graduated to the use of full-sized spears when their strength enabled them to hunt as adolescents.

Reeds were used to cover huts, to make baskets and fishing nets, and the roots were a source of flour.

Hunting.

REINCARNATION. The doctrine of reincarnation was fundamental to religious belief. It followed logically from the doctrine of pre-existence. The ancestral heroes left behind them spirit children who are born afresh in the people of successive generations. Some tribes believed that certain of their number were reincarnations of the ancestor, that they represented part of his qualities, and that through them the ancestor was kept alive. They received totemic names which were usually kept secret and which preserved the actions and characteristics of the spirit ancestor.

Life was never lost. It began in the Dreamtime, and after life in the flesh returned in spirit form to the spirit centre, whence it might return to be reincarnated. Such centres were usually water-places, but might be trees or standing stones. The spirits lived in trees and entered into the bodies of women who ventured near them. An unusual belief, held by one tribe, was that after death the spirit, Yalmuru, stayed with the corpse and produced a "double" which was called Iwaiyu, and which entered the body of a man or woman, thus reincarnating itself. The Yalmuru watched over the living person constantly. When that person died the old Iwaiyu, that is the portion of the spirit inhabiting the body, became the new Yalmuru, which in turn produced a new Iwaiyu, which sought a new home, thus perpetuating itself eternally.

Babies, Conception, Pre-existence, Religious beliefs, Totemism.

RELATIONSHIPS. The system of kinship comprising the family, clan, and tribe was the basis of social organisation, but is so complex that few laymen understand it. Its importance in the appreciation of matters such as permissible degrees of relationship in marriage, attitudes of people one to another, and to the whole structure of tribal life and custom cannot be overestimated. It requires the training of a qualified anthropologist to penetrate the ramifications of kinship in Aboriginal life and tribal lore.

Essentially, everyone with whom a person came in contact was a relation. Prescribed rules had to be observed in speech and in their mutual attitudes. "Aboriginal society is kin-based; and so, consequently, is its law," writes R. M. Berndt.* "In any given conflict situation, as in those where co-operation is stressed, a person can, ideally, depend on a number of others to defend or assist him. The kinship system, with its set of conventional behavioural patterns, provides a frame of reference for this. It constitutes a blueprint for social action, a guide to which people are expected to conform—not strictly, but within a range which does not strain those relationships, nor jeopardise the fulfilment of obligation."

When two people met, their first obligation was to discover their degree of kinship so that they would know how to act towards each other. It might be thought that this would involve an unlimited number of relationship terms, especially in a large tribe, but the system was simplified by classifying relations, no matter how distant, within certain degrees of consanguinity and marriage, extending over three generations (grandparents to grandchildren) and laterally as far as second cousins. Yet the complexity of classification within this range could be considerable. Elkin discusses the matter in detail,† showing how the system can be broken down to four main classifications in which relationships stem from parents, grandparents, brothers, sisters, uncles, and aunts. To go further than this and to understand exceptions and sub-classifications the student is referred to Elkin's chapter devoted to "The Family and Other Relations", and to many other anthropologists whose work must be studied closely if a better understanding is required.

The four broad groups of kinship were as follows:

1. The immediate blood relationships from grandparent to grandchild, extending in the middle generation to brothers and sisters of both husband and wife, and to their parents and children.

2. As a first simplification it should be noted

* *Aboriginal Man in Australia*, page 169.

† *The Australian Aborigines*, pages 84-90.

that all brothers were equivalent to each other, and sisters to each other. Thus a mother's sister was regarded as equivalent to a mother and was so called. However, the first degree of kinship existed between mother's brothers, not with sisters. Similarly, a father's brother was a father, therefore the sons of father's brothers were also brothers, not as we know them, cousins. Conversely, a nephew who was the son of a brother and not a nephew but a son.

3. As a result of the above classifications the children of a man's sisters were not sons and daughters but nephews and nieces. His sister's children regarded him not as a father but as an uncle because he was their mother's brother. Her sister's children, however, were their brothers and sisters. The same principle extended back a further generation. From it emerges the entity of the "family", more closely knit yet more extensive than in the European definition of a family. The Aboriginal family belonged to the "country". It was a group, a clan, a local subdivision of the tribe, varying enormously in size but consisting essentially of a father, his brothers and sisters, his father's brother's children, and such of the parents and children as came within the same pattern of relationships.

4. Relations by marriage were classified within the terminology of blood relationship.

Here then was a basic structure for society, enormously complicated not only within itself, but also by reason of moieties, individual, and group totemic relationships.

As the system extended in ever wider circles to cover the relationships of a tribe of several hundred people and, in the cases of inter-tribal marriage, of more than one tribe, there were occasions when people who met for the first time were unable to discover their exact relationship. It was essential that it should be stated, and it was determined by their age and generation, totemic affiliations, and the territorial and social groupings to which they belonged. In the absence of sufficient information the last resort was to declare a newcomer the brother of the person who introduced him to the group.

R. M. and C. H. Berndt sum up this complex and puzzling system succinctly: "In Aboriginal Australia kinship is the articulating force for all social interaction. The kinship system of a particular tribe or language unit is in effect a shorthand statement about the network of interpersonal relations within that unit—a blueprint to guide its members. It does not reflect, except in ideal terms, the actuality of that situation; but it does provide a code of action which those members cannot ignore if they are to live in relative harmony with one another. And kinship, in this situation, pervades all aspects of social living. We cannot understand or appreciate traditional life in Australia without knowing something, at least, of its social organisation and structure—of which kinship is the major integrating element, or, to put it another way, the fine mesh which holds the society together."*

And from this point onwards it is possible to pursue such a fascinating subject only in the company of the anthropologists.

Families, Tabus, Totemism.

RELIGIOUS BELIEFS. Living in a harsh environment and dependent on the clemency of the elements even in the most fertile regions, the Aborigines strove to strengthen the links with the Eternal Dreamtime by ritual and ceremony, and devoted much time and energy to this purpose. The first Europeans who came to Australia were ready to believe that the Aborigines had no religion, or else that it was directed into bestial, degrading patterns. This gross misconception no doubt arose from the absence of places of worship, and from the grosser material manifestations of the initiatory tests the young people were called on to endure.

During the past hundred years, and particularly throughout the present century, patient and sympathetic investigation has revealed the fact that the Aboriginal was a deeply religious person with insight into the deep mysteries of his faith. It is no exaggeration to say that his devotion to, and sense of kinship with, unseen reality were more sincere and occupied a much larger part of his life than is experienced by the average European. Sacred and secular life were indivisible.

* *The World of the First Australians*, Ure Smith, page 91.

There were no separated, dedicated exponents of religion. The medicine man and the rain-maker had some specialised knowledge of supernatural matters, but the realm of the spirit world was open to all men and to a lesser degree to women. The initiation ceremonies gave a first insight into the ever-present reality of the Dreamtime, and as a man gained experience he penetrated more deeply into the mysteries that enfolded him and controlled the environment in which he lived.

Proof of the pervading influence of spiritual life is found in the pages of every book written about the Aborigines. Without some understanding of the power of the "other life" there can be no appreciation of the how or why of any aspect of traditional life in Australia. Belief in culture heroes, the sanctity of totemic sites, the reality of the Dreamtime, the necessity for increase and initiation rites, the preservation of tribal lore, the authority of the elders, all point to the pervasive influence of religion.

In the eastern part of the continent the cult of the sky-hero or god was predominant; in the far north-west Kimberleys the allied Wondjina or Rainbow Spirit reigned; in the western part of the 'Arnhem Land Peninsula region the people believed in the Mother Goddess, the personification of fertility, and in the Rainbow Serpent; in north-western Australia the Two Brothers were important creators; elsewhere the totemic heroes of spirit cults were the principal element in religious belief. In spite of the difference between belief in an All-Father, a Fertility Mother, and a totemic ancestor, there were common elements: first, the recognition of a friendly attitude towards man by the cult-heroes who formed the world and endowed it, even in the most unpromising environment, with the gifts that he required for his survival; second, the fact that the actions of these spiritual beings continued ceaselessly in an Eternal Dreamtime; third, that they did not occur spontaneously but required the active participation of mankind, manifested through ritual practice, to ensure that Nature continued to provide them with the on-going life that was essential for their survival. There was a spiritual kinship between the ancestral divinities and the human beings who were their spiritual children, and an equal affinity with different forms of animal life. The ancestors were known to them both as men and in varying animal forms, providing an explanation of the creation of animal life as well as the means of perpetuating it.

The Aborigines were actors in the never-ending drama of the spiritual life. Their physical needs could be met only by full participation in the rites that linked them with spiritual forces and spiritual beings. The material domain was entirely dependent on the potency of the Dreaming. Initiation rites were the disciplines which men had to undergo in order to qualify them as channels of the Dreaming; the carved and painted churinga and designs on rocks, earth, bark, and on their own bodies, were the symbols that brought men into sacramental contact with the Dreaming; dance, ballet, song, and mime were visible and audible links with the Dreamtime and an acceptance of divine providence; and the recurrence of the annual miracle of spring was the assurance that the Dreaming was ever-present. In painting, carving, and ritual observances the traditional past was perpetuated and life was understandable in terms of a divine purpose.

There was no conception of heaven or hell, but simply a fulfilment of the purpose and destiny of the soul of man, sustained through its mortal life by the eternal cycle of reincarnation, or by the ultimate reunion with the forces of life in an eternal but ill-defined state of future existence.

The Rev. Father E. A. Worms provides a summary of the original elements of south-eastern Australian belief and custom:*

1. The absence of esoteric doctrine; it should however be noted that initiation ritual was confined to males;
2. belief in a personal sky-being;
3. belief in auxiliary spirit-beings—most often a son of the sky-being—who are the tutors in sacred rites and the donors of sacred instruments;
4. the existence of holy objects left behind by the sky-being, which represent him and contain all his power;
5. the use of liturgical drama to renew

* Professor Elkin holds the opinion that real understanding of Aboriginal beliefs comes only through an Oriental (Indian and Tibetan) approach in which the concept of the "Eternal Now" is basic.

and symbolise the creative actions of the being;
6. initiation, excluding corporal operations for both sexes, but including tests of hardship, usually involving plucking of the hair;
7. traces of sacrifice and prayer, in the widest sense of the words; and
8. the existence of a leading liturgist, or medicine man.

To the list Father Worms adds the following "accidental accretions":

1. The appearance of secondary beings—ancestor spirits, hero spirits—and of wander myths;
2. the introduction of esoteric practices which exclude women;
3. the appearance of stronger symbolism, especially in regard to the serpent and other animals;
4. the expansion of circumcision and sub-incision with the retention of older and lighter mutilations such as hair plucking, tooth cutting, scars and defloration, and of test by fire;
5. numerous increase ceremonies, bilocation, thread cross, incantation, and the element of fear;
6. second burial, variations of attitude towards life after death, etc.;
7. the development of art, geometric, abstract, or realistic, on tjurungas and in cave paintings and rock carvings; and
8. the idea of spirit children.*

These elements of religious belief are treated in some detail under appropriate headings in the present work. In addition to the "essentials" and "accidental accretions" (the two categories may be disputed), Father Worms adds the effect of foreign influences, imports, and the changing nature of religion from the earliest times until the coming of the white man.

Dreamtime, Gods, Initiation, Magic, Mythology, Pre-existence, Reincarnation, Spirits, Totemism.

REST. The Aboriginal had an immense capa-

* *Australian Aboriginal Studies*, pages 232-5.

city for complete relaxation. It was part of his training and explained his feats of endurance when hunting and on strenuous walkabouts. When the need for activity was over the relaxing of muscles was necessary to restore energy. Allied to physical relaxation was an equally important ability—the art of submission to the Eternal Dreamtime. Communion with the ancestral beings brought freedom from anxiety and assisted in conserving energy which could be released with explosive force when the need arose.

Hunting, Walkabout.

REVENGE. Any act which wronged another demanded revenge. The principal wrong was the death of an individual caused by bone pointing or some similar act of black magic. Personal suffering could be avenged by the victim, but the avenging of death was a group or tribal responsibility. A revenge expedition was preceded by an inquest, during which responsibility for the evil deed was fixed on one person or on a group of people, nearly always folk belonging to another clan.

During the mourning period and subsequent inquest, feeling ran high. Some responsibility fell to the elders to allow the natural indignation and crowd hysteria to evaporate. During a corroboree, when several tribes gathered together, was the time for discussions and settling disputes which sometimes flared up into open conflict, but more frequently were settled by compromise.

Vengeance tended to be governed by the importance of the victim. A fight between two groups or tribes could be a serious matter. Responsible elders realised the danger to the unity and peace of the tribe and were often responsible for diverting the feelings of their people into harmless channels such as empty, threatening gestures, or demonstrations of magical acts which satisfied them and did no harm to their intended victims. Mrs Daisy Bates records that when a duel took place between brothers and a slight wound had been inflicted as punishment, food would be shared and the quarrel forgotten. "Thigh-spearing and duelling were frequent, but I knew the dangerous sounds, and I casually asked them to tell me when they wanted to fight. They laughed and said, 'We will tell you, Kabbarli, if a spear is thrown to hit.' "*

Satisfaction for personal injuries, including alienation of a wife's affections, could be obtained in a ceremonial fashion in the presence of the whole group. The offender stood with a shield or spear-thrower and allowed his victim and his friends to hurl spears at him with the intention of wounding him. If the aim were bad, either because of poor judgment or because of animosity, and his opponent was killed, the whole routine of mourning, inquest, and revenge would begin again.

Fighting, Inquests, Punishment, Shoes.

RIVERS. It was natural that creeks and rivers should become centres of occupation. Along the Murray and other rivers the banks became the territory of many tribes. This concentration of population was supported by the fish, wildfowl, and vegetable products that were obtainable in such areas. The tribes were self-contained units with strictly defined boundaries. Because of the fertility of the land the tribesmen had more leisure than the nomadic peoples of the interior and developed their art forms to a much greater degree.

Art, Food, Hunting.

ROCKS. Rocks, trees, creeks, and waterholes were important in fixing clan and tribal boundaries. On many parts of the desert rocks had a peculiar significance because they had been placed in position by the totemic ancestors. Observance of ritual ensured an adequate water supply at points that were well known and preserved as part of tribal lore. Certain rock quarries that provided grinding stones were jealously preserved.

Paintings, rock.

ROOTS. Yam roots, dug from the ground by women with their digging-sticks, formed a staple article of diet. The roots were eaten raw, cooked, or ground into flour. Waterlily roots from lakes or billabongs were sought for as another popular article in the diet, and also bracken and reeds.

Poisons, Yams.

* *The Passing of the Aborigines*, page 197.

ROPE.
Cord.

RUNNING. Foot racing was a popular sport among boys and young men. No special train-ing was required, but hunters needed to be fleet of foot, and competitive sports of this kind helped to give the speed and endurance they needed.
Competitions, Hunting.

S

SACRED OBJECTS. Churinga, the flat, sacred boards and stones bearing incised or painted designs, were used in Central Australia, Northern Territory, and Western Australia, but their names and uses varied widely. Churinga was the name given by Spencer and Gillen for the Aranda (Arunta) tribe of Central Australia. A modern spelling is tjurunga or tjuringa. They were material, symbolic representations closely associated with the ancestors of the Dreamtime, bringing the forces of spiritual life into the everyday world. They were part of the secret life, their mysteries being revealed only to those who were initiated into the Dreamtime. Women and children regarded them with awe, and were not permitted to see or handle them. As part of the Dreamtime they were themselves a Dreaming, instinct with mysterious power and with a life of their own which came direct from the ancestors. Communally owned and also as personal possessions (in the latter case they were decorated or incised with the totemic symbols of the owner), the churinga brought life and strength to individuals and fertility from the mythological being whose spirit animated a particular area.

Lending of a personal churinga was a high honour and a token of friendship. Rubbing it over a sick person brought health and strength, enduing him with the vitality of the eternal spirits. Churinga taken on a hunting trip endowed the owner's weapons with mysterious power; but the game that was killed in this way became sacred food which could be eaten only by men. The display and use of churinga in increase rites and on other sacred occasions was the element which made the ritual most effective and brought the participants into the midst of that other-world which inspired and sustained the tribe.

When the churinga was stored in a hut or secret hiding place, a man's spirit remained close to it giving vitality even when he was performing his usual daily tasks. Similarly, the tribal churinga ensured the perpetuation of plant and animal life needed for the support of the people.

The permanent types of churinga were bullroarers, ceremonial poles, and sacred boards and stones, but ground paintings, headgear, and mounds which were not necessarily permanent objects were considered to be of equal sanctity. Sacred boards were of all sizes up to 17 feet in length, carved with totemic symbols on one side and stored in secret hiding places which might not be approached by uninitiated persons. Smaller churinga were made of stone, carved or painted, and preserved by rubbing with fat. Poles and posts in the northern regions served the same purpose.

The word tjurunga and its equivalents in the different tribes had a wide range of meanings, and it is likely that the conception varied amongst the tribes. The Aranda tribe, for instance, applied the term to sacred ceremonies, myths, songs, and dances of a sacred character. When a churinga was first revealed to an initiate he

TJURUNGA

was told that it was his ancestor in visible form, or that it had been made by the ancestor and that its spirit form remained in the churinga itself. In this way there was a spiritual bond between the unseen Dreamtime and the Dreamtime of the material world. No matter what theological variations were held, the churinga was always the material representation of powerful spiritual forces that pervaded every part of the life of man and his environment.

Bull-roarers of stone and wood, swung at the end of a cord, were the voice as well as the presence of the ancestor. They were an important item in religious ceremonies, and an object of dread to those who had not been admitted to the mysteries of the secret life. However, some bull-roarers and similar objects were not necessarily part of the religious ritual, but were used more light-heartedly.

Art, Boards (sacred), Bull-roarers, Religious beliefs, Tabus.

SANDALS.
Shoes.

SCARS.
It was customary for men and women to be "ornamented" with raised scars on various parts of their bodies. There was no uniformity in the practice or purpose of cicatrisation. In some tribes the scars were regarded as purely ornamental; usually the making of scars was a part of the initiation rites of both men and women. They marked age-grades and initiation stages, the number being increased with status, and sometimes at marriage. An individual's age-grade was revealed to others by the pattern of scars. Cutting the flesh was often a sign of mourning. Over a widespread region the flesh was cut with sharp stones, ashes being rubbed into the wounds to heal them and to raise the scars that were so universally admired.

Men were often proud of the scars caused by fighting because they were indications of their manhood, and were also proud of those caused as a result of jealousies aroused by their amorous adventures. The infliction of long, deep cuts in the flesh was a widespread practice amongst mourners, the number and severity of the wounds being governed by the closeness of relationship.

The degree of cicatrisation varied with its purpose. Amongst the Melville and Bathurst Islanders, where the custom was purely decorative, there were extensive scars on the face as well as on the thighs and arms, with horizontal lines across the chest, and vertical and horizontal lines on the back. This custom was more pronounced in the northern areas than in central and southern Australia.

An interesting theory has been advanced that the cicatrices braced and tightened the tissues which would normally become loose in middle age, as was the habit of the Scythians and Nomades mentioned by Hippocrates, but the theory may be untenable, because the strenuous life of the Aborigines kept them at a peak of physical fitness.

The raised welts, which were of course beautiful in Aboriginal eyes, were made by rubbing the gashes with clay, ashes, ochre, or grease, thus causing excessive granulation and producing artificial ridges in the flesh. Some men had groups of scars $\frac{3}{4}$in. high on the stomach and back.

Circumcision, Mourning.

SCENT.
While scent was not usually employed, even by young women, it has been reported that the people of Central Australia occasionally wore wreaths of sweet-scented cassia flowers.

SEASONS.
To a people who lived so close to Nature and depended on it so directly for food and water, the signs of the recurring seasons were closely observed. Varying in number in different parts of the continent, the seasons were all-important in their lives. The first signs of each season were carefully noted in preparation for the adaptation of life to the changing conditions. Owing to the wide range of climatic conditions, the seasons had different effects upon the people who lived in various parts of the continent.

Two major events were heralded by the coming of spring—the need to prepare for a new cycle of food-collecting; and ritual activities which in some places provided an opportunity for families and scattered sections of a tribe, or for several tribes, to come together. There was a double purpose in these ceremonies; firstly, the increase rites that would ensure a recurrence of the growth cycle; secondly, the rites and social gatherings associated with the abun-

dance of food that could be enjoyed in a fruitful season.

The time for enjoyment of the bounties that
the ancestral spirits brought each year varied
tremendously in different places. In the southern regions spring was the most important
time of the year. The whole landscape became
green and refreshing, and colourful with flowers,
and there was promise of abundant food supplies, provided that the increase ceremonies
were correctly performed. The tribes gathered
together for this celebration. It was a time for
rejoicing, love-making, and the cementing of
social alliances by corroborees as well as for the
more serious business of initiation ceremonies.
In the northern regions autumn, or the beginning of the dry season, was the time for such
observances. After the hot, wet summer season the genial sun brought a harvest of fruit
and vegetables, and birds and animals were in
good supply. In the western deserts summer
and autumn were succeeded by cold, sunny winter weather when rain could be expected, and
the enervating heat was over. People looked forward to the replenishment of the dried up
waterholes. Desert areas did not provide the
abundance of food that encouraged the gathering of the tribes, but life became easier and
freer of the strenuous activities of the sterile
aridity of the desert.

The appearance of new constellations,
flowers, birds, and insects was the first sign of
the coming of the fruitful season of the year
when fish and animals would become more
plentiful, and nuts and roots would be ready
for the probing digging-sticks. The flowering of
the wattle tree preceded the appearance of geese
on their trans-continental flight; blooms on the
corkwood tree indicated that the yams were
ready for digging; the cry of the stormbird
foretold the coming of rain and the fruiting of
the wild plum tree; these and a thousand other
signs were observed in the calendar of the food-
gatherer.

The year was divided into seasons according
to the range of temperature, wet and dry periods, direction of the wind, or the supply of
food. In some areas five to nine of these "seasons" were recognised. In the western deserts,
for example, the Aborigines noted the windy
season, followed by the heat of summer, storm
clouds, cold cloudy weather with easterly winds,

fair weather clouds from the south, rainbows
and storm clouds, winter weather, and then the
coming of spring once more with windy weather. Above all else, the variations in the food
supplies were the basis of the local yearly
calendar.

Astronomical knowledge.

SECRET LIFE. The secret life of the Aboriginal was simply a part of the Dreamtime existence. Consciousness of a life beyond the immediate needs of the body, hunting, eating,
sleeping, and sex, and pervading each of these
activities, was the most distinctive feature of
Aboriginal life. It could never be escaped because existence depended on it. The sight of a
man's totemic animal linked him with the
mythical being who created it. The animal was
the totem, the man himself, his spirit, and his
ancestor. The pervasiveness of this other-world
was such that the art of contemplation (for
want of a better word) was highly developed.

It was at the time of the initiation rites that
the secret life was explored and entered into
most fully. The very meaning of these rites was
death to common life and rebirth in the secret
life that man shared with his ancestors.

*Dreamtime, Initiation ceremonies, Mytho-
logy, Religion.*

SEEDS. Grass and other seeds were collected,
winnowed, and ground to make flour, mixed
to a paste with water, and baked in the ashes
of a fire. The winnowing was usually done in
shallow coolamons, separating the husks and
foreign matter from the grain. Seed cakes were
a staple diet of the inland tribes. Grindstones
were among the few treasured possessions of
the Aboriginal woman. There were quarries that
were noted for the quality of their stone, and
grindstones that came from these quarries were
traded for other supplies over a considerable
distance. Women sometimes husked the grain
by rubbing it with their feet in a natural or
artificial hollow in rocks.

Amongst the groves of kurrajong trees south
of the Mann Ranges, flocks of crows descended
to eat the grass seed and then quenched their
thirst at waterholes, where the seeds were
ejected. Great masses of seed accumulated on
the rocks in this manner during the harvest
season. When the tribes on walkabout came to

these places they gathered the seed from the rocks round the waterholes and winnowed it. Hot coals were placed with the seed in the coolamons and shaken till it was thoroughly dry and roasted. The seed was winnowed from the dead coal, ground, mixed into cakes with water, and baked in the hot ashes.

Cooking, Grinding stones.

SEWING. Where tribes were comfortably settled in well-watered country and had the opportunity of adding to the amenities of camp life, a certain amount of sewing was done by the women. Hair, animal fur, and sinew were rolled and twisted to a thread and sewn with a bone or wooden needle. Bags were stitched together in this way, and occasionally sandals, bark canoes, and the miniature "canoes" that were called pitchi and used as cradles for babies. It was a primitive operation, but part of a girl's training. Needles were rare in Australia. In sewing skins to make a cloak, the ends of bark canoes, or the sides of bark baskets, a hole was made with a bone awl and the twine or cane pushed through.

SEX. In the intimacy of camp life it was impossible for sexual matters to remain secret. There was nothing inhibited about relationships, even among children, who played at being "mothers and fathers". Discussions between the sexes were frank and caused much enjoyment. Even after marriage, especially when a young woman was married to a much older man, illicit relations took place, but there was public disapproval of blatant display. Though the affair might be known to everyone, it could be disregarded provided that it was conducted discreetly. But though the group might condone the misdemeanour, the victimised husband would probably take the law into his own hands. When tribal dignity was offended the erring woman might be forced into intercourse with many males to cure her of her promiscuity, and the male offender punished by physical means.

Men "lent" their wives to others on occasion, but although this might appear to indicate a completely amoral attitude towards sex and marriage, there were rules to guide their behaviour. A man acting as a host to a visitor of the correct totem made his wife available to

him. Interchange of wives between contending parties on an expedition of revenge was a recognised method of settling differences without recourse to fighting. Similarly, a tribe or clan that was about to be attacked by another might divert its opponents by sending women to them. If they were accepted peace was proclaimed, but if their advances were rejected it was a sign that the fighting would presently begin. After the battle was over, wives would be exchanged. On occasions of intense emotional excitement the laws governing marriage (with the exception of incest) were broken with impunity. Religious rites were also a time of regulated sexual freedom, especially during increase ceremonies.

Hospitality, Marriage, Love magic, Love songs, Pre-existence.

SHELLS. Shells were used as ornaments and traded from the Kimberley and Cape York coastal regions to many parts of the interior, even to the southern coast of the continent. Pearl shell, incised with geometrical designs, and which came mainly from the Kimberleys, was valued above all others. Melo shell (oval) ornaments, also used to decorate spear-throwers, were traded from Cape York into southern Queensland and beyond. The shells were worn as pendants or pubic decorations, sometimes by men and women, but often only by men after initiation; or by clever-men as a part of their magic performances. Pearl shell was also scraped to powder by rain-makers.

Carving, Rain-making.

SHIELDS. Great variety of shape and design was exhibited in the shields made in different parts of the country. Parrying shields to deflect spears were narrow hardwood forms and used in south-eastern Australia. Broad shields to stop spears, clubs, and boomerangs were used in south-eastern Australia, Queensland, Central Australia and Northern Territory, and Western Australia, the largest being the figtree shields of north-eastern Queensland, which are up to 5 feet in length. They were either incised or painted, or painted over the incised design, their decoration being a feature of Aboriginal art.

In New South Wales the shield was called a

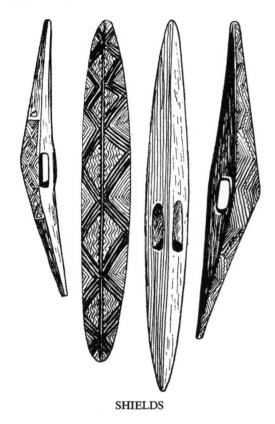

SHIELDS

hielaman.* T. L. Mitchell wrote in 1839: "There is much originality in the shield or hieleman of these people. It is merely a piece of wood of little thickness, and two feet eight inches long, tapering to each end, cut to an edge outwards, and having a handle or hole in the middle, behind the thickest part."†

SHOES. The Aboriginal seldom needed shoes or sandals to protect his feet. They were hardened by going barefoot, the toes flexible and capable of acting almost like fingers. With hands and feet men scaled trees as easily as if walking on the ground. Nevertheless in some parts of the Northern Territory and adjoining desert country a primitive form of footgear was made from cord or bark to protect the feet.

The shoes that were known and feared amongst many of the tribes in Central Australia were called kurdaitcha, coordaitcha, or

* Also rendered as elimang, e-lee-mong, and hilaman.

† *Three Expeditions into the Interior of Eastern Australia*, Vol. 2, page 239.

goditcha, though it is said that the real name was interlinga or urtathurta (there were no doubt many other names), and that kurdaitcha was the man who wore them.

These shoes were made of emu feathers tied with fur or human hair string, with both ends the same shape. It has been said that no one could tell from the footprints in which direction the wearer was travelling, but the Aborigines were so skilled in tracking that they would certainly not be deceived by shoes that were pointed at both ends. But kurdaitcha shoes had magical properties, and it was believed by the Aborigines that they left no tracks at all.

The emu or kurdaitcha shoes were used for several purposes. They were supposed to have been worn by fugitives to obliterate their tracks. Their principal purpose was to assist in acts of sorcery and revenge. The kurdaitcha man was in a sense the tribal executioner, killing those who offended against the unwritten tribal laws.

The shoes or slippers were matted together with human blood. Before wearing them the kurdaitcha man's little toes were dislocated in such a way that they protruded from holes in the shoes. They were thought of as "eyes", enabling him to see his way in the dark. If the kurdaitcha man was not a sorcerer, he was accompanied by the worker of black magic. When on the trail he carried churinga which were supposed to make him invisible. As he approached his victim he performed the usual procedures of bone pointing or injecting of magic crystals and healing of the wound so that the afflicted man might go about for several days before succumbing to the magic operation.

SICKNESS. Severe and unexpected illness was ascribed to the machinations of the sorcerer. Minor ailments, aches and pains, colds, sore eyes, headaches, and wounds were accepted as ills to which the flesh was heir. As they were natural and understandable, practical remedies could be applied. There were some herbal remedies, the product of centuries of experiment, poultices, liniments, treatment by heat, and bandages made of paperbark or leaves for gaping wounds.

Those who suffered from physical deformities—the lame, blind, and deaf—and from incurable diseases such as leprosy and yaws, were cared for by their relatives. Even when their disabilities prevented them from hunting or contributing to the welfare of the group, they were assured of their portion of the common food supply. Only when the existence of the group was imperilled by drought and famine was there any danger of the weakest ones being left to die.

Magic, Medicine, Medicine men.

SIGN LANGUAGE. Sign language was highly developed for two reasons. Hunters and warriors needed to communicate with one another without warning their quarry. A few simple hand signals conveyed what they meant to their companions. The second need arose because of tabus of silence that were imposed for a number of reasons. There were many occasions when speech was forbidden to a man or woman—sometimes during or after mourning ceremonies, during initiation rites, and between a man and his mother-in-law. In some places the restriction applied only to everyday speech, a separate vocabulary having been evolved for sacerdotal purposes, or to overcome the prohibition; but where the tabu was on speech in any form, sign language became the medium of communication.

Sign language was also employed in dances. The name given to the subject is finguistics. It is the systematic study of the grammatical structure of sign language, and is complementary to mimetics, the study of movements of the body and limbs that express definite ideas, actions, and objects, readily understood by the participants and those who watched. Finguistics and mimetics were not standard throughout Australia, but varied almost as much as language. W. E. Roth recorded 213 such signs in Queensland.

Languages, Mothers-in-law, Tabus.

SINGING. To "sing" magic into a shield or other weapon, or into a person, is a technical term in anthropology, not to be confused with "singing" in its normal sense.

Magic, Pointing bones.

SITTING. It was usual for Aborigines to sit on the ground rather than on rocks and logs. This they did gracefully, in four different ways: crouched, with the knees in the armpits; with

one leg straight and one bent, with the knee in the crutch; with both legs straight; or with the feet crossed.

SKY.
Gods.

SLEDGES. Ion Idriess has described a kind of sledge or ski which was used by boys in the far north.* A piece of bark a foot wide and about 3 feet long was selected, heated over a fire, bent upwards at the tip, and the underside polished with hot ashes and resin. Standing on the small sledge and propelling it with one foot as though it was a scooter, boys were able to slide over soft mud at a tremendous pace.

Sledges were not known apart from this simple plaything.

SLEEP. Sleeping habits varied a great deal owing to the range of climatic conditions. In the wet regions of northern Queensland it was customary to erect sleeping stages (sometimes with a hut built on top) over a smoky fire to keep off the mosquitoes. Huts were used occasionally in most areas with a hair rope round them to induce sleep, but although these huts were needed for protection in inclement weather, the Aborigines preferred to sleep in the open air, and were usually content to lie in the shelter of a windbreak some two feet in height, made of bark, brushwood or branches of trees.

The nights were cold in winter. In the desert the night air was often chilly even after a hot day. Sleeping places were hollowed out and fires lit between them. Depending on the temperature, several methods were used to combat the cold. When frosts were expected fires were lit on the ground to warm it before retiring. After the evening meal fat saved from the meat was mixed and rubbed over the body; and in the middle of winter it was not unknown for the Aborigines to go to sleep buried in the sand with only their heads above ground. In spite of fires to keep them warm, their sleep was broken on account of the cold and the need to keep the fires replenished throughout the night. Babies and young children slept next to their mothers, and it was not unusual for a man to lie back to back with his wife, a fire on

* *Our Living Stone Age*, page 32.

each side of them which each one stoked when necessary.

Families slept together when the children were young. The time for boys and girls to leave their families varied a great deal. Sometimes it occurred before puberty, when they played and slept in two separate groups. Elsewhere the girls stayed with their parents until initiation and marriage, while the boys went to a camp with other young men at the time of circumcision, subincision, or initiation. It was not uncommon for a girl to join her future husband's camp before puberty in order to become fully acquainted with his people.

Camps, Huts, Mats.

SMOKE. Information has been recorded at various times about the sending of messages by means of smoke signals, but it seems that they were not used in this way except by a hunter to lead his people to the hill and to the encampment for the night where the meal would be eaten, or to give warning of arrival in "foreign" territory. A man who had occasion to leave his tribal grounds to visit other tribes would be regarded with suspicion. It was far better for him to announce his arrival openly by lighting a fire when he camped. This gave warning of his coming and confirmed the fact that it was a friendly visit. It is said that in flat country a signal fire of this kind could be seen for nearly a hundred miles, thus giving notice that a stranger was coming three days before his actual arrival.

Smoky fires were made to keep mosquitoes at bay in some parts of the country. On the plains scrub fires were lit by hunters to drive out game.

SOCIAL GROUPINGS. The many ways in which Aborigines were grouped is an intricate pattern, varying widely among the tribes, and seems complicated to Europeans. Throughout the present book the broad term "group" has been used to indicate any of these divisions, which can only be applied specifically when the full circumstances are known. The local group or horde was the most important economic, political, and social group.

It is not possible to survey a subject of such complexity here. For a brief survey the student is recommended to study "Social Groups",

Chapter Five in *The Australian Aborigines*, fourth edition, by A. P. Elkin. The following notes serve only to introduce the subject without penetrating it in depth. It should be noted, however, that there can be no proper understanding of Aboriginal society or marriage customs without some knowledge of this subject.

It is difficult to define the term "tribe", but frequently it was a linguistic unit, a collection of "groups" speaking the same language, and recognising territory as belonging to the tribe as a whole, performing a series of ceremonies linked by the ancestral spirit and totemic myths, and by a series of art designs associated with them, and governed by the same laws and social groupings. Many tribes had common affinities of other kinds with their neighbours. Such a grouping of tribes was known as a nation in early literature.

Within an aggregate of tribes there was a constant type of social organisation. The tribes were divided into local groups, each of which possessed some part of the tribal territory and of the ancestral spirit and totemic myth which in its entirety was common to the tribe. Social totemic clans were direct lines, usually of matrilineal descent. Territorial clans were patrilineal, and were usually cult groups, as well as having a social aspect; they possessed their own territory together with a part of the ancestral myth common to the tribe. This local group was in effect an enlarged family group. Being patrilocal as well as patrilineal, a woman was required to marry outside her own territory to a man of another local group or "country" and to live with him there. Nevertheless she would continue to live within the tribal territory.

While the social and territorial clans can be regarded as the main structure of tribal organisation, there were many other social groups of equal importance governing social behaviour and institutions. Of great significance was the division of the tribe into two, four, or eight groups, called moieties, sections, and subsections. One or other of these were in existence in the majority of tribes. It amounted to a dual organisation, being both a social and a ceremonial or ritual grouping, totemic in nature and existing within the framework of the clan system.

The other all-important factor was that of

totemism, which is discussed under that heading. Men, women and children were not only related to each other but to the one or more natural species that were their totem. The totem animal was a man's food, his friend, and his guardian. It was in effect himself, and he was not permitted to marry a woman of the same totem, as this would have been equivalent to incest.

Sections, subsections and semi-moieties had the function of grouping types of relatives and incidentally served to regularise marriage.

Dr M. J. Meggitt* divides social organisation into four main categories:

1. Systems of kinship and marriage.
2. Descent groupings, i.e. moieties, clans, lineages, sections, and subsections.
3. Local groupings from the small family unit up to the full tribe.
4. Other less enduring groupings, i.e. age classes, common language associations, and ceremonial exchange partnerships.

Families, Marriage, Moieties, Pre-existence, Totemism, Tribal organisation.

SONGMEN. Song composers, singers verging on professionalism, were known in the far north where the struggle for existence was not so pronounced as in less favoured localities. As a result the arts flourished and songmen who inherited the position from their fathers were kept by the rest of the community. They were able to specialise in conducting the musical activities of the group to which they belonged. The songman inherited not only the position but also the songs. To them he added others of his own composition, usually woven around events that occurred in the tribe. He was the leader of the small "orchestra", tapping the time with sticks to give the lead to the players of the didgeridoo as well as the singers and dancers. He was paid for his work with presents of food and other gifts. There was less community singing in the northern regions than in more southerly districts. Often the songman was the only singer, the dancers and the women who played the clapping-sticks or smote their thighs with open palms providing the accompaniment.

* *Australian Aboriginal Studies*, page 211.

These specialists were necessary in Arnhem Land, where the big hero and fertility cult ceremonies were attended by two or more songmen, and many hundreds of songs were sung. Each man, however, could sing only the songs of his own clan. There is evidence that they also existed in the Cape York Peninsula, where big hero-cult rituals were performed, and where song and corroboree composers were highly respected. Despite their status, they still had to hunt and fish, make implements, and take part in the normal duties of the group.

SONGS. Singing was very close to the heart of the Aboriginal. In song and dance, men and women found entertainment and education; their mythological stories and religious beliefs were preserved in song; in song they exchanged the daily gossip of the camp, warned evildoers that their faults were known, released the tensions of life, and became one with the Eternal Dreamtime. It was the best method of teaching, both for children and adults. In song they used the fewest possible words. There was only a small range of tunes, but words and music were sufficient to convey their meaning, emphasised by the strong rhythm, movements of the body, and the accompaniment of dance steps and simple instruments such as clapping-sticks and didgeridoos.

Mr N. B. Tindale classified the songs of the south-eastern portion of South Australia into eight groups, most of which could be found in other parts of the continent, as follows:

Dream songs which told the adventures of ancestral beings.
Magical songs.
Songs which were associated with sickness and death.
Totemic songs, allied to Dreamtime songs.
Hunting songs.
Dramatic songs and epics.
Fighting songs.
Songs that were a means of expression of public opinion.

To these we might add lullabies which mothers sang to their babies.

Covering every circumstance of life and death, songs were the newspaper and theatre, school and church and public forum of the Aborigines. After the hardships of the day they could retreat into the Dreamworld and live a new, carefree life that went on through the long hours of the night until they were overcome with exhaustion. As the songs were very old and passed from one generation to another, they were often couched in archaic language, the meaning of which had been lost.

In Arnhem Land there were "hymns" that came from emotional urges ending with a long drawn out e-i, which Elkin says left no doubt of their sacred character. At the other extreme the songman sang ribald, topical songs, commonly called gossip songs, which penetrated all defences and exposed people to ridicule without mentioning their names. Part of the fun lay in identifying the victims.

One of the most effective ways of bewitching people was through song. It was really a form of chant, pregnant with power and difficult to combat. It was sung by a group of people, whereas the sorcerer who chanted over his pointing bone did so in secret. Much sacred singing was done in secret, though the secrecy stemmed from the evil action rather than from the singing itself, because if it were overheard the magic might be turned back against the singers.

As songs took so many forms it is advisable to find a definition which will satisfy the requirements of musicians. Mr Trevor Jones defines a song as "an isolable stretch of music, separated from the preceding and following 'song' by silence. Such a 'song' may consist of several melodic descents separated by continuing stick beats or other instrumental interlude, or it may comprise but one short phrase . . ."*

Terms for these separated and complete "songs" in a song cycle include song-descent, verse, or round, but the extended definition given above is the only one that clearly conveys what is intended by the use of the word song.

The structure of songs of course varied in different tribes. Some were exceedingly simple, being confined to intoned recitatives, but in a territory with a well-developed culture, such as parts of Arnhem Land, there was a rich harmony. A basic type in this area consisted of four descending glides from an upper note,

* *Aboriginal Man in Australia*, page 289.

each beginning and ending at a lower pitch than the preceding one. In this part of the country there were duets in which the songman took the principal part.

The range of song words varied as much as the music. The simplest consisted only of syllables, others having a much more extensive vocabulary and range of thought. In gossip songs there was a considerable element of improvisation, though a songman would maintain that the words had been put into him in dreams. In incidental singing of this kind freedom and variety were permitted, but in the inherited songs of remote times the words and music were sacred. No change was allowed even when the words had lost all or most of their meaning to the singers. In the former case the songs were an effective method of influencing public opinion, just as the sanctity of the latter ensured that the mythology and lore of the tribe would remain unchanged.

A curious feature of singing was that the songs could be inherited by individuals, sold, and used in trade. According to their degree of sanctity, so the words would remain secret or would be adapted to the needs of the new owner, possibly with the change or addition of names. There was also a secret vocabulary in which words that were quite different to those of ordinary speech were used in relating matters that came within the compass of the Dreamtime.

Though it is usual to think of songs as a communal activity, solos were sung by the tribal songman in northern regions, the tribespeople taking part by providing the rhythmic accompaniment of tapping and dancing. The elaborate structure both of words and music may have been responsible for this practice, which makes a great contrast with the simpler music of the south where solo singing was confined to the crooning and singing of individuals, just as the European will express satisfaction with life by singing at his work or in his bath. Conversely, a man who was absent from the land that was his spiritual home would comfort himself by singing his totemic songs. But there were no rigid divisions between solo and choral singing. In Arnhem Land there were occasions when everyone joined in the singing, just as on occasion there were individual solos further south. It is simply that the institution of the professional songman was confined to the northern tribes.

The difference between incidental and sacred singing should be emphasised. In the latter the song was the property of the tribe and pregnant with meaning. A single word, unknown in normal speech, might have overtones that conveyed a volume of meaning to those who knew the secret message. In this connection the importance of the moiety system is apparent. The members of a moiety that possessed its own version of mythological lore also owned the particular "music"—the rhythm, the melody, the pattern of words.

Light-hearted singing was a feature of camp life. As darkness fell the fires twinkled, and a tiny world was compressed into the circle of firelight surrounded by a vast unseen emptiness. Then someone would begin to sing. The words were known to them all. Others joined in the compulsive rhythm of song and dance. Some would be content to remain seated, watching and slapping their thighs to keep time, others shuffled their feet and began the circling dance that kept close to the firelight. They were no longer individuals but a family, secure and happy, with minds attuned to each other in a shared experience.

The purpose and meaning of song are well summed up in a quotation from R. M. and C. H. Berndt which expresses the attitude of an Aboriginal woman to the place of song in her life:

"When we sing about chickenhawk eggs, and snake eggs, things like that, we want that chickenhawk, that snake, to have plenty of eggs, plenty of young: and women too, plenty of babies. If some women want to sing of sweethearts, they can sing. But some want to sing for Dreaming: well, they can sing for Dreaming. Some of us don't want to sing for sweet hearts all the time, we like to sing for Dreaming."*

The most representative collection of songs ever recorded was made by Professor Elkin from 1949 to 1958. They contain a wealth of material which has now been preserved for posterity.

* *The World of the First Australians*, pages 227-8.

Chants, Children, Love songs, Mourning, Music, Pointing bones.

SORCERY.
Magic.

SOULS.
Spirits.

SPEARS. The throwing-spear was the most frequently used weapon in the Aboriginal's armoury. It was both a fighting and a hunting weapon, usually of considerable length, thrown by hand or by means of the woomera or spearthrower with force and accuracy. A short spear was also used by some tribes for fighting at close quarters. Pointed sticks about 3 to 5 feet in length were used for training boys and young men, when discs of bark or wood were bowled along the ground and the spears thrown at the moving target.

Over 30 different kinds of plain, barbed, stone, and bone heads existed, and in each local region there was a special range of types, such as a single length of hardwood, a hollow grass-tree stem, a bamboo or other hollow stem with a hardwood point up to 2 feet in length, or with a stone blade. There was one type that consisted of three sections. The longest and heaviest spears were made of hardwood with long pointed barbs cut in the head and used in Bathurst and Melville Islands. Beautifully shaped stone points were set in gum on Kimberley spears; long pointed quartzite blades were mounted in the same way from Arnhem Land to Central Australia, but nowhere else. Bone points and barbs were common along the east coast.

The "death spear" had tiny stone or shell fragments set in gum along the pointed end. These remained in the wound when the spear was extracted. Governor Philip was wounded by such a spear at Port Jackson. In the Cape York area a large number of stingray barbs were set in a lump of gum on the head of a special type of spear that had magical properties.

Fish spears, about 9 feet in length, had two or more sharply pointed wooden prongs tied to the shaft with fibre. Reed spears, about 5 feet long, slender, and with wooden points,

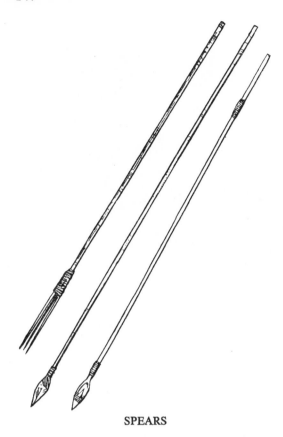

SPEARS

spearheads, and quartzite was commonly used to make flaked and serrated blades. Stone heads were attached to the shaft by gum or wax, this being an important development in the evolution of the weapon. The sharp edge of a stone blade enabled it to penetrate the flesh. After the coming of the white man the Stone Age was ended, and a considerable degree of ingenuity was shown in using broken conductors from the Overland Telegraph Line (a sore trial to the pioneer linesmen), nails, and other metal objects, of which the best known is the shovel-headed iron head. Glass and telegraph insulators are still used in the Kimberleys.

The making of a spearpoint was a skilled operation. There were many types, ranging from the more primitive forms in which the point was simply a sharpened end of the shaft, sometimes barbed, to those in which a separate head of stone, wood, or bone was attached to it. Some blades were triangular, others shovel-shaped with a straight cutting edge, or serrated and barbed.

The stages in the manufacture of a flaked stone blade were as follow. Long, pointed stone blades were struck off a core with a hammer stone and sometimes partly chipped along the edges. The biface points were flaked into the approximate shape then pressure-trimmed with a bone or wooden fabricator. The edge that was being worked was rubbed on a stone to flatten it and so produce a platform for pressing off the small flakes. A row of teeth was shaped along both edges by pressure-trimming.

To make a spear shaft the Aboriginal chose a long, straight, slender stem of suitable timber and peeled off the bark. Any irregularities were removed with a stone chisel. It was then passed backwards and forwards over a hot fire or placed in the warm ashes to make it pliable, the curves being kneaded out of the wood by bending it between the hands or teeth, or over a stone. It was then smoothed and polished by rubbing with an abrading stone, and sometimes greased to make it smooth and to prevent the wood from splitting. The final act was to lash the wooden or stone head to the shaft or to fasten it in place with hot gum.

As all human life depended on the effectiveness of his limited armoury, the Aboriginal cared for his weapons. On hot, dry after-

were carried on hunting or fighting expeditions in bundles.

In addition to the ordinary hunting, fighting, fishing, and practice spears, others were decorated for ceremonial purposes. There was an example of a spear made especially for a sorcerer to use against a person who had violated tribal law. It was prepared by being thrust into the body of a corpse to absorb the spirit of the dead man. Impregnated with magic it was effective against any violation of the law and, as an object of vengeance, could be depended on to reveal the will of the ancestral beings. In Arnhem Land ceremonial spears with ornately carved and pointed heads were never used for practical purposes.

The delicate leaf-shaped pirri form of blade (a pre-historic uniface stone point) and the later sharp-edged blades were formed by pressure-flaking. The biface stone point with dentated edges, the finest of all the spearpoints, is still made in the Kimberleys. There were quarries for the supply of stone for manufacturing noons he greased the shaft, sharpened the blade, and made sure that the lashings were taut, or that the head was firmly fastened with gum.

The final development was the woomera or spear-thrower which added force to the thrust of the weapon. With its aid a hunter who was able to get within 20 to 30 yards of his quarry could be certain of his kill.

Fishing, Games, Hunting, Knives, Reeds, Spear-throwers.

SPEAR-THROWERS. The spear-thrower is well known by its Aboriginal name of woomera or wommera. The word appears in early records. In 1793 Governor Hunter recorded in a vocabulary: "*Womar*—a throwing stick," and in 1798 D. Collins, "Wo-mer-ra—throwing stick." In both cases the translation was misleading. A good description of the southeastern Australian type was given by J. Fraser in 1892: "The 'womara' is an instrument of wood, from 24 to 30 inches long, and a little thicker than a spear. Unlike the spear, it is not thrown at the enemy in battle, but remains always in the black man's hand . . . he ornaments it profusely, back and front. . . . The point is turned up, exactly like the point of a lady's crochet needle. . . . The spears have a dimpled hole worked in their butt end, which holes receives the point of the hook end of the 'throw-stick'."*

The woomera was the lever that projected spears with greater force than by arm movement alone. It increased the range and speed of the spear, but made it more difficult to aim. It therefore required much practice before the user became adept, but was in fact used with considerable skill.

There were many variations in shape, some being long and narrow, or like a small paddle, others more like a shallow dish, and used for this purpose; but in all cases there was a barb or peg of wood or bone at one end into which the butt of the spear was fitted. When thrown with great force the spear tended to rotate on its axis in flight, giving greater accuracy to the weapon.

As a tool the woomera had many uses. In the central desert regions the end opposite the

* *Aborigines of New South Wales*, page 73.

WOOMERA

handle had a specially shaped chisel or pointed stone fastened to the implement, and this acted as a chisel, knife and graver. It was invaluable in making and decorating other weapons and implements. The woomera was also used as a lever to prise the bark from trees when searching for grubs, as a digging-stick, a knife for cutting cooked meat and, by using the edge, as a saw for kindling fire. The broader ones served as mortars for colouring feather down, and the concave type for holding blood in rituals.

Fire-making, Spears.

SPELLS.
Magic.

SPIRITS. Belief in spirits that inhabited the bodies of men and women, and others who were homeless and exercised an evil influence on mankind, was practically universal. Ancestral beings, whether sky heroes or totemic creatures, had the attributes of spirits as well as being anthropomorphous by nature. Baiame, the

Great Father, was also the Great Spirit, and the same could be said of his counterparts amongst other tribes. There was also a belief in malevolent or destructive beings who opposed the will of gods and men. This, however, does not imply any widespread conception of strongly opposed forces of good and evil.

The usual belief was that spirits emanated or were descended from ancestral beings. They came into being as a result of activity by the cult-heroes, usually during their legendary journeys, and were therefore associated with particular places. Everyone knew the locality of the homes of the spirits and was careful to avoid them except for definite purposes. These places were life centres, the places where the perpetuation of the human race and of all living creatures was assured. A tribe that departed from the place where its portion of the myth originated, and where it was recreated by proper ritual, was in danger of extinction.

Even to walk innocently beneath a grove of trees which was a life centre would be sufficient to make an unwary woman conceive. Brought there in the Dreamtime, the spirit waited for such an opportunity. It became the life force of the child. When death finally came the spirit was released. If correct burial and mourning rites were not carried out it lingered in the vicinity causing harm to human beings. As a lost spirit it would never return to its spirit home. Increase rites were a potent factor in assisting the spirits to animate successive generations of babies.

This did not mean that the Aborigines were unaware of the part played by the parents, but they believed that without the presence of the spirit the flesh could not become animated. The unborn spirits were visible under certain conditions, but were homeless until they took human form. They were not necessarily malicious by nature in the unborn state, but without a mortal home they could cause harm, especially for a short period after the death of their hosts. In this state they were unsettled and perhaps jealous of others. This gave rise to a fear of evil spirits and even in some cases to a belief in the Evil One and to "devil-devils".

There was even a belief in a trinity of spirits amongst some tribes. After death one spirit went to the spirit world, another to the Dreaming or life centre to await rebirth, the third becoming an unmaterialised spirit which caused much trouble in the world. But duality of spirits was the usual doctrine. One was instantly reincarnated, the secondary one becoming dangerous to mankind. In Central Australia there was a belief that of the two spirits, one resided in the churinga, the other acting as its guardian until reincarnation. In other places a trickster spirit protected the real one from danger. In south-eastern Australia dummy graves were dug to protect the real grave and its spirit.

There was no uniformity of belief, but there is no doubt that spirit forces were recognised as the essential element in continuing life and essential to the welfare of men and women.

There were also spirits that lived in rocks, in special parts of the bush, in caves, on mountains, and at waterholes. They were folklore spirits connected neither with the ancestral creator spirits nor with fertility and increase rites.

The ancestral creator spirits originated in the sky in the south-east and part of the northwest, in the sea in Arnhem Land and the Kimberleys, in the bush in Cape York Peninsula, and as travelling bands of spirits in the central region. Some came out of the ground and returned to it at the end of their travels. All but the sky heroes and heroines went into the ground or water, turned into a rock or tree, or into a painting (such as the Wondjina of the Kimberleys).

Ancestors, Babies, Burial, Death, Evil, Medicine men, Pre-existence, Reincarnation, Spirit worlds.

SPIRIT WORLDS. Unlike the clear-cut beliefs of Polynesians and other native races in an underworld and overworld that were precise and well defined, the beliefs of the Aborigines were diverse and often inconsistent. The only subject on which there was general agreement was that there was some form of continuing life after death. All mortuary rites emphasised this common creed. Death was not the end but a transition from one state of life to another. Frequently the released spirit entered another living being; sometimes it became temporarily homeless and potentially dangerous to mankind; less frequently it went to another stage and place of existence, usually in the sky. Amongst the northern tribes in particular this view was held. In a wider sphere it was thought that, no matter how often it might be reincarnated, the spirit eventually found its home in the spirit world. This vague place, on a mountain, or at a waterhole, sometimes to the west or on a distant island, was a region of eternal life lived in the company of the sky or other cult-heroic beings. There was no punishment for wrongdoing, nor reward for virtue. The spirit simply reached its eternal home and regained the gift of eternal youth.

The spirit which managed to escape from earth frequently arrived at a "jumping off place"—a mountain or riverbank. Here we come to a variety of legendary accounts of the journey of the soul to its final home. The following account may not be typical and is certainly not an adequate foundation for philosophical and religious belief, but is used to illustrate the type of fireside tale that would be told in some parts of the continent. The legend is supposed to be told by the spirit of a man who had died and returned to the land of the living:*

"I travelled across a wide plain," he said. "In the distance I saw the gleam of running water and knew that I would have to cross the river. When I came close to it, I saw that the banks were steep, and that no man could hope to live in the rushing torrent. But the way was made plain. There is a giant tortoise by which the souls of men may cross. On the far shore the shell of the tortoise rises up like a mountain, and its head is as big as a small hill. Its mouth is full of sharp white teeth, and its eyes gleam like fire.

"There is no other way to cross. I stepped on to the tail and ran across as quickly as I could, but I had not gone half the distance when the tortoise wriggled and I fell into the river. I was tossed about like a twig and carried into a dark tunnel. I thought I would have died a second time, because I was dashed against rocks, and bruised and cut by their sharp edges. . . .

"Presently I was carried into the daylight again, and I saw many people playing by the banks of the river, hunting, and gathering

* From "How the Tortoise Lost his Tail", in *Aboriginal Fables and Legendary Tales*, Reed, pages 78-9.

firewood. Some of them were our own people who have died, but I do not think that the river is the true land of spirits. It may be that they are still resting before they continue their journey.

"The river swept me past them and carried me into the ocean, where I was battered by the waves, and the salt water stung my wounds. . . . After a long time I was thrown up on a sandy beach. When my strength returned I kept the sun on my left side, crossing wide plains and high mountains, until at last I reached my home. . . ." *Spirits.*

SPORTS.
Balls, Boomerangs, Children, Competitions, Games, Hunting, Running, Wrestling.

SPRING. The season of new life and growth when corroborees, and fertility and initiation rites were held.
Seasons.

STANDING. When standing, men often placed one foot against the opposite knee, adopting the shape of the figure 4, balancing themselves by leaning on a spear or woomera. Children naturally imitated the same position from an early age.

STICKS.
Clapping-sticks, Digging-sticks.

STIMULANTS. Water was the natural beverage of the Aboriginal, who was not addicted to stimulants. The pituri or pitcheri, the leaf of a *Duboisia*, was sometimes chewed as a stimulant. The plant grew in south-western Queensland, its main source being the Mulligan River. It was traded widely in all directions, the dried stems and leaves being broken up and carried in special string bags.

In *Proceedings of the Royal Society of Van Diemen's Land*, April 1863, the following description is given: " 'Pitcherry', a narcotic plant brought by King, the explorer, from the interior of Australia, where it is used by the natives to produce intoxication. . . . In appearance it resembled the stem and leaves of a small plant rubbed into a coarse powder. . . . On one occasion Mr King swallowed a small pinch of the powder, and described its effects as being almost identical with those produced by a large quantity of spirits."

The leaves were used in Central Australia to poison waterholes for the purpose of catching emus.

Wild tobacco was chewed in the Central Australian region. Tobacco smoking was introduced into Arnhem Land by Indonesians, and to the Cape York Peninsula by the Torres Strait islanders. An intoxicating drink called mangaitj was made in south-western Australia by fermenting grass-tree cones in a bark trough.

STONES. Heavy stones were the hammers and anvils of the Aborigines. Hard, water-worn stones were used to smash bones in order to extract the marrow. It was from stone that knives and spearheads were made, and stones were used as knapping tools. Millstones were essential for grinding grass seed to obtain flour, while larger stone slabs were sometimes used as churinga. Others were set up as memorial posts or to mark important events.

There were several legends that related how men and women were transformed into stone as a punishment for their misdeeds, or for offences against the spirits. Stones denoted the sites of increase ceremonies and in fact were employed in many ways in daily life.

Blood, Increase rites, Initiation ceremonies, Grinding, Knives, Sacred objects, Spears, Tools.

STOREHOUSES. Storehouses such as crevices in rocks, shelves in caves, thick bushy trees, clumps of spinifex grass, and waterholes were in use in the Central Australian regions. Between their ritual uses, rangga were placed in storehouses in northern areas.

Sacred objects.

STRING. The preparation of cord or twine was often women's work, but was not confined to women. Using human hair, animal fur, strips of pandanus and other leaves and fibres from many kinds of grass and bark, they fed it from one hand to the other, rolling it dexterously on their thighs and then on to a spindle. Twine made in this way was usually two-ply. There were endless uses for string, the principal one being the making of nets and dilly bags, bindings on weapons and sacred objects, and for ornaments and fishing and canoe lines.

Baskets, Belts, Cord, Nets.

STRING FIGURES. String games have been played by the native inhabitants of many countries, and the art was not unknown in Australia. In the Northern Territory and Queensland especially it was a favourite pastime among women, who made hundreds of designs. Even during the performance of songs and dances they stretched the string between their hands and made some of the more intricate designs of the "cat's cradle", as it is known in other lands. Kangaroo sinew was sometimes used in place of string. The string was carefully protected by the women, for its use for purposes of magic was not allowed.

String.

SUN. The sun was frequently personified as a woman. As Yhi, in some legends, she helped Baiame in the creation of the world, and persecuted Bahloo, the Moon God, as a result of an unrequited passion.

SUNBURN. The skin of babies was practically white at birth, and liable to be affected by sunburn. In fact Aborigines of all ages suffered from sunburn under certain conditions, but the dark skin did not show the effects as it does in a white person. Aboriginal mothers rubbed their babies with a mixture of their own milk and grease or ashes, protecting the skin, which quickly became pigmented. The dark colour of Aboriginal skin is largely due to the sun. Without long-continued exposure it fades to a very pale brownish-white. In intermarriage with whites the dark colour disappears after a few generations.

SWIMMING. Where large expanses of water were reasonably accessible the Aboriginal was a good swimmer and, when necessary, could travel considerable distances in this manner, usually with a one-arm or rough breast-stroke action, or with the aid of a floating log.

SWINGS. Lawyer vines and stronger cable vines of the rain forests provided natural swings for boys and girls. Some would be looped and ready to use, others needed the free end to be attached to a tree to make a proper swing with a seat. Small boys could be taunted by their companions into climbing high into the branches of a tree by means of one of the long vines.

Where heavy cable vines were growing, older girls and their mothers with babies could join in the fun. The cables were strong enough to hold several people at one time as they swung backwards and forwards. Babies held on to their mothers with a vice-like grip and laughed as the great vines swung to and fro with their heavy burdens.

Climbing.

T

TABUS. Amongst primitive peoples tabus act both as law and as a police force to preserve the peace and welfare of the community. What may at first appear to be perverse and senseless proves, on further investigation, a purposive regulation based on a sound knowledge of the problems of family and communal life. Tabus or prohibitions of any kind were a form of control, the breaking of which incurred severe penalties.

One of the most frequent forms of tabu was that imposed on speech. It was a fairly general rule at some time during the initiation rites of boys, and was also directed at the mother and sisters, who were not allowed to speak above a whisper at that time. After the death of her husband a widow might have to keep silent for some time and to observe other tabus. A widespread custom dictated that a man and his mother-in-law were not permitted to speak to each other. She was required to avoid him as much as possible. When it was imperative to make a request or to convey information it was done in a recognised sign language or through a third person. To a lesser degree the same prohibition was directed at brothers and sisters. Once childhood was past they seldom spoke to each other and took care to turn away while doing so. After a girl was married her brother was careful to avoid her, and when he needed to speak to his brother-in-law he sat with his back to her. It was not unusual for him to avoid mentioning her name and the name of her totem.

Elkin suggests that this peculiar restriction may have been designed to avoid the possibility of incest. There is no doubt that many common tabus were applied to family, moiety, and social relationships. Just as degrees of kinship were known exactly and resulted in certain types of social behaviour, so they governed the regulation of tabus, even to the disposition of seating arrangements in a camp. It has often been noticed that families adopted definite arrangements when seated on the ground at mealtimes. The son-in-law/mother-in-law avoidance has already been noticed. To this may be added several degrees of avoidance of relatives.

Knowledge of this delicately balanced, intricate code of permission and restriction was part of the training of children from their earliest years, so that they were able to differentiate between their relatives and those who might some day stand in this relationship to them.

Restrictions placed on girls during their puberty rites were of equal severity to those which boys were required to endure. In some districts there were food tabus which prohibited the eating of certain flesh foods, the underlying thought being that the fertility of the animals would be affected by the girls at such a time; or the avoidance of plants which grew in or near water lest the Rainbow Snake should visit vengeance on the group.

Outside the restrictions imposed during initiation rites, death brought the most rigid tabus, and the severest penalties for infringement. Spirits had been released at this time and powerful influences were at work. The closest relatives of the deceased were subject to binding restrictions on speech and food until the spirit had been left behind, and often for an even longer period. Tabus were also associated with pregnancy and birth for husband and wife, and on communal hunting and fishing ventures, at times of warfare and rain-making in drought times.

As the tabus had been devised long ago by the ancestral spirits, they were related to the secret life. It was of the greatest importance that churinga and the storehouses in which they were kept should be guarded from deliberate or accidental intrusion. Within a radius of a mile or more hunting and food-gathering were prohibited, and anyone who offended suffered horrible torments. When it was necessary to take the sacred objects away for a ceremony the most elaborate ritual had to be observed by the fully initiated men who were authorised to remove them.

Birth, Names, Sickness, Mothers-in-law.

TASMANIANS. The extinct native people of Tasmania are a subject of debate amongst anthropologists and ethnologists. There are three distinct theories to account for their origin:

1. That they were the original inhabitants of the mainland who were driven southwards by later migrations and eventually took refuge in Tasmania. At the time of their arrival there were a number of islands in Bass Strait, and it would have been possible for them to have travelled from one to another by canoes or raft until they found a final refuge.
2. That they were castaways from New Caledonia and other islands of Melanesia. As these were members of a seafaring race with ocean-going canoes, the theory of drift voyages would no doubt be tenable. This theory, however, requires an explanation of their subsequent abandonment of canoes.
3. That they had come originally from the mainland, but that drift voyages from Melanesia supplemented the population, resulting in a race of mixed blood.

Archaeological evidence now indicates that they lived in Tasmania when the sea level in Bass Strait was much lower, and that they migrated to Tasmania about 12,000 years ago. Existing theories recognise them as either of Negrito stock driven southwards by the Australoids, or as an early offshoot of the Australoids who developed into a local Tasmanian geographical sub-race.

Evidence to support these theories is taken from their physical characteristics, language, and artifacts. They possessed dark skins, woolly or spirally curly hair, were short in stature, and apparently had the features and build of Papuans and Melanesians, all of which pointed to a mixed origin. They lacked ground-edge axes and other advanced stone implements, the boomerang, spear-thrower, shield, netting techniques, and many other advanced traits of the mainland that were not in existence when they settled in Tasmania. Their language had some affinity with that of the Aborigines of Victoria. The puzzle of their origin has not yet been solved, but it is certain that they were a primitive people of great antiquity.

TEACHERS. In the mythology of many tribes the ancestral spirits sent messengers or emissaries to teach people the mysteries of religion, to expound tribal lore, and to ensure their welfare. Nurunderi and Chirr-bookie were examples of such notable messengers and teachers; Nurunderi was regarded as a god by some of the tribes. In addition there were a number of famous god-like warriors who, in the remote past, fought against giants and monsters to protect those who were unable to defend themselves.

TEETH. The Aborigines were noted for their well-preserved teeth and powerful jaws. The bite of a man or a woman was sufficient to crush the head of a snake or lizard, or to assist in straightening a heat-softened sapling when making a spear. In old age the teeth became worn, but were rarely subject to decay. They were cleaned with the tip of the tongue or with the fingers.

A widely observed custom was what has been known as tooth evulsion—the forcible extraction of a tooth—as part of one of the preliminary tests at the time of initiation. Like circumcision and subincision it was in many regions a ceremony of religious significance, not merely a test of the initiate's capacity to bear pain. The gum was pushed back from the tooth with the fingernail or a splinter of wood, and the tooth hammered out with a stone hammer and wooden stick. Up to four of the upper and lower incisor teeth were extracted.

Shark teeth were set in knives in the Cape York Peninsula, necklaces and forehead bands of kangaroo teeth were worn by men and women, and kangaroo teeth were set in gum as breast pendants. They were also used as scrapers in Cape York. Dugong teeth were employed as chisels in Arnhem Land, while the lower jaws of various animals such as kangaroos, wallabies, and possums, with a tooth at the end, were used as scrapers and borers.

THATCH. Wet-weather huts in northern Queensland were thatched with the broad leaves of the banana tree in order to keep out the rain. Grass thatch was used in many parts of Australia, also reeds.

THEFT. Theft was practically unknown amongst the Aborigines. Their possessions were few and easily identified. The only common type of theft was a ritual performance, recognised as a social obligation, and confined to only a few tribes. One example amongst the northern tribes was that of the "collection man" who was carried from one hut to another, articles being "collected" with or without the consent of the owners. This custom should not really be defined as theft, but rather as a form of distribution and communal ownership, because the bereft owner was sure to obtain some equivalent article when he took part in a "collection" at a later date.

Possessions.

THROWING-STICKS. The throwing-stick was a primitive weapon, a precursor of the boomerang, which was not used in all parts of the continent. A stout piece of wood, it was used in warfare and in hunting, and was hurled with considerable force. It was capable of breaking limbs. A stick which turned over and over in its flight created a wider path of destruction, and was more likely to strike a man or an animal than a spear which could so easily miss its mark.

They were carefully-shaped and well-balanced missiles used to kill lizards, bandicoots, possums, other small animals, and birds. They were especially effective when thrown into a flock of birds. In Western Australia a slightly curved round stick 2 feet long was used; in eastern Australia there was a variety of small clubs with round or conical heads; on Bathurst and Melville Islands short hardwood clubs had thick, pointed, or divided heads. They were thrown with great accuracy up to 20 yards or less, often by a hunter concealed in grass or rushes, or as he stalked his prey through the bush.

Boomerangs, Fighting, Hunting.

TJURUNGA.
Sacred objects.

TOOLS. Materials used in the manufacture of tools were confined to wood, stone, teeth, and bone. Kangaroo teeth were mounted in woomeras as chisels. The nature of the implement was determined by the materials that were available locally. They became objects of trade to tribes living at a considerable distance. In quartzite regions chipped and flaked tools were made; where diorite could be procured they were ground to a fine edge.

Stone implements were used for cutting, grinding, and pounding. Axes, knives, adzes, chisels, and spearheads were all cutting tools or weapons. They ranged from blunt instruments to delicate, sharp-edged blades. One outstanding development in Australia was the use of gum or wax to provide a handgrip for small tools and to attach stone blades to wooden shafts.

Flat or round stones were used for grinding grass seed; and suitable types of stone were in keen demand. Occasionally a pounding stone was used inside the hollow of another stone as a pestle and mortar.

In the arid parts of the continent tools were reduced to a minimum, a single implement serving several different purposes. In more settled regions it was natural to find a much wider range of specialised instruments.

Most tools were ruggedly made and seldom decorated. When a treasured implement was decorated with incised designs, the work was done with possum or kangaroo teeth, pieces of quartz crystal or flint, or the sharp edges of cockle shells. An interesting type of plane was made by breaking the centre out of a shell and using the sharp edge to smooth the wooden handle of a spear or any other weapon or tool. Shark skin provided "sandpaper" for the same purpose among the coastal tribes.

One peculiar fact must be recorded. The art of making pirri and microliths, the most delicate cutting implements, lasted for thousands of years and then declined. This was particularly the case in Victoria where there was a dearth of stone tools.

Artifacts that have been preserved show that wood, bone, teeth, reeds, and shells, all of which could most easily be fashioned into tools, were the basic materials used in making implements.

Axes, Barter, Chisels, Digging-sticks, Grinding stones, Knives, Possessions, Stones.

TORCHES. Torches or flares were made of paperbark, and were used to provide light for spearing fish in northern and eastern Australia. As a rule the open fire provided the only source of illumination at night. A bundle of dried pandanus leaves or grass thrown on the fire gave a sudden blaze whenever it was required. At corroborees the fires were built up to illumine the

whole dancing ground. Hollow logs full of combustible materials were sometimes used for the same purpose. Torches of various kinds were a feature of some of the Arnhem Land rituals.
Fires.

TOTEMISM. Totemism is a term that is used in many different ways, for different purposes, and with different shades of meaning. The beliefs and practices that were associated with it varied according to the form of totemism. The subject is complex and there is no simple method of understanding or explaining it, but to the Aboriginal it was of supreme importance, as can be shown by two well-known definitions provided by Professor A. P. Elkin, the doyen of anthropologists. It is "a view of nature and life, of the universe and man, which colours and influences the Aborigines' social groupings and mythologies, inspires their rituals and links them to the past. It unites them with nature's activities and species in a bond of mutual life-giving . . .";* and again: "[It] is our key to the understanding of the Aboriginal philosophy and universe—a philosophy which regards man and nature as one corporate whole for social, ceremonial, and religious purposes, a philosophy which from one aspect is pre-animistic, but from another is animistic, a philosophy which is historical, being formed on the heroic acts of the past which provide the sanctions for the present, a philosophy which, indeed, passes into the realm of religion and provides that faith, hope and courage in the face of his daily needs which man must have if he is to persevere and persist, both as an individual and a social being."†

To understand any aspect of Aboriginal thought or behaviour, it is necessary to go back to the creative Dreamtime, and this is as true of totemism as of any other subject. The world was created by the ancestral spirit heroes and heroines who on their journeys distributed their spirit totems in different places. These were mostly human, and ultimately became transformed into totem animals. The ancestral spirits were able to become composite human and animal creatures which represented the to-

tems. Some of the ancestral beings remained human in character throughout the whole period of their journeys. The Wandjina, Two Brothers, Kunapipi, and the Earth Mother were depicted as gigantic human spirits. Others like Baiame and Daramulun were depicted in both human and human-animal form. Some are described as giant kangaroos, snakes, dingoes, and emus, but apart from the celebrated Rainbow Serpent, these are usually subsidiary ancestral spirits who created specific objects such as ochre mines, etc.

The totemic ancestors travelled everywhere, and on their journeys they made life centres where spirit children lingered while waiting for entrance into the bodies of their mothers. The spirit took its life form and from the moment of conception the totemic animal which in fact was part of the personality of the ancestor was part of the child. It was his or her totem, linking the baby with the Dreamtime and, as it grew older, imposing social restraints and obligations.

There are many aspects of totemism, some more complex than others, which will be referred to later. But in essence every person had the spirit of some animal inside him—a spirit which bound him closely to the totem animal, made him a brother to others of the same totem, prevented marriage between men and women of the same totem (for that would be incest), and either prevented him from killing that animal, or ensuring that he did so! The situation was confused (to the European but not to the Aboriginal) by the fact that a kangaroo man might possess the spirit or totem of a lizard, and therefore Kangaroo and Lizard were totemic brothers. The confusion is increased when we attempt to survey the whole subject, but it will be recognised that any one group or tribe was concerned only with the practices which they believed to have come to them from their own ancestor.

Totemism was a mystical bond between the ancestor and the individual which was expressed by a symbol. The symbol was the animal or the sacred design by which it was represented. A baby accepted and contained the totemic representation which was the essence, the life form of the locality where the ancestor had bestowed his spirit, and which had entered the child's body at the moment of conception.

* *The Australian Aborigines*, page 165.

† Quoted by Dr W. E. H. Stanner in *Aboriginal Man in Australia*, page 224.

His whole welfare depended on this union, not only as an individual linked to the ancestral being, but also through his group totem, which would again be different.

That which appears at first to be perfectly straightforward, i.e. that every person was possessed of a totemic spirit which took the form of an animal linking him with the Dreamtime, becomes more involved as we enter the realm of social and ritual totemism. There have been many attempts to classify these concepts, e.g. group, sex, and individual totems; social (matrilineal) cult or ceremonial (patrilineal) and magical totems; or social and ritual totems.

A division into two categories appears to be most satisfactory, provided that there is recognition of the fact that there may be many sub-classifications.

1. *Social totemism*: A woman was not permitted to marry a person of the same totemic affiliation, nor were people permitted to kill or eat their totemic animal (they might be permitted to hunt and kill the animal for sacerdotal purposes). The origin of this form of totemism was through the group, usually though not always by descent through the female line. If a man became a fugitive and was forced to enter the territory of another tribe, he was not content until he found one who shared his totem and that of his mother. Having done so he could safely claim brotherhood with these people. All members of a social clan were related to each other and to their totems which were their "flesh and meat".

2. *Ritual totemism*: The totemic animals in this case were not usually regarded in the same manner as those that were personal and social. A man could kill and eat his ritual totem (i.e. the animal). There was a strong link between the human and supernatural worlds. The totem symbolised the bond between the ancestor of the Dreamtime and the ordinary activities of life.

The following types of totemism are generally recognised. They do not imply that any one person or group shared them all; rather they indicate the varieties that were to be found in different places.

Conception totemism: One of the most common forms, and similar to local totemism. The totem was usually conferred at the time the mother conceived. When she became pregnant it was necessary for her to remember the place and circumstances of conception in order that the totemic spirit could be identified. As it had occurred at a specific place, usually hallowed by mythological influences, and because it was a place at which the ancestor had performed some deed in the Dreamtime, the animal could readily be identified.

Birth totemism: There were places where the identification was delayed until the birth of the child rather than at conception.

Local totemism: This form is allied to conception totemism, and was influenced by the ancestor in one particular locality.

Dream totemism: This is a symbol of a person in the dreams of others. It might be revealed in a dream either to the father or mother; or might be the mother's brother's totem, or the person's own cult totem.

Individual totemism: A guardian and assistant species related to an individual (normally a medicine man).

Sex totemism: A common totem shared by all members of one sex in a group, providing a ritual distinction between men and women.

Clan or group totemism: Allied to local totemism, the totemic symbol of the clan was an integrating force that preserved the close relationship with and dependence on the territory that was shared with the ancestor.

Moiety totemism: As the moiety was a well-defined category outside family, hereditary, and sex relationships, so its members were bound together by a common totemic symbol.

Section and subsection totemism: Within the compass of clan or moiety, all the four sections or eight subsections had certain totems in common. Each major totem included a number of other totems, and formed a system of classification.

Totemism regulated social relationships, was at the centre of ritual, entering largely into the initiation ceremonies, and had a tremendous influence on art. Paintings and carvings of every kind, the decoration and painting of the body, the symbols on churinga and weapons, the arrangement of feathers and colours on the tall headgear used at corroborees and ceremonies, were nearly always representative of totems, and of the ancestral spirits who created them.

During the 1961 Research Conference of the Australian Institute of Aboriginal Studies, Professor J. B. Cleland remarked that Sir George Grey had identified Australian totemism 30 years before McLennan "invented" it in 1869. The name was adopted when it was realised that the totemism of the North American Indians was of the same nature as the religious beliefs of the Australian Aborigines.

A significant statement has been made by Dr W. E. H. Stanner: "Most of the choir and furniture of heaven and earth are regarded by the Aborigines as a vast sign-system. Anyone who, understandingly, has moved in the Australian bush with Aboriginal associates becomes aware of the fact. He moves, not in a landscape, but in a humanised realm saturated with significations. Here 'something happened'; there 'something portends'."*

It was this awareness that was at the heart of totemism.

TRACKING. Although it has often been said that the Aborigines were "born trackers" they possessed no greater instinctive ability than any other people. Their survival often depended on the skill with which they could pick up a faint track, hours or even days old, and follow it across stony ground as well as on soft sand.

Training began at the very earliest age. When babies began to crawl they followed the tracks of insects and small reptiles. Older people caught insects and small lizards and used them to teach the toddlers how to recognise their tracks. The paws of animals and the feet of birds were impressed on soft earth or clay or ashes and the children were taught to distinguish between one animal or bird and another, to know the direction in which it was going, whether it was walking or running, and many other facts simply from the impression made by the feet. Mother and father, guardians and friends, patiently drew diagrams of tracks

* *Aboriginal Man in Australia*, page 227.

in the sand and explained them to children. Bush scents had to be recognised—the faint smell of a distant fire, the smell of a snake or of fat on a human body, which denoted a hidden enemy, the smell of water—all these abilities needed to be learned at an early age if a boy was to do his part as a hunter when he became a man, a girl as a food-gatherer when she became a woman.

Constant observation and lightning deduction were practised assiduously until an almost uncanny ability was attained. The footprint of every member of the tribe could be recognised, so that those of strangers would be immediately identified. The disturbance of earth or foliage meant something to the hunter. In passing through grass, animals brushed it in one direction; a pebble displaced was always forwards, sideways, or backwards; the sand at each bend of a snake's body was always pushed in a certain direction; these and a thousand other signs were recognised by the skilful tracker, leading him unerringly to his prey.

He did not follow the trail with his eyes on the ground. He thought as an animal does, putting himself in its place, looking ahead, knowing where it was going. Only occasionally did he look down to see that the trail was still visible. If he lost it he made casts to right and left until he picked it up again. If the animal had turned on its tracks on stony ground he was quick to detect the almost indistinguishable signs that indicated the new direction, or he circled round until he found the track again. He used light at the best angle to show up disturbances on the faint trail. These were the accumulated skills of years of training that became second nature to the Aboriginal hunter and tracker.

Hunting.

TRADING.
    Barter.

TRAVELLING.
    Walkabout. _____

TREES. The Aboriginal made every possible use of trees in his daily life. His spears, clubs, digging-sticks, bowls, and handles of stone weapons were made of timber. Trees and bushes provided material for huts and windbreaks, fuel for the oven and for the camp fires at night. Canoes were fashioned from hollow logs or from large sheets of bark stripped from trees and stitched together at the ends. The bark sheets had many uses: folded in two they made efficient and easily constructed huts; flattened and scraped they were used as canvases for painting in the far north; and in all parts of the continent bark or timber provided the bowls known as coolamons. Weapons and implements were made of wood. Posts were used to mark burial grounds, and corpses were placed on wooden platforms.

Tree climbing was one of the accomplishments of the Aborigines. Women as well as men were able to romp up seemingly inaccessible trees as though they were running on a flat surface, in search of the nests of honey ants and bees, or the nests of goannas. A vertical, branchless bole was climbed by means of a cord held round the trunk and jerked upwards as the climber ascended.

In eastern Australia trees had designs carved in them for ritual purposes.

Camps, Canoes, Climbing, Huts, Painting.

TRIBAL NAMES.
See Appendix A.

TRIBAL ORGANISATION. Variations in the size of tribes in different regions were largely due to climatic conditions. In the desert and arid interior the environment was insufficiently productive to support a large number of people. Each tribe occupied a large area of country and in fact had more numbers as a rule than the lesser tribes in good country. This led to fragmentation of tribes into small family units that were self-supporting and seldom came into contact with others except during ceremonies. In more favourable locations the teeming wild life and plant growth encouraged permanent encampments with a larger total population, but with smaller tribal areas and numbers of members.

Families, Moieties, Relationships, Social groupings, Totemism.

TRIBES. It is generally agreed that before the first white settlers came to Australia the continent was occupied by some 500 to 700 tribes whose territories ranged from about 150 square miles in fertile areas to as much as 40,000 square miles in arid regions.

A tribe did not necessarily consist of a band of people living and moving together. In many places it was only the local group or horde, or expanded family unit, or a clan in some areas, that was able to survive in this way. Such groups wandered far from others in the tribal territory reserved for them by their mythical ancestors. They had little or no contact with distant clans and sometimes even spoke a different dialect. For these reasons it is difficult to find an adequate definition of a tribe. A fairly common conception has been a collection of groups which formed one linguistic unit. While this is usually satisfactory, there were a number of tribes in which more than one dialect or language was spoken by the component groups.

The tribe must therefore be recognised by one or more of several criteria, the following being those usually accepted:

1. A group or groups of people who had definite territorial rights, who were related, no matter how distantly, and who were governed by a common tribal law.
2. Those who shared a common language.
3. People who had a common tribal name. Many tribes, however, had no specific name for themselves, and were given more than one name by their neighbours.
4. A collection of groups which had social and ritual identity in common, one which was not shared by neighbouring tribes.

Although the common language was one of the more important elements, we have seen that it cannot be depended upon as a decisive factor in defining the tribe. Ritual and law which distinguished one group or collection of groups from others was equally important. Often a sub-tribe seemed to possess all the qualifications of a tribe except for some essential feature.

Classifications within the tribe were as follow: family units or local groups linked by kinship, religious, and territorial rights; age-groups amongst which the elders formed a recognised component; the two sexes; totemic clans as distinct from family groups; and, in many tribes, moieties. In some tribes there were sections and subsections. Sections and subsections were correlated with moieties if these exist, but they were not in themselves subdivisions of moieties. The tribe was normally recognised as a group which claimed descent from a common ancestor and where totemic affiliations were of paramount importance.

A list of Aboriginal tribes and their locations appears in Appendix A, pages 168-71.

TRUMPETS.
Didgeridoos.

TUCKONIES. Tribes in some of the well-timbered areas believed in the existence of quaint little people who lived among the trees and sometimes interfered in the ways of men. They were called Tuckonies. They were guardians of living things in tribal legends, such as the story of how the Crow attacked the young Pelicans, which were saved in a novel fashion by the Tuckonies; or the tale in which water was given to the thirty wives of the Goannas. In this story they were headed by a leader,

their bodies were striped with red ochre and pipeclay, and their heads decorated with white cockatoo feathers.

TURTLES. The dozens of eggs which a turtle laid in the sand provided a satisfying meal for several people. In hunting the turtle for food an ingenious method was sometimes adopted. A sucker-fish was caught and tethered to a long cord. When it was released near a turtle the fish attached itself to it, and the big creature could easily be towed ashore by means of the line. Turtles were caught on beaches and turned on their backs or were captured from canoes by throwing a harpoon with a detachable wooden head on a cord.

TWINS. No stigma normally attached to a mother who gave birth to twins; but one was nearly always killed, for the mother could handle only one baby at a time. It might happen on very rare occasions that one was given to another woman.

U

UNCLES. A mother's brother had the responsibility of choosing a husband for his niece. In effect she was his child. He was a very important relative for a boy. He became his guardian, and often steered him through initiation and instructed him in tribal lore. He was repaid with food and other gifts.
Marriage, Relationships.

V

VENGEANCE.
Revenge.

VISITORS. Except when messengers were sent to another tribe when it was time to call the clans together for a ceremony in the spring, when food and water failed completely in their own territory, or when trading journeys were made to an adjacent tribe, little visiting was done. The man who left his own tribal territory was a stranger in a strange land, separated from the comforting guardianship of his own kin and of totemic ancestors. Nevertheless there were such occasions and they had their own etiquette. As a protective measure the visitor sent up smoke signals to announce his coming in peace well in advance of his arrival. When he reached the camp he did not speak until spoken to, nor did he enter until he was invited to do so.

W

WADDIES. A word that has probably been adopted from the Aboriginal into the English language; but it is not certain whether it was originally an Aboriginal name, or whether it is simply a corruption of the word "wood". Strictly speaking, a waddy was a club made from the stem and root of a certain kind of mallee, but it has been applied to all wooden striking weapons. It was a favourite type of club amongst young men and boys, who used it to kill small animals; it was also a weapon used by men in fighting and hunting. At close quarters and in the hands of an experienced hunter it could be thrown at large animals such as kangaroos to crush their heads while they were in flight.

In 1830 R. Dawson wrote: "It is formed like a large kitchen poker, and nearly as heavy, only much shorter in the handle. The ironbark wood, of which it is made, is very hard, and nearly as heavy as iron."*

WALKABOUT. Walkabout is the English

WADDY

* *The Present State of Australia*, page 66.

equivalent of an expressive word which describes the nomadic habits of the large numbers of tribes inhabiting the drier parts of Australia. It was not a compulsive urge but dire necessity which forced them to spend the dry season wandering from one waterhole to another in search of game, vegetable food, and water. They sometimes established scores of camps and travelled hundreds of miles; and it must be remembered that each group included elderly people, pregnant mothers, young children, and babies born on the journey, as well as young men and women and full-grown hunters, and that they had to carry all their possessions with them.

Thousands of years of adaptation had equipped them for this unending ordeal. Waterholes were often widely spaced and contained little water, while game and vegetable food were scarce. It was seldom that they could camp for more than one night in the height of summer, for the scanty water supply was soon exhausted. In times of prolonged drought it might be necessary for a group to seek food in the territory of a neighbouring tribe. This was a great tribulation because strict laws governed their behaviour, and they had lost the protective powers of their spirit ancestor. Even when their hosts possessed part of the legend of the same totemic being, the neighbouring territory did not belong to them in the sense that their own lands did. They were strangers in a spiritual as well as material desert.

Old people were required to keep up with the younger ones. Although they were treated well and shared the meagre supplies of food and water while making little contribution to them, they had to be put to death or abandoned to die of thirst if they fell behind. The welfare of the group was paramount and could not be sacrificed to the needs of those who were unfit. In spite of the affection and tolerance displayed to children, babies were mercifully put to death if the mother's milk was insufficient to support them.

It might be thought that under these cruel conditions life would become almost unbearable, but it was borne with confidence and cheerfulness. The travellers were seldom anxious. They had an uncanny knowledge of the location of every waterhole, and could find the hidden rocks in an unrelieved expanse of scrub.

Their average daily journey was only about 10 miles. When not hunting they were perfectly relaxed, and it was this that saved them from thirst and exhaustion. When the burning sun and parched desert made it impossible to travel by day, their journeys were made at night. As the heat died away they were able to travel much further in search of water.

But the journey was usually made during the hours of daylight in order that the spoor of game could be picked up and every scrap of vegetable insect food gathered while on the march. The last drops of water were drunk at dawn and frequently without a meal if the food supplies had been exhausted the previous night. Once again the tiny, determined cavalcade set off for the next waterhole. The young men went first, eager to capture any game they came across, followed by the older men who were ready to join them at any time, yet strategically placed to keep the women and children, who travelled behind, under observation. The women were burdened with dilly bags and coolamons, and in fact everything except spears and clubs, leaving the men free to spring to instant action if game was sighted. Their progress was slower because of the need to seek food, for the evening meal might depend solely on the efforts of the women.

At night the women cooked the meal while the men made windbreaks and greased and repaired their weapons. Their bodies were rubbed with fat and ashes to keep out the cold, and finally they settled in their shelters to sleep brokenly throughout the long, cold night.

Carrying, Food, Hunting, Rest, Waterholes, Women.

WANINGA.
   Art, Head ornaments.

WARFARE.
   Fighting.

WATER. In coastal districts where permanent camps were built close to streams and billabongs, and amongst river tribes, water was no problem. Even in unusually dry seasons it could be found by digging or tapping supplies which were stored in certain trees, such as the bottle tree and the baobab. But in the vast interior the search for water was an unending quest.

In places where a white man would die of thirst the Aboriginal was quietly confident of his ability to find sufficient to meet his needs. He did not squander it. It was unthinkable to use it for washing when skin, hair, and beard provided ready-made towels for greasy fingers. Nor was it something to be poured lavishly down a thirsty throat. Water was the pre-eminent gift of the ancestral spirits, to be husbanded and used for its proper purpose—to support the body of man, which was the living home of the eternal spirit.

Every waterhole in his private territory was known to the Aboriginal, every depression in the ground where water might collect and seep through the sandy soil to a place where a few drops could be obtained by digging. Even when surface moisture and natural reservoirs were dried up by the fierce sun, he knew of other sources of supply, no matter how small they might be. Although the air might seem dry, dew collected on plants during the cold night. Women went out in the chill dawn, working quickly to shake the precious drops from hairy plants into a bowl before the sun evaporated them. There were trees with long roots—kurrajong, needlebush, some wattles and gum trees, even the ubiquitous mallee scrub which drew supplies from deep in the soil. They were dug up, cut into short lengths, and drained into coolamons. Similarly, branches of some trees and young saplings could be drained of their moisture, the process being assisted by blowing at one end of the cut branch.

The site of a swamp, long ago dried up by drought to a hard, unyielding surface could add to the supply. Faint signs revealed the presence of frogs underground. They had drunk water when the ground was swampy until their bodies were swollen like oranges, and then buried themselves in the mud to survive the long drought. When exhumed their bodies were pressed, yielding a supply of fresh, wholesome water.

The captain of HMS *Beagle* recorded that tribes bordering the Gulf of Carpentaria had accustomed themselves to drink salt water because of the scarcity of streams and pools, but this report has not been confirmed.

There was a scarcity of drinking vessels.

Shells, coolamons, and even skulls were used for this purpose, but when on walkabout the need was not to carry water but to quench the thirst at the beginning and end of a long day, and if possible to leave a supply for others who might follow. As for the fortunate people who lived beside lakes and rivers, the human hand was the perfect drinking vessel.

Drink, Walkabout, Waterholes.

WATERHOLES. The lifeline of scores of desert tribes was a tenuous chain of tiny waterholes and soaks stretching for hundreds of miles across the continent. They were on the sacred routes of the ancestral spirits, and each place had its own name. Without the limestone formations that were scattered through the scrub, life would have been insupportable. The largest rock holes seldom contained more than a hundred gallons, even after heavy rain. In the smaller ones assiduous baling and soaking up of water with pads of dried grass yielded only a few mouthfuls of the precious liquid.

COLLECTING WATER FROM
A WATERHOLE

It was part of the training of young men to learn the location and name of every waterhole in the tribal territory, together with the legend of the ancestor who made it, so that he could find it without hesitation. On the rare occasions when the group was forced to abandon its own territory, the larger waterholes could be discovered by the flight of birds or the tracks of animals. Fortunate was the hunter who found an ample supply and was able to kill a wallaby that frequented the hole. A more careful search amongst the rocks might reveal a procession of ants creeping into a crack and emerging with swollen bodies. Then, with primitive stone tools the track would be enlarged until the tiny reservoir was reached.

In the deserts of Western Australia especially, the soaks were cared for diligently. The openings of ngama (usually pronounced ngamma) were covered over with loose stones and vegetation to stop animals from drinking the water, and to prevent evaporation. These holes were frequently bottle-shaped with a narrow neck, and there was always a danger of birds and small animals being unable to escape, thereby drowning and polluting the water. The ngama were often kept as a last resource. Tiny bark bowls were lowered at the end of a cord to bale out the water when the ngama was deep and narrow, or spongy grass balls were tied to a stick and lowered into the pit.

Walkabout, Water.

WEAPONS.
Axes, Boomerangs, Clubs, Lil-lils, Nulla Nullas, Shields, Spears, Spear-throwers, Throwing-sticks, Waddies.

WIDOWS AND WIDOWERS. At the death of her husband a widow lived an unenviable existence for some time. The mourning period extended over several months, during which she returned to her mother, and smeared herself with white clay as a sign of grief. Mourning with delayed disposal of the bones could take up to three years. Clay widows' caps were worn in the area from western New South Wales to the Lake Eyre district. After the period of seclusion the widow was free to marry again, usually to one of her husband's brothers. If she was still young and capable of

bearing children she would have plenty of suitors.

A widower was free to take any eligible woman. When he had children and no other wives to take care of them, he soon selected a new wife or else handed the children to relatives.

Marriage, Mourning.

WINNOWING.
Cooking, Seeds.

WITCHCRAFT and WITCH DOCTORS.
Magic, Medicine men, Pointing bones, Rainmaking, Ropes.

WITCHETTY GRUBS.
Grubs.

WOMEN. Besides giving birth to children and caring for them, a woman's main task was to provide vegetable food and small game for her family. When in a permanent camp her time was occupied in gathering and cooking food during the daylight hours; on walkabout the small stock of possessions had to be carried by the women while the men concentrated on hunting. They lagged behind their husbands gathering food on the way. Plant foods included yams, yelka, nuts, fruit, berries, seeds, and roots. Sugar exudations from eucalyptus trees, grubs, honey ants, lizards, snakes, and goannas were all material for their dilly bags or coolamons. It was a hard life, but had its times of relaxation and enjoyment at night.

They were not admitted to the council of the elders, nor were the secret parts of tribal legend releaved to them, and they had no part in male initiation ceremonies. Nevertheless women in some parts claimed to have been the first possessors of sacred mysteries which were later taken from them by men; but they retained their own ritual which was hidden from the men, and sometimes possessed their own churinga, although they did not see them. It is to be hoped that further research will reveal how they lost their dominant position in religious matters. Girls were required to undergo painful ordeals, but were spared the severer tests which young men had to endure.

Two Aboriginal words were borrowed by early settlers and applied to women—gin and lubra. Edward E. Morris states that "gin was a native word for an aboriginal woman, and used, though rarely, even for a female kangaroo. . . ." "Lubra, *n.* aboriginal name for a black woman. The name comes from Tasmania. . . . It is probably a compound of the Tasmania words *loa* or *lowa*, a woman, and *proi* (with variants), big. In Victoria, the use of the word began at the Hopkins River and the vicinity, having been introduced by settlers from Tasmania, but it was generally adopted south of the Murray. North of the Murray the native women were called *Gins*. Both words are now used indiscriminately."*

Food, Initiation ceremonies, Men, Possessions.

WOOMERAS.
Spear-throwers.

WORK.
There was no privileged class in primitive Australia. Everyone was a worker, whether at the normal daily tasks of hunting, food-gathering, and cooking, or in the more specialised operations such as painting, carving, and leading songs and chants. Apart from the

* *Austral English*, Macmillan, 1898, pages 161 and 274.

songman, sorcerers and medicine men, who were semi-professionals and supplied with food and gifts for their services, no members of the tribe were paid for their work. Most of the skilled crafts and occupations were engaged in by the majority of the tribe.

WOUNDS.
The Aboriginal was able to survive blows and wounds of great severity. Clay or mud was commonly put over wounds. Gaping wounds were roughly bandaged and in some cases bathed and covered with the ashes of burnt mulga wood, which was believed to have a healing effect. A mixture of fat, hot ashes, and powdered kaolin clay were used as a poultice. Spiders' webs were used to staunch the blood from an open wound.

WRESTLING.
Wrestling was a common sport amongst young men and boys, and was indulged in to develop agility. Lively contests, in which the bodies of the contenders were smeared with fat or oil, were held between equally matched groups of young men. It has been recorded that prizes such as newly made boomerangs and other weapons were awarded, the victor being required to match himself against a succession of opponents in order to win the prize.

Y

YAMS.
There were many wild varieties of yam in Australia, amongst them several desert species, which were an important food stand-by. They varied in shape from thin branching species to long and round varieties. A well-known one which grows to the size of a football is called Blackfellows' Bread.

YEAR.
The new year began with the rising of the Pleiades, as it did for so many peoples of the Southern Hemisphere. This was in the spring when the most important ceremonies were held. In the tropical north of Australia the year was divided into wet and dry seasons.
Seasons, Spring.

APPENDIX A

ABORIGINAL TRIBES AND THEIR LOCATION

The list of tribes that follows is a preliminary working list, from which alternative names are excluded, supplied by the Australian Institute of Aboriginal Studies, Canberra, which is carrying out a survey of Australian tribes and the spelling of their names.

Abodja	Qld	Bandjima	WA	Buluguda	WA
Adidingidigh	Qld	Ba:nggala	SA	Buluwai	Qld
Ajabadha	Qld	Banjgaranj	Vic	Bunaba	WA
Aji	Qld	Baraba-Baraba	Vic. NSW	Buna:ra	WA
Alawa	NT	Baraban	Qld	Bundhamara	Qld
Alja:wara	NT	Barada	Qld	Buneidja	NT
Alngid	Qld	Baramangg	SA	Bungandidj	SA. Vic
Alura	NT	Baranbinja	NSW	Bunggura	WA
Amangu	WA	Ba:rangu	NT	Bunwurung	Vic
Amarag	NT	Barbaram	Qld	Burada	NT
Ambara	Qld	Bard	WA	Bural-Bural	NT
Ami	NT	Barunggama	Qld	Buranadjini	NT
Anaiwan	NSW	Bawududjara	WA	Burara	NT
Andagerebina	NT	Bemba	WA		
Andagirinja	SA	Biangil	Vic	Dadi-Dadi	Vic
Andidja	WA	Bibalman	WA	Dadungalung	Vic
Andiljaugwa	NT	Bida-Bida	Qld	Dagalag	Qld
Andjingid	Qld	Bidia	Qld	Dagoman	NT
Anggamudi	Qld	Bidjandjadjara	NT. SA	Daguda	WA
Angudimi	Qld	Bidjara	Qld	Dai	NT
'Araba	Qld	Bidungo	WA	Dainiguid	Qld
Arabana	SA	Bigambul	Qld. NSW	Dajoror	NT
A'ragu	Qld	Biladaba	SA	Dal:a	Qld
Aragwal	NSW	Bilamandji	NT	Dalabon	NT
Aranda	NT	Binbinga	NT	Dalandji	WA
Arawari	WA	Bindaga	Qld	Dalwangu	NT
Aridingidigh	Qld	Bindel	Qld	'Damala	WA
Arnga	WA	Bindjarub	WA	Danganegald	SA
Awabagal	NSW	Bindubi	NT	Dangbon	NT
Awarai	NT	Binggu	Qld	Danggadi	NSW
		Bin-Gongina	NT	Danggali	NSW
Badimara	WA	Binigura	WA	Darambal	Qld
Badjala	Qld	Birbai	NSW	Dargari	WA
Badjari	Qld	Birdawal	Vic	Darginjung	NSW
Baganambia	Qld	Biria	Qld	Dargudi	WA
Baganu	Qld	Birniridjara	WA	Daribalang	Qld
Bagu	WA	Bodaruwidj	SA	Darmaramiri	NT
Ba:gundji	NSW	Bolali	NSW	Daungwurung	Vic
Bajali	Qld	Bondynj	Qld	Debidigh	Qld
Bajungu	WA	Bongo-Bongo	NT	Denma	WA
Balamumu	NT	Bordawulung	SA	Dharawa:l	NSW
Balardung	WA	Brabirawilung	Vic	Dharug	NSW
Balgalu	Qld	Brada:wulung	Vic	Dharumba	NSW
Baljgu	WA	Brajagawulung	Vic	Dhawa	NSW. Vic
Balmawi	NT	Buan	NT	Dhu:rga	NSW
Ba:na	Qld	Buduna	WA	Dieri	SA
Banambila	Qld	Bugangidja	NT	Dijogoi	NT
Ba:nbai	NSW	Bugula	NT	Diraila	Qld
Bandjagali	NSW	Buibadjali	Vic	Dirari	SA
Bandjalong	NSW	Bujibada	Qld	Djabadja	Qld
Bandji	Qld	Bulinara	NT	Djaber-Djaber	WA

Djabu	NT	Galwangug	NT	Gugada	SA
Djabugai	Qld	Gamaraigal	NSW	Gugadji	Qld
Djabwurung	Vic	Gambre	WA	Gugadja	NT. WA
Djadjala	Vic	Gambuwal	Qld. NSW	Gujambal	Qld. NSW
Djadjawurung	Vic	Gamilaroi	NSW	Gujangal	Vic. NSW
Djagaraga	Qld	Gamor	NT	Gujani	SA
Djagunda	Qld	'Ganajang	WA	Gujula	NT
Djalaguru	NT	Ganalbwingu	NT	Gulnggai	Qld
Djalgandi	WA	Gan'dangara	NSW	Gulumali	Qld
Djambarwingu	NT	Gandju	Qld	Gulunggor	NT
Djamindjung	NT	Gan-Ganda	Qld	Guluwarin	WA
Djandnandi	Qld	Ganggalida	Qld	Gumadji	NT
Djarawala	NT	Gangulu	Qld	Gumbainggar	NSW
Djarlwa:g	NT	Garadjari	WA	Gunaidbe	NT
Djarn	NT	'Garama	NT	Gunavidji	NT
Djaru	WA	Garanggaba	NSW	Gunba:lang	NT
Djawanj	NT	Garanguru	SA	Gundara	Qld
Djawi	WA	Garanja	Qld	Gundeidjeme	NT
Djeradj	NT	'Garawa	NT	Gundudj	NT
Djerag	WA	Gardudjara	WA	Gunei	NT
Djeraridjal	WA	Garendala	Qld	Gungadidji	Qld
Djerimanga	NT	Gariera	WA	Gungaragan	NT
Djial	NT	Garingbal	Qld	Gungari	Qld
Djidjijamba	WA	Garmalangga	NT	Gunggalenja	Qld
Djinang	NT	Garundi	Qld	Gunggara	Qld
Djinba	NT	Garuwali	Qld	Gunggarbara	Qld
Djingili	NT	Gaurna	SA	Gunggari	Qld
Djirbal	Qld	Gawambarai	Qld. NSW	'Gungorogone	NT
Djiringanj	Vic	Geawegal	NSW	Gunian	WA
Djiru	Qld	Geinjan	Qld. NSW	Gunindiri	NT
Djiwali	WA	Gia	Qld	Gu:nja	Qld
Djonggandji	Qld	Giabal	Qld	Gunjbarai	NSW
Djowei	NT	Giadjara	WA	Gunwinggu	NT
Djuban	WA	Gidabal	NSW	Guradjara	WA
Djugan	WA	Gidja	WA	Gurama	WA
Djulngai	Qld	Gidjingali	NT	Gurang-Gurang	Qld
Djungurdja	WA	Gigi	NT	Gure:ndji	NSW
Djuroro	WA	Gingana	WA	Gurindji	NT
Do:dj	Qld	Giraiwurung	Vic	Gurnai	Vic
Duduruwa	Vic	Giramai	Qld	'Gurndidj'mara	Vic
Dulua	Qld	Goa	Qld	Gu:rnu	NSW
Dungidjau	Qld	Goara	WA	Gurung	Vic
Durilji	NT	Gobabwingu	NT	Gurungada	NSW
		Gobadeindamiri	NT	Guwamu	Qld
Gabalbara	Qld	Gogai	Qld	Guwidj	WA
Gabi	Qld	Goinbal	Qld	Gwandera	Qld
Gadhang	NSW	Going	Qld	Gwijamil	NT
Gadjerawang	NT	Go:la	WA	Gwini	WA
Gadjerong	NT	Golagngad	Vic		
Gagadju	NT	Gona'ni:n	Qld	Ibarga	WA
Gaididj	NT	Gongabula	Qld	Idindji	Qld
Gairi	Qld	Gonggandji	Qld	I:lba	Qld
Gajardild	Qld	Gonin	WA	Inawonga	WA
Gala:gu	WA	Gonjmal	Qld	Indjilinji	Qld
Galali	Qld	Goreng	WA	Inggarda	WA
Galamai	WA	Gorlba	NT	Iningai	Qld
Galawlwan	NT	Grawadungalung	Vic	Iora	NSW
Galbu	NT	Gudabal	Qld	Iuwalarai	NSW
Galgadung	Qld	Gudanda	Qld		
Galibal	NSW	Gudandji	NT	Jabula-Jabula	Vic
Galibamu	Qld	Gudjala	Qld	Jadhaigana	Qld
Galumburu	WA	Gudjalavia	NT	Jadjmadang	Vic
Galwa	NT	Gudjandju	Qld	Jadliaura	SA

Name	Loc	Name	Loc	Name	Loc
Jagalingu	Qld	Lewuru	Vic	Mining	WA
Jagara	Qld	Liagalawumiri	NT	Minjangbal	Qld
Jalanga	Qld	Liagojomir	NT	Miriwun	WA
Jalugal	NT	Ludigh	Qld	Mirning	WA
Jambina	Qld	Lul:marangu	NT	Moil	NT
Janari	WA	Luridja	NT	Mudalga	WA
Janda	Qld			Mudbura	NT
Jandruwanda	SA	Mabuiag	Qld	Mudhi-mudhi	NSW
Janga	Qld	Madhirdirl	Qld	Mudumui	Qld
Jangga	Qld	Madngela	NT	Mugarganalmiri	NT
Janggondju	Qld	Madoidja	WA	Muliara	WA
Jangman	NT	Maidhargari	Qld	Mun-Narngo	NT
Jan-Gundjara	SA	Maigudung	Qld	Munumburu	WA
Janjango	NT	Maigulung	Qld	Murinbada	NT
Janjula	NT	Maja	WA	Murunidja	WA
Jaralde	SA	Majabi	Qld		
Jardwa	Vic	Majali	NT	Nagara	NT
Jari-Jari	Vic	Majuli	Qld	Nalawgi	NT
Jarnangu	NT	Malag-Malag	NT	Nambuguja	NT
Jaroinga	Qld	Malara	NT	Nanda	WA
Jauor	WA	Malarbardjuradj	NT	Nanduwara	?
Jawaraworga	SA	Maldjana	WA	Nangadadjara	WA
Jeidji	WA	Maljangaba	SA. NSW	Nanggumiri	NT
Jeljendi	Qld	Malngin	NT	Nangiblerbi	NT
Jida-Jida	NSW	Mamangidigh	Qld	Nangor	NT
Jiduwa	NT	Mamu	Qld	Narangga	SA
Ji:gara	NSW	Mamwura	Qld. NSW	Nargalundju	Qld
Jilngali	NT	Mandandanji	Qld	Nari-Nari	NSW
Jiman	Qld	Mangala	WA	Narrinjeri	SA
Jindjibanji	WA	Mangeri	NT	'Nawagi	Qld
Jinwum	Qld	Manggalili	NT	Nawalgu	NSW
Jirawirung	SA	Manggarai	NT	Nawo	SA
Jirgandji	Qld	Mangu	WA	Ndorndorin	Qld
Jir:randali	Qld	Mangula	WA	Ndra:angid	Qld
Jiwadja	NT	Manu	NT	Nemarang	Qld
Joda-Joda	NSW. Vic	Manungu	WA	Ngadhugudi	Qld
Juad	WA	Mara	NT	Ngadjen	Qld
Ju'gaiwadha	Qld	Maradanggimiri	NT	Ngadjunma	WA
Jugambal	NSW	Maragulu	NT	Ngadjuri	SA
Jugul	NT	Maramanindji	NT	Ngagu	NSW
Jugula	Qld	Maranunggu	NT	Ngaiawang	SA
Jugumbir	Qld	Mararba	NT	Ngalado	NT
Ju-Ju	NSW	Marawa	WA	Ngalagan	NT
Julbaridja	WA	Mara:Wara	NSW	Ngalia	SA
Jumu	NT	Marawari	Qld. NSW	Ngaliwuru	NT
Ju:ngai	NSW	Mardidjali	SA	Ngamba	NSW
Junggor	NT	Mardudhunira	WA	Ngamini	SA
Juru	Qld	Marganj	Qld	Ngandangara	Qld
Juwalarai	NSW	Margu	NT	Ngandi	NT
Juwibara	Qld	Maridhiel	NT	Ngangurugu	SA
Juwin	NSW	Mariung	NT	Ngaralda	SA
Juwula	Qld	Marulda	Qld	Ngardog	NT
		Maung	NT	Ngargad	SA
Kaura:reg	Qld	'Mawula	Qld	Ngarigu	Vic
Koko	Qld	Mbalidjan	Qld	Ngarinjin	WA
Kulin	Vic	Mbambylmu	Qld	Ngarinman	NT
		Mbo:aru	Qld	Ngarla	WA
Ladamngid	Qld	Meindangg	SA	Ngarluma	WA
Ladji-Ladji	Vic	Mian	Qld	Ngaro	Qld
Lamumiri	NT	Midhaga	Qld	Ngarug	NT
Laragia	NT	Midjamba	Qld	Ngawadj	SA
Lardil	Qld	Milamada	WA	Nga:wun	Qld
Lenngidigh	Qld	Min-gin	Qld	Ngengenwuru	Vic

Name	Location	Name	Location	Name	Location
Ngewin	NT	Umbuigamu	Qld	Wardal	WA
Nggerigudi	Qld	Ungawangadi	Qld	Warda:man	NT
Nggod	Qld	Unggumi	WA	Wardibara	Qld
Ngindadj	SA. Vic. NSW	Unjadi	Qld	Warejdbug	NT
Ngjamba	NSW	Urningangg	NT	Warga-Warga	Vic
Ngoborundji	Qld			Wargi	SA
Ngoera	Qld	Wad:a	NT	Warianga	WA
Ngoori	Qld	Wada-Wurung	NSW	Warrai	NT
Ngormbal	WA	Wadigali	SA. NSW	Warungu	Qld
Ngormbur	NT	Wadi-Wadi	Vic. NSW	Warwa	WA
Ngugi	Qld	Wadjabangai	Qld	Wawilja	NT
Ngunawal	NSW	Wadjalang	Qld	Wawula	WA
Ngu:rand	Qld	Wadjandi	WA	Wembria	WA
Ngurawola	SA. Qld	Wadjari	WA	Wengej	NT
Nguri	Qld	Wadjigi:n	NT	Widagari	WA
Ngurlu	WA	Wadjug	WA	Widi	WA
Nimanburu	WA	Wagaja	NT	Widjabal	NSW
Njagi-Njagi	WA	Wagaman	Qld	Widjandja	WA
Njamal	WA	Waga-Waga	Qld	Widjilg	NT
Njangga	NT	Wagelag	NT	Wik-	Qld
Njangumarda	WA	Wagoman	NT	Wila-Wila	WA
Njegudi	Qld	Waiangara	WA	Wilingura	NT
Njigina	WA	Waidjinga	SA	Wiljagali	SA. Qld. NSW
Njijabali	WA	Waigur	Qld	Wiljali	Qld
Njining	WA	Wailbi	SA	Wiljara	WA
Njirma	Qld	Waladjangari	WA	Wi:lman	WA
Njul-Njul	WA	Walangama	Qld	Wimarangga	Qld
Njuwadhai	Qld	Walar	WA	Wiradhuri	NSW
Noala	WA	Walbanga	NSW	Wirajarai	NSW. Qld
Nordanimin	NT	Wal'Boram	Qld	Wirangu	SA
Norweilimil	NT	Walgi	WA	Wirdinja	WA
Nugunu	SA	Waljbiri	NT	Wiri	Qld
Nundjulbi	NT	Waljen	WA	Wirngir	WA
Nungali	NT	Waljwan	NSW	Wogadj	NT
Nungara	WA	Walmadjari	WA	Woiwurung	Vic
Nunggubuju	NT	Walmanba	NT	Wolamangu	NT
Nunugal	Qld	Walmbarddha	Qld	Wolgal	NSW
		Walmbaria	Qld	Wolgara	NT
Obulgara	NT	Walu	NT	Wol'jamidi	WA
Ogerliga	Qld	Wambaja	NT	Wonarua	NSW
Oidbi	NT	Wamba-Wamba	Vic. NSW	Wongaibon	NSW
		Wanamara	Qld	Wonganja	Qld
Raggaja	Qld	Wandarang	NT	Wonggadjara	Qld
Ramindjari	SA	Wandjira	NT	Wonggaman	Qld
Ranjbarngu	NT	Wan-gan	Qld	Woralul	NT
Rereri	NT	Wanggaji	WA	Worgabunga	Qld
Ridarngu	NT	Wanggamala	NT	Worora	WA
Ringu-Ringu	Qld	Wangganguru	SA	Wudjari	WA
Riraidjangu	NT	Wanggara	Qld	Wudjubalug	Vic
		Wanggumara	Qld	Wulagi	NT
Saibai	Qld	Wan:guri	NT	Wulamba	NT
		Wa:nji	Qld	Wulbudji'bur	Qld
Tiwi	NT	Wan:guri	NT	Wulgurugaba	Qld
Tutu	Qld	Wanjwalgu	NSW	Wulu	WA
		Wanman	WA	Wulwulam	NT
Ug'windjila	Qld	Wanujara	WA	Wunambal	WA
Ulaolinja	Qld	Waragumai	Qld	Wurangu	NT
Ulwawadjana	Qld	Waramanga	NT	Wurangung	Qld
Umbila	Qld	Waramiri	NT	Wurungugu	NT
Umbindhamu	Qld	Wardandi	WA		

APPENDIX B

A READING LIST

ABORIGINAL MAN IN SOUTH AND CENTRAL AUSTRALIA. Part 1. Authors selected by the Board for Anthropological Research, University of Adelaide. B. C. Cotton, ed. Adelaide, Government Printer, 1966. (Handbook of the flora and fauna of South Australia).

AMERICAN-AUSTRALIAN SCIENTIFIC EXPEDITION TO ARNHEM LAND, 1948. Records. Melbourne, Melbourne University Press, 1956-1964. 4 vols.

BASEDOW, H. *The Australian Aboriginal.* Adelaide, Preece, 1925.

BATES, Daisy. *The Passing of the Aborigines,* 2nd edn. Heinemann and Murray, 1966.

BERNDT, Ronald M., ed. *Australian Aboriginal Art.* With chapters by R. M. Berndt, A. P. Elkin, F. D. McCarthy (and others), Sydney, Ure Smith, 1964.
Djunggawul. Melbourne, Cheshire, 1951.
Kunapipi. Melbourne, Cheshire, 1950.

BERNDT, Ronald M. and Catherine H. *The World of the First Australians, an introduction to the traditional life of the Australian Aborigines.* Sydney, Ure Smith, 1964.

BERNDT, Ronald M. and Catherine H., ed. *Aboriginal Man in Australia; Essays in honour of A. P. Elkin.* Sydney, Angus and Robertson, 1965.

BLACK, Roman. *Old and New Australian Aboriginal Art.* Sydney, Angus and Robertson, 1964.

BLEAKLEY, John William. *The Aborigines of Australia; their History, their Habits, their Assimilation.* Brisbane, Jacaranda Press, 1961.

BUHLER, Alfred, T. Barrow and C. P. Mountford. *Oceania and Australia; the Art of the South Seas.* London, Methuen, 1962.

CHASELING, W. *Yulengor: Nomads of Arnhem Land.* London, Epworth, 1959.

CONFERENCE ON ABORIGINAL STUDIES, *Australian National University, 1961. Australian Aboriginal Studies; a Symposium of Papers presented at the 1961 Research Conference.* W. E. H. Stanner, convener and chairman, Helen Sheils, ed. Melbourne, Oxford University Press, 1963.

CRAIG, B. P., compiler. *Arnhem Land Peninsular Region (including Bathurst and Melville Islands).* Canberra, Australian Institute of Aboriginal Studies, 1966. (Occasional papers in Aboriginal studies no. 8. Bibliography series no. 1.)

DOCKER, E. G. *Simply Human Beings.* Brisbane, Jacaranda Press, 1964.

DRAKE-BROCKMAN, H. Y. F. *Australian Legendary Tales.* Sydney, Angus and Robertson, 1939.

DUGUID, Charles. *No Dying Race.* Adelaide, Rigby, 1963.

DUNCAN-KEMP, A. M. *Where Strange Paths Go Down.* Brisbane, Smith and Paterson, 1964.

ELKIN, Adolphus Peter. *Aboriginal Men of High Degree.* Sydney, Oceania, 1946.
The Australian Aborigines, How to Understand Them, 4th edn. Sydney, Angus and Robertson, 1964.

ELKIN, A. P., and BERNDT, R. M. and C. *Art in Arnhem Land.* Melbourne, Cheshire, 1950.

ELKIN, A. P., and HARNEY, W. E. *Songs of the Songmen.* Melbourne, Cheshire, 1949.

ELLIS, Catherine J. *Aboriginal Music-Making; a Study of Central Australian Music.* Adelaide, Libraries Board of South Australia, 1964.

FALKENBERG, Johannes. *Kin and Totem; Group Relations of Australian Aborigines in the Port Keats District.* Oslo, Oslo University Press, Allen and Unwin, 1962.

GALE, G. F. *A Study of Assimilation; Part-Aborigines in South Australia.* Adelaide, Libraries Board of South Australia, 1964.

HARNEY, W. E. *Life Among the Aborigines.* London, Hale, 1959.
Tales from the Aborigines. London, Hale, 1960.

HIATT, L. R. *Kinship and conflict; a Study of an Aboriginal Community in Northern Arnhem Land.* Canberra, Australian National University, 1965.

HOWITT, A. W. *The Native Tribes of South-east Australia.* Adelaide, Libraries Board of South Australia, *forthcoming.* Facsimile reprint. (Australian facsimile editions no. A50.) First published London, Macmillan, 1904.

IDRIESS, Ion L. *Our Living Stone Age.* Sydney, Angus and Robertson, 1963.

KABERRY, Phyllis M. *Aboriginal Women.* London, Routledge, 1939.

KUPKA, Karel. *Dawn of Art; Painting and Sculpture of Australian Aborigines.* Sydney, Angus and Robertson, 1965.

LARNACH, S. L. and N. W. G. Macintosh. *The Craniology of the Aborigines of Coastal New South Wales.* Sydney, University of Sydney, 1966. (Oceania monograph no. 13.)

LINDSAY, H. A. See TINDALE and LINDSAY.

LOCKWOOD, Douglas. *The Lizard Eaters.* Melbourne, Cassell, 1964.
We, the Aborigines. Melbourne, Cassell, 1963.

McCARTHY, Frederick David. *Australian Aboriginal Decorative Art,* 7th edn. Sydney, Australian Museum, 1966.
Australian Aboriginal Rock Art, 2nd edn. Sydney, Australian Museum, 1962.

Australia's Aborigines, Their Life and Culture. Melbourne, Colorgravure Publications, 1957.

Australian Aboriginal Stone Implements. Sydney, Australian Museum, 1967.

MACINTOSH, N. W. G. and BARKER, B. C. W. *The Osteology of Aboriginal Man in Tasmania.* Sydney, University of Sydney, 1965. (Oceania monograph no. 12.)

MALINOWSKI, Bronislaw. *The Family Among the Australian Aborigines.* New York, Schocken Books, 1963. First published 1913.

MEGGITT, Mervyn John. *Desert People; A Study of the Walbiri Aborigines of Central Australia.* Sydney, Angus and Robertson, 1962. Chicago, University of Chicago Press, 1965.

MITCHELL, S. R. *Stone Age Craftsmen.* Melbourne, Bread and Cheese Club, 1949.

MOUNTFORD, Charles Pearcy. *Aboriginal Paintings from Australia.* London, Collins, 1964. (Fontana Unesco art books.)

Ayers Rock, Its People, Their Beliefs and Their Art. Sydney, Angus and Robertson, 1965.

The Dreamtime; Australian Aboriginal Myths in Paintings by Ainslie Roberts, with text by Charles P. Mountford. Adelaide, Rigby, 1965.

MOYLE, A. M. *A Handlist of Field Collections of Recorded Music in Australia and Torres Strait.* Canberra, Australian Institute of Aboriginal Studies, 1966. (Occasional papers in Aboriginal studies no. 6. Ethnomusicology series no. 1.)

NORLEDGE, Mildred. *Aboriginal legends from Eastern Australia: The Richmond-Mary River region.* Sydney, Reed, 1967.

PARKER, Mrs K. Langloh. See DRAKE-BROCK-MAN, H. F. Y.

REAY, Marie, ed. *Aborigines Now; New Perspectives in the Study of Aboriginal Communities.* Sydney, Angus and Robertson, 1964.

REED, A. W. *Aboriginal Fables and Legendary Tales.* Sydney, Reed, 1965.

Aboriginal Place Names and their Meanings. Sydney, Reed, 1967.

Aboriginal Words of Australia. Sydney, Reed, 1965.

Myths and Legends of Australia. Sydney, Reed, 1965.

ROBINSON, G. A. *Friendly Mission; the Tasmanian Journals and Papers of George Augustus Robinson, 1829-1834.* N. J. B. Plomley, ed. Hobart, Tasmanian Historical Research Association, 1966.

ROBINSON, Roland. *Aboriginal Myths and Legends.* Melbourne, Sun Books, 1966.

The Australian Aborigines in Colour. Sydney, Reed, 1968.

The Feathered Serpent. Sydney, Edwards and Shaw, 1956.

The Man who Sold his Dreaming. Sydney, Currawong Publishing Co., 1965.

ROSE, F. G. G. *The Wind of Change in Central Australia; the Aborigines at Angas Downs, 1962.* Berlin, Akademie Verlag, 1965.

SEMINAR OF THE PROBLEMS OF ABORIGINAL EMPLOYMENT, WAGES AND TRAINING, Monash University, 1966.

Aborigines in the Economy; Employment, Wages and Training. Edited by Ian G. Sharp and Colin M. Tatz. Melbourne, Jacaranda, 1966.

SIMPSON, Colin. *Adam in Ochre; Inside Aboriginal Australia,* 5th edn. Sydney, Angus and Robertson, 1962.

SMITH, W. R. *Myths and Legends of the Australian Aborigines.* London, Harrap, 1930.

SPENCER, Sir Walter Baldwin. *Native Tribes of the Northern Territory of Australia.* London, Macmillan, 1914.

Wanderings in Wild Australia. London, Macmillan, 1928.

SPENCER, Sir Walter Baldwin and F. J. Gillen. *Across Australia.* London, Macmillan, 1912.

The Arunta; A Study of a Stone Age People. London, Macmillan, 1927.

The Native Tribes of Central Australia. London, Macmillan, 1899.

The Northern Tribes of Central Australia. London, Macmillan, 1904.

STREHLOW, T. G. *Aranda Traditions.* Melbourne University Press, 1947.

TINDALE, Norman and LINDSAY, H. A. *Aboriginal Australians.* Brisbane, Jacaranda Press, 1963.

WARNER, William Lloyd. *A Black Civilization; A Social Study of an Australian Tribe,* revised edn. New York, Harper and Bros., 1958.

PERIODICALS

ARCHAEOLOGY AND PHYSICAL ANTHROPOLOGY IN OCEANIA. vol. 1, no. 1-. Apr. 1966-. Sydney, University of Sydney.

AUSTRALIAN ABORIGINAL STUDIES. Nos. 1 —, 1963 —.

MANKIND. vol. 1, no. 1-. 1931-. Sydney, Anthropological Society of New South Wales. (C/o Australian Museum, College Street, Sydney.)

OCEANIA, vol. 1, no. 1-. 1930-. Sydney, University of Sydney.

OTHER REED BOOKS

Aboriginal Words of Australia. This book is more than an authoritative dictionary; it is also entertaining reading. As well as alphabetically, words are listed under such headings as birds, reptiles, weapons, etc. Indications of the locations where the words are used are included. This is invaluable, since tribal languages differ enormously between one part of the continent and another. In addition, there is an entertaining short section of phrases and sentences. Illustrated, 144 pages, paperback.

Aboriginal Place Names by A. W. Reed. Australia possesses a heritage of place names which pays tribute to the lively imagination of her Aboriginal inhabitants. These names have a curious fascination for Europeans and in this book A. W. Reed has compiled a comprehensive collection, with meanings collected from all parts of Australia, which throws light on the customs and way of life of the Aborigines. So, the imagination of an older people remains alive to gladden the hearts of their totemic ancestors. 144 pages, paperback.

Altjeringa and other Aboriginal Poems by Roland Robinson. Robinson, one of Australia's leading poets, understands the mind and attitudes of the Aboriginal as few other Europeans do. In the first part of Altjeringa, Robinson has recorded the songs, chants and narrative poems of his Aboriginal friends and has translated them into English verse. They reflect the sad and haunting spirit of a displaced people. The second part — Robinson's own poems — evokes more personally but just as effectively the spirit of the original Australians and the atmosphere of the inland places where wandering tribes continue to live the life of old. 80 pages, cased.

Myths and Legends of Australia by A. W. Reed. There is a rich heritage of Aboriginal myths and legends, in which the Aborigines, observing the mysteries of sun and stars, bird and animal, man and woman, life and death, have woven a magic fabric. From this fascinating material A. W. Reed has selected fifty five tales — each story a classic of the Aboriginal repertoire. By retelling them simply and without the distortions of European dramatisation, the author has preserved the authentic strength and colour of the original myth or legend. 256 pages, cased.

Aboriginal Fables and Legendary Tales by A. W. Reed. This book is a companion volume to *Myths and Legends of Australia*. Here the author has collected the shorter stories of the Aborigines rather than the longer myths and legends. These shorter stories share the same basis of belief in which the original spirit of the Dreamtime is part of the mythological tradition. The many line illustrations by Roger Hart are a happy supplement to a text that will engage the interest of children and adults alike. 256 pages, illustrated, cased.